THE COMPLETE IDIOT'S GUIDE® TO

Search Engine Optimization

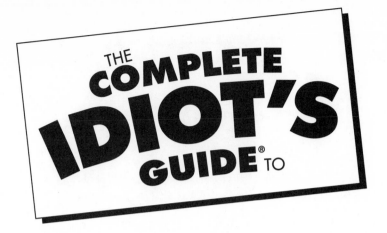

THE COMPLETE IDIOT'S GUIDE® TO

Search Engine Optimization

by Michael Miller

ALPHA

A member of Penguin Group (USA) Inc.

To Sherry: My search is over.

ALPHA BOOKS

Published by the Penguin Group

Penguin Group (USA) Inc., 375 Hudson Street, New York, New York 10014, USA

Penguin Group (Canada), 90 Eglinton Avenue East, Suite 700, Toronto, Ontario M4P 2Y3, Canada (a division of Pearson Penguin Canada Inc.)

Penguin Books Ltd., 80 Strand, London WC2R 0RL, England

Penguin Ireland, 25 St. Stephen's Green, Dublin 2, Ireland (a division of Penguin Books Ltd.)

Penguin Group (Australia), 250 Camberwell Road, Camberwell, Victoria 3124, Australia (a division of Pearson Australia Group Pty. Ltd.)

Penguin Books India Pvt. Ltd., 11 Community Centre, Panchsheel Park, New Delhi—110 017, India

Penguin Group (NZ), 67 Apollo Drive, Rosedale, North Shore, Auckland 1311, New Zealand (a division of Pearson New Zealand Ltd.)

Penguin Books (South Africa) (Pty.) Ltd., 24 Sturdee Avenue, Rosebank, Johannesburg 2196, South Africa

Penguin Books Ltd., Registered Offices: 80 Strand, London WC2R 0RL, England

International Standard Book Number: 978-1-59257-835-1
Library of Congress Catalog Card Number: 2008933155

11   10   09   8   7   6   5   4   3   2   1

Interpretation of the printing code: The rightmost number of the first series of numbers is the year of the book's printing; the rightmost number of the second series of numbers is the number of the book's printing. For example, a printing code of 09-1 shows that the first printing occurred in 2009.

Printed in the United States of America

Note: This publication contains the opinions and ideas of its author. It is intended to provide helpful and informative material on the subject matter covered. It is sold with the understanding that the author and publisher are not engaged in rendering professional services in the book. If the reader requires personal assistance or advice, a competent professional should be consulted.

The author and publisher specifically disclaim any responsibility for any liability, loss, or risk, personal or otherwise, which is incurred as a consequence, directly or indirectly, of the use and application of any of the contents of this book.

Most Alpha books are available at special quantity discounts for bulk purchases for sales promotions, premiums, fundraising, or educational use. Special books, or book excerpts, can also be created to fit specific needs.

For details, write: Special Markets, Alpha Books, 375 Hudson Street, New York, NY 10014.

Publisher: *Marie Butler-Knight*
Editorial Director: *Mike Sanders*
Senior Managing Editor: *Billy Fields*
Acquisitions Editor: *Tom Stevens*
Development Editor: *Michael Thomas*
Production Editor: *Kayla Dugger*
Copy Editor: *Krista Hansing Editorial Services, Inc.*

Cartoonist: *Chris Sabatino*
Cover Designer: *Bill Thomas*
Book Designer: *Trina Wurst*
Indexer: *Johnna Vanhoose Dinse*
Layout: *Ayanna Lacey*
Proofreader: *Laura Caddell*

Contents at a Glance

Contents

Introduction

Search engine optimization.

That's a mouthful of a phrase to describe a deceptively simple concept—finding ways to make your website pop up higher in Google and Yahoo!'s search results.

I don't need to tell you about Google and Yahoo! (and, to a lesser degree, Microsoft's Live Search) and why they're important for driving traffic to your website. The fact is, most people find your site by searching for something. If your site appears near the top of the search results, many of them will click through to your page; if your site doesn't appear on the first page of results, you may not get anyone clicking at all.

This is why you need to do everything you can to fight your way to the top of the search rankings. This is what search engine optimization, or SEO, is all about.

Of course, SEO isn't one big thing; it's a lot of little things. But each little thing is important and works in conjunction with all the other little things. It's not a quick and easy job.

What little things are we talking about? Well, effective SEO involves working with things like keywords, HTML tags, inbound links, and your site's overall content and navigation. It's something anyone can do—if you know what to do.

That's why I wrote this book. *The Complete Idiot's Guide to Search Engine Optimization* covers everything you need to know to optimize your site and improve your search engine rankings. But it covers more than that; I also walk you through optimizing your site for local and mobile search, and for social networks and bookmarking. There are even a few chapters that help you integrate your SEO efforts with the other components of your online marketing plan—something every online marketer needs to know.

When you're done with this book, you'll know exactly what you need to do to make your site rank higher. And that's a very good thing.

Who This Book Is For

The Complete Idiot's Guide to Search Engine Optimization is written for anyone who wants their site to rank higher with Google, Yahoo!, Live Search, and the other search engines and directories. You don't need a technical background to understand what's going on, although it would help if you knew just a teensy bit about some basic HTML tags. And although this book has a definite marketing or business bent, the techniques presented here apply to any type of website.

What You'll Find in This Book

The business of optimizing a website is a fairly straightforward affair. That said, to best optimize your site, it helps to know how Google and the other search engines rank the sites in their search results. It also helps to know how SEO fits in with all the other types of online marketing you could be doing.

To that end, I've presented a lot of interrelated information in this book, divided into five major sections.

Part 1, "Understanding Search Engines and SEO," starts at the beginning—by explaining how Google, Yahoo!, and the other search engines work. You'll also learn how SEO works and which of the major search engines are worth targeting.

Part 2, "Optimizing Your Website for Search Engines," walks you step-by-step through all the aspects of the SEO process. You'll learn how to optimize your site's content, keywords, HTML tags, design and navigation, inbound links, and images and videos. You'll also learn how to submit your site to the major search engines and how to improve your ranking by creating a sitemap.

Part 3, "Other Types of Optimization," goes beyond simple website SEO to discuss optimizing your site for local search, mobile search, and social media. You'll also learn how to optimize your blog for search.

Part 4, "Analyzing Your Site's Performance," shows you how to track the success of your SEO efforts. You'll learn how to use the search engine's analysis tools, choose third-party SEO tools, avoid the most common search engine mistakes, and maintain your SEO on an ongoing basis.

Part 5, "Managing a Complete Search Engine Marketing Plan," is written for anyone marketing a business on the web. You'll learn how to create an SEO strategy for your site, integrate SEO into your overall online marketing plan, integrate shopping directories and pay-per-click advertising into your plan, and evaluate the performance of your online marketing plan.

The Complete Idiot's Guide to Search Engine Optimization concludes with a glossary of SEO terms which is a great reference even after you've read the rest of the book!

How to Get the Most Out of This Book

To get the most out of this book, you should know how it is designed. I've tried to put things together to make reading the book and learning how to conduct an SEO campaign both rewarding and fun.

In addition to the main text, you'll find a number of little text boxes (what we in publishing call *margin notes*) that present additional advice and information. These elements enhance your knowledge or point out important pitfalls to avoid, and they look like this:

> ### Search Note
>
> These boxes contain additional information about the topic at hand.

 Stop!

These boxes contain important warnings about what *not* to do.

 SEO Tip

These boxes provide additional tips and advice beyond what's present in the main text.

Let Me Know What You Think

I always love to hear from my readers. Feel free to e-mail me at seo@molehillgroup.com. I can't promise that I'll answer every e-mail, but I will promise that I'll read each one!

And, just in case a few mistakes happen to creep into the printed book, you can find a list of any corrections or clarifications on my website (www.molehillgroup.com). That's also where you can find a list of my other books, so feel free to look around—and maybe do a little online shopping!

Acknowledgments

Thanks to the usual suspects at Alpha, including Tom Stevens, Michael Thomas, Laura Caddell, Ayanna Lacey, Kayla Dugger, Krista Hansing, and Marie Butler-Knight, for helping to turn my manuscript into a printed book.

Special Thanks to the Technical Reviewer

Speaking of that technical reviewer, *The Complete Idiot's Guide to Search Engine Optimization* was reviewed by an expert who double-checked the accuracy of what you'll learn here. Special thanks are extended to Rolf A. Crozier for his review and comments in this regard.

Trademarks

All terms mentioned in this book that are known to be or are suspected of being trademarks or service marks have been appropriately capitalized. Alpha Books and Penguin Group (USA) Inc. cannot attest to the accuracy of this information. Use of a term in this book should not be regarded as affecting the validity of any trademark or service mark.

Part 1

Understanding Search Engines and SEO

Want to know how search engines work? Then this is the place to start. These chapters provide a basic understanding of the major search engines (Google, Live Search, and Yahoo!) and of the search engine optimization process.

How Search Engines Work

In This Chapter

- ◆ Storing information on the web

- ◆ Remembering the old ways to search—Gopher, Archie, Veronica, and WAIS

- ◆ Exploring new ways to search—directories and search engines

- ◆ How search engines work

- ◆ What pages search engines have trouble indexing

Search engines are an essential part of any company or website's online marketing plan. Yes, you can purchase banner ads and pay-per-click ads, but you'll still get a majority of links from good old-fashioned search engine results. That's right, despite the best efforts of web advertising firms, most users continue to find the sites they want by searching for them.

That's why you've bought this book, after all—to improve your placement in those search engine results. But to know how to make your site more search-friendly, you first need to know how those search engines find your site and rank it. In other words, you need to know how search engines work.

How Information Is Stored on the Web

To understand the nature of web search, it helps to know a little bit about what the search engines search for—and why.

You see, the Internet is not an orderly place. The sites on the web are kind of like a bunch of file cabinets in a great big office. You can walk from file cabinet to file cabinet (surf from website to website), rifle through the file folders in any particular file drawer (browse through the pages on any site), and scan the papers within any individual folder (read the contents of any individual web page). And, after all that work, you still might not be able to find what you were looking for.

Think about it: How many times have you tried to find a specific piece of information in your office—and failed? Did you always go to the right file cabinet? Did you always find the right folder? Were the folders always organized the way you thought they'd be organized? Did the folders you looked in always contain the papers you thought would be there? And did the papers you read always contain the information you wanted—worded in precisely the manner you expected?

Of course not. Papers and folders and files are all created and organized by human beings, and human beings (1) are not perfect, (2) seldom think perfectly logically, and (3) rarely think alike.

Guess what? It's the same way on the web. Human beings create web pages, and human beings assemble multiple pages into websites—lots of websites. It's been estimated that the web contains somewhere in excess of 150 million websites and close to 1 trillion individual pages, and those pages aren't assembled in any organized fashion; each website has its own unique logic and organizational scheme. In other words, the web is nothing more than barely organized chaos—and a lot of it.

All of which explains the difficulty of searching and indexing all the information that comprises the Internet—which is exactly the challenge faced by Google, Yahoo!, and the other major search engines.

The Old Ways to Search

The problem of finding and retrieving data from the Internet is not a new one. Almost from the very beginning of the Internet, users have needed to find information that was not readily visible. What search tools did they use then—and what tools are available today?

Well, before there was the World Wide Web (pre-1994), there was the Internet. (The Internet itself has been around since the 1970s, in one form or another.) Even in those pre-web days, lots of information was stored on Internet servers around the globe, and lots of users needed to find specific bits of that information.

How did they do it?

Remember that the pre-web Internet didn't have fancy graphics and clickable hyperlinks, so it should come as no surprise that all the data back then existed in text format only. That text was stored in various file formats on various computers, and four main tools were available for getting at those text files:

◆ **Gopher** was a tool for organizing files on dedicated servers, extremely popular in universities across the United States. Each Gopher server contained lists of files and other information, both at that specific site and at other Gopher sites around the world. As you can see in Figure 1.1, Gopher worked similarly to the hierarchical file tree used in Windows Explorer; users clicked folder links to see their contents and then navigated up and down through various folders and subfolders.

Figure 1.1

Gopher, a simple way to search the pre-web Internet.

◆ **Veronica** was a server-based tool used to search multiple Gopher sites for information. Veronica worked somewhat similarly to today's web search engines—users entered a query and clicked a Search button, which generated a list of matching documents.

◆ **WAIS,** which stands for *wide area information server,* used the old text-based Telnet protocol to perform full-text document searches of Internet servers. WAIS was

> **Search Note**
>
> Gopher was created at the University of Minnesota, home of the Golden Gophers—hence the system's name. And yes, Archie and Veronica were not-so-veiled references to characters from the *Archie* comic books.

more powerful than Veronica but was quickly superseded by the web and web-based search tools.

◆ **Archie** was a tool for searching FTP sites—Internet servers that store files for downloading. Archie was used to hunt for specific files to download.

Of course, after the web came along, these old tools went the way of the horse carriage and buggy whip. Although you still find a few old Gopher servers up and running on one college campus or another, very little new information has been added to these servers since 1994. For that reason, they're mentioned here purely for their historical and curiosity value.

The New Ways to Search

With the advent of the World Wide Web in 1994 (or thereabouts), data started migrating from Gopher and FTP servers to web servers. Boring old text documents got dusted off and spruced up with graphics and hyperlinks, and Microsoft and Netscape started battling back and forth about who had the better web browser. In short, the Internet was stood on its head as the web became the dominant infrastructure—and as millions of new users flooded the Internet monthly.

As the number of individual web pages grew from tens of thousands to hundreds of thousands, to millions, to billions, it became imperative for people to quickly and easily find their way around all those pages. With the explosion of the web, then, came a new industry of cataloging and indexing the web, via search engines and directories.

Manual Organization with Web Directories

One approach to organizing the web is to physically look at each web page and stick each one into a hand-picked category. Once you get enough web pages collected, you have something called a *directory*, which organizes its collection of websites into a variety of easy-to-browse categories. A directory doesn't search the web—in fact, a directory catalogs only a very small part of the web. But a directory is very organized and very easy to use.

Directories—such as the original Yahoo! directory—were, in the early days of the web, the most popular way to find sites and information. In fact, there are still some very popular directories today, including Best of the Web (www.botw.org) and the Open Directory (www.dmoz.org), shown in Figure 1.2. But directories are hindered by their manual nature; no group of editors can work fast enough to catalog anything but a small percentage of all existing websites. For this reason, web directories have suffered in comparison with today's most popular way of organizing the web—via search engine index.

Figure 1.2

The Open Directory—not a search engine!

Automatic Organization with Search Engines

It's important to note that a directory is *not* a search engine. A *search engine* is not powered by human hands, as a directory is; instead, a search engine uses a special type of software program (called a *spider* or *crawler*) to roam the web automatically, feeding what it finds back to a massive bank of computers. These computers hold *indexes* of the web—in some cases, entire web pages are indexed; in other cases, only the titles and important words on a page are indexed. (Different search engines operate differently.)

In any case, as the spiders and crawlers operate like little robot web surfers, the computers back at home base create a huge index (or database) of what was found. Some search engines' indexes contain tens of billions of entries, which provide a larger base of results than is capable with even the largest web directory. It's the quantity of results that attracts the majority of web searchers—although the best search

> **Search Note**
>
> Another popular directory is the Google Directory (directory. google.com), which is simply a Google-branded version of the Open Directory.

engines (from Google, Yahoo!, and Microsoft) also return high-quality results in terms of relevance and accuracy.

How Search Engines Index the Web

Now that you have a better idea of *what* search engines and directories do, let's take a look at *how* search engines do their thing. There's a lot of sophisticated technology behind even the simplest search.

How a Typical Search Works

Searching a site like Google or Yahoo! is deceptively simple. The user enters a search query, clicks the Search button, and then waits for the site to display a list of matching results.

A typical search of this type takes less than half a second to complete. That's because all the searching takes place on the search engine site's own web servers. That's right; a user may think that he's searching the web, but in effect he's searching a huge index of websites stored on the search site's servers. That index was created previously, over a period of time; because the user is searching only a server, not the entire web, his searches can be completed in the blink of an eye.

Search Note

As an example, Google uses close to a half-million servers, located in clusters in its technology centers around the world. All of these servers run the Linux operating system. Google uses three types of servers: *web servers* (which host Google's public website), *index servers* (which hold the searchable index to the bigger document database), and *document servers* (which house copies of all the individual web pages in Google's database).

So what happens when a user enters a query into the search site's search box? It's a process that looks something like this:

1. When the user clicks the Search button, his query is transmitted over the Internet to the site's web server.

2. The search site's web server sends the query to the company's array of index servers. These computers hold a searchable index to the site's database of web pages.

3. The query is matched to listings in the site's search index—that is, the index servers determine which actual web pages contain words that match the query.

4. The search site now passes the query to its document servers, which store all the assembled web listings (documents) in the database.

5. The document servers assemble the results page for the query by pasting together snippets of the appropriate stored documents.

6. The document servers send the assembled results page back to the main web server.

7. The search site's web server sends the results page across the Internet to the user's web browser, where he views those results.

> ### Search Note
>
> The search site's document servers store the full text of each web page in the site's database. Snippets of each page are extracted to create the page listings on the search results pages. In addition, these stored documents provide the cached pages that are linked to from the search results page.

Of course, the user is unaware of all this behind-the-scenes activity. He simply types his query into the search box on the search site's main web page, clicks the Search button, and then views the search results page when it appears. All the shuffling of data from server to server is invisible.

How a Search Site Builds Its Database—and Assembles Its Index

At the heart of a search engine's system is the database of web pages stored on the site's document servers. These servers hold literally billions of individual web pages—not the entire web, but a good portion of it.

How does a search site determine which web pages to index and store on its servers? It's a complex process with several components.

First and foremost, most of the pages in the site's database are found by special *spider* or *crawler* software. This is software that automatically crawls the web, looking for new and updated web pages. Most sites' spiders not only search for new web pages (by exploring links to other pages on the pages it already knows about), but also periodically recrawl pages already in the database, checking for changes and updates. A complete recrawling of the web pages in a search site's database typically takes place every few weeks, so no individual page is more than a few weeks out-of-date.

Search Note

Google's spider software is known as GoogleBot. It's smart enough about how it updates the Google database that web pages that are known to be frequently updated are crawled more frequently than other pages. For example, pages on a news site might be crawled hourly, whereas more static pages on a reference site might be crawled once every few weeks.

The search engine's spider reads each page it encounters, much like a web browser does. It follows every link on every page until all the links have been followed. This is how new pages are added to the site's database, by following those links the spider hasn't seen before.

The pages the spider discovers are copied verbatim onto the search site's document servers—and copied over each time they're updated. These web pages are used to compile the page summaries that appear on search results pages.

To search its database, the search site creates an index to all the stored web pages. This search engine index is much like the index found in the back of this book; it contains a list of all the important words used on every stored web page in the database. Once the index has been compiled, it's easy enough to search for a particular word and return a list of all the web pages on which that word appears.

And that's exactly how a search index and database work to serve your search queries. You enter one or more words in your query, the search engine searches its index for those words, and then those web pages that contain those words are returned as search results. Fairly simple in concept, but much more complex in execution—especially since each search engine indexes all the words on several billion web pages.

Ranking Search Results (Google Version)

As a website owner, you care less about how Google or Yahoo! searches the web than you do about how high up you appear in that search engine's results pages. What makes a search engine rank a particular site high in its search results and a similar site much lower?

Each search engine has its own particular algorithm for ranking the pages in its search index. In general, though, they follow similar methodology; similar factors are important to all the major search engines. To that end, it's instructional to look at Google, the web's largest and most popular search engine, to observe how it ranks its results.

Google, like all the other search engines, attempts to serve its users by ranking the most important or relevant pages listed first, and ranking less-relevant pages lower in the results. How does Google determine which web pages are the best match to a given query?

While Google keeps its precise methodology under lock and key, for competitive reasons, we do know that there are three primary components to its results rankings:

- **Text analysis.** Google looks not only for matching words on a web page, but also for how those words are used. That means examining font size, usage, proximity, and more than a hundred other factors to help determine relevance. Google also analyzes the content of neighboring pages on the same website to ensure that the selected page is the best match.

- **Links and link text.** Google then looks at the links (and the text for those links) on the web page, making sure that they link to pages that are relevant to the searcher's query.

- **PageRank.** Finally, Google relies on its own proprietary PageRank technology to give an objective measurement of web page importance and popularity. PageRank determines a page's importance by counting the number of other pages that link to that page. The more pages that link to a page, the higher that page's PageRank—and the higher it will appear in the search results. The PageRank is a numerical ranking from 0 to 10, expressed as PR0, PR1, PR2, and so forth—the higher, the better.

Although the other factors are important, PageRank is the secret sauce behind Google's page rankings. The theory is that the more popular a page is, the higher that page's ultimate value. While this sounds a little like a popularity contest (and it is), it's surprising how often this approach delivers high-quality results.

The actual formula PageRank uses (called the *PageRank algorithm*) is super-duper top-secret classified, but by all accounts, it's calculated using a combination of quantity and quality of the links pointing to a particular web page. In essence, the PageRank algorithm considers the importance of each page that initiates a link, figuring (rightly so) that some pages have greater value than others. The higher the PageRank of the pages pointing to a given page, the higher the PageRank will be of the linked-to page. It's entirely possible that a page with fewer, higher-ranked pages linking to it will have a higher PageRank than a similar page with more (but lower-ranked) pages linking to it.

> **Search Note**
>
> PageRank is page specific, not site specific. This means that the PageRank of the individual pages on a website can (and probably will) vary from page to page.

The PageRank factor on the linking page is also affected by the number of total outbound links on that page. That is, a page with a lot of outbound links will contribute a lower PageRank to each of its linked-to pages than will a page with just a few outbound links. As an example, a page with a PageRank of PR8 that has 100 outbound links will boost a linked-to page's PageRank less than a similar PR8 page with just 10 outbound links.

It's important to note that Google's determination of a page's rank is completely automated. There is no human subjectivity involved, and no person or company can pay to increase the ranking of its listings. It's all about the math.

What Search Engines Have Trouble Finding

As big as the databases at Google and Yahoo! are, there are still lots of web pages that don't make it into those databases. What kinds of web pages are difficult for the search engines to index—and why?

Dynamic Pages

In particular, most search engines today don't do a good job of searching the "deep web," those web pages generated on the fly from big database-driven websites—that is, pages that result when you fill in a form or enter a query on a specific website. Similarly, search engines don't always find pages served by the big news sites, pages housed on web forums and discussion groups, blog pages, and the like.

What's the common factor behind these hard-to-index web pages? They all contain "dynamic" content that changes frequently, and the pages themselves don't always have a fixed URL. With most dynamic web pages, the URL—and the page itself—is generated on the fly, typically as a result of a search within the site itself.

Search Note
Dynamically generated pages constitute what is called the *invisible web*, thought to be over 550 billion pages in size—and growing.

This lack of a permanent URL makes these pages difficult, if not impossible, for a search engine spider to find. That's because a spider, unlike a human being, can't enter a query into a site's search box and click the Search button. It has to use those pages that it finds, typically the site's fixed home page. The dynamically generated pages slip through the cracks, so to speak.

This is why it's possible to search for a page that you know exists (you've seen it yourself!) and not find it listed in a search engine's search results. It's not a trivial problem; more and more of the web is moving to dynamically generated content, leaving at least half the Internet beyond the capability of search engine spiders. While Google and Yahoo! have technicians working on this challenge, it's a big enough challenge that you shouldn't expect big improvements anytime soon.

> **Search Note**
>
> Google has been exploring ways for its GoogleBot spider to automatically enter common text into any web form it finds when crawling the web. This is an attempt to mimic common queries users might enter and then capture the URLs for the subsequent dynamically generated web pages.

Images and Media

There's another type of web page that search engines don't like—and there are a lot of them on the web. I'm talking about pages that consist solely of images or other non-text content. This may include picture pages (without text captions), video pages, or those annoying Flash animations that pop up on many sites' introductory pages.

What all these media types have in common is that they don't contain any text. And since text is what search engines index, the search engines don't index these pages. In effect, a web page without text is invisible to the search spiders!

That's right, the search engines completely ignore images, videos, audio files, and Flash animations; they focus on the text and nothing but the text. So if your website relies heavily on images, animations, and other media, it may be affecting your search rankings. Better to replace those pretty pictures with boring—but more effective—text content!

> **Search Note**
>
> While search engines ignore images, they can and do index the images' file names and anchor text, as well as any text surrounding the images.

The Least You Need to Know

- ◆ Information on the web is organized into web pages and websites.
- ◆ A directory manually organizes a small number of websites into easily browsable categories.

◆ A search engine uses spider technology to find web pages, which are then stored in a large database.

◆ When a user queries a search engine, the query searches an index of the site's database.

◆ Search engines rank their results based on a combination of relevance and popularity.

◆ Search engines index only text, not images, animations, or other media.

How Search Engine Optimization Works

In This Chapter

- ◆ Discover what search engines look for
- ◆ Learn how to improve your search rankings
- ◆ Determine who should optimize your site
- ◆ Find out when your optimization is complete

You've been charged with increasing your website's traffic. You know that search engines drive a majority of traffic to your site, so you want to ensure that your site ranks as highly as possible in the results for all the major search engines. How do you do this?

The key to increasing your search engine rankings is to optimize your site for search—that is, to give the search engines what they're looking for. Search engine optimization can involve everything from the design of your site to the text you place on each page to those sites that link back to your site. You have to optimize all of these factors if you want to place near the top of the first page when someone is searching for what you have to offer.

What Search Engines Look For

To know how to optimize your site for search, you need to know what, exactly, search engines look for when ranking sites in their search results. Fortunately for anyone doing the optimization, a few key factors control the results—and they're pretty much the same factors for every major search engine.

Behind all these factors, however, is one overriding goal: each of the search engines wants to provide more accurate results to its users. The search engines don't care so much about you and your site; they care about giving their users a more effective and efficient search experience. The better the results they deliver, the happier their users will be.

When a search engine ranks search results, then, it's with the intent of delivering the one best answer to that particular user's query. They use every tool in their arsenal to determine the content of a website and then to match that content to what the user is searching for.

Ideally, then, if someone is searching for a particular topic, those sites that best cover that topic will rise to the top of the search results. Or, think of it another way: if your site *doesn't* cover a particular topic, it won't appear in the search results for that topic. That's only logical. You have to cover what people are searching for, and cover it as well as you can.

Stop! ⎯⎯⎯⎯⎯⎯⎯⎯⎯⎯⎯⎯⎯⎯⎯⎯⎯⎯⎯⎯⎯⎯

Remember, for a searchbot to notice the content of your site, that content must be textual. Today's search engines have yet to develop a means of evaluating the content of nontext objects—images, videos, Flash animations, and the like. In fact, to most search engines, if it's not text, it might as well not exist; a site with all its content in graphics is pretty much invisible to Google, Yahoo!, and the like.

With this in mind, how does a search engine determine how appropriate your content is to a given query? There are a number of ways, although none involving actually reading and interpreting your site's text.

Let me explain.

Keywords

A search engine doesn't yet have the human capacity to read sentences and paragraphs and understand what it reads. Technology lets the search engine look for specific words and phrases within a block of text, but that's about it; it can't tell how well those words and phrases are used.

What a search engine can do is look for and determine how important a keyword or phrase is on your page. It does this by seeing where on the page the keyword is used, and how many times. A site with a keyword buried near the bottom of a page will rank lower than one with the keyword placed near the top or used repeatedly in the page's text. It's not a foolproof way of determining importance and appropriateness, but it's a good first stab at it.

Remember, the keyword or phrase is what the user is searching for. If someone is searching for "hammers" and your site includes the keyword *hammers* (or *hammer*, singular) in a prominent position—in the first sentence of the first paragraph, for example—then your site is a good match for that search. If, on the other hand, your site doesn't include the word *hammers* at all, or includes it only near the bottom of the page, then the search engines will determine that your site *isn't* a good match for that searcher. It doesn't matter if you have a big picture of a hammer at the top of your page (search engines can't read images, remember); unless you use the keyword prominently and relatively often, you won't rank highly for that particular search.

So when the various search engines examine your page, they look for the most important words—those words used in the site's title or headings, those words that appear in the opening paragraph, and those words that are repeated throughout the page. The more often and more prominently you include a word on your page, the more important a search engine will think it is to your site.

Stop! _____

Giving prominent placement to the wrong words can hurt your search rankings, by providing less relevant results. If your site is about power tools but you include the words *boot* and *leather* multiple times on the page for some reason, your site will likely be viewed as a site about leather boots. This not only drives the wrong visitors to your site, but it also lowers your search ranking in general, because you're now one of the less-useful leather boot sites listed.

HTML Tags

A search engine looks not just to the text that visitors see when trying to determine the content of your site. Also important is the presence of keywords in your site's title, which is determined by the metadata in your site's HTML code.

This metadata includes your site's name and keyword "content," which is specified within the **<META>** tag. This tag appears in the head of your HTML document, before the **<BODY>** tag and its contents.

A typical **<META>** tag looks something like this:

```
<META NAME="KEYWORDS" CONTENT="keyword1, keyword2, keyword3">
```

It's easy enough for a search engine to locate the **<META>** tag and read the data contained within. If a site's metadata is properly indicated, this gives the search engine a good first idea of what content is included on this page.

That said, the **<META>** tag isn't the only HTML tag that searchbots look for. For example, the **<TITLE>** tag is just as important as the **<META>** tag—which is why you shouldn't fall into the trap of assigning only your site name to the tag. Instead, the **<TITLE>** tag should contain two to three important keywords, followed by the site name. Most search engines place major importance on the **<TITLE>** tag when determining a site's content; you want to make sure that your site's most important content is listed within this tag.

Searchbots also seek out the heading tags in your HTML code—**<H1>, <H2>, <H3>,** and so forth. For this reason, you should use traditional heading tags (instead of newer Cascading Style Sheet coding) to emphasize key content on your page.

The only problem with HTML metadata, of course, is that it doesn't have to represent the page's real content. That is, a webmaster can falsify the metadata to make the site look like it's about one thing when it's really about another. For example, one could have a site about something boring like biology but describe it, via the **<META>** tag, with keywords like *adult* and *sexy*. And if it *can* be done, it *has* been done.

For this reason, search engines don't rely solely on metadata to index a page. They also rely on keyword placement within the page's text, as discussed previously, and on additional elements—including how relevant other sites think your site is.

Links to Your Site

The folks at Google first realized that web rankings could be somewhat of a popularity contest—that is, if a site got a lot of traffic, there was probably a good reason for that. A useless site wouldn't attract a lot of visitors (at least, not long term), nor would it inspire other sites to link to it.

So if a site has a lot of other sites linking back to it, it's probably because that site offers useful information relevant to the site doing the linking. The more links to a given site, the more useful it probably is.

Google took this to heart and developed its own algorithm, dubbed PageRank, which is based first and foremost on the number and quality of sites that link to a particular page. If your site has a hundred sites linking to it, for example, it should rank higher in Google's search results than a similar site with only 10 sites linking to it. Yes, it's a popularity contest, but one that has proven uncannily accurate in providing relevant results to Google's users.

And it's not just the quantity of links; it's also the quality. That is, a site that includes content that is relative to your page is more important than some random site that links to your page. For example, if you have a site about NASCAR racing, you'll get more oomph with a link from another NASCAR-related site than you would with a link from a site about Barbie dolls. Relevance matters.

 SEO Tip

Google uses links to a site rather than site traffic because the number of links is relatively easy to determine with some degree of accuracy; site traffic, less so.

Search Note

These aren't the only factors that determine how high a site is ranked, of course. Google, for example, says it considers more than 200 different factors when ranking a site—none of which it publicly discloses.

Ten Key Factors for Improving Your Search Rankings

Search engine optimization is about more than just improving your search rankings; it's ultimately about increasing the volume and improving the quality of the traffic that those search rankings drive to your website. You want more than just increased traffic; you also want more qualified traffic.

This last factor requires you to do more than adapt to the algorithms the various search sites use. You also need to know what people are searching for. It won't do to have a site about "cars" if people are searching for "transportation"; the more you get inside the heads of your potential customers, the better you can fine-tune your site's content and keywords to match what they're looking for.

With that in mind, I now present 10 key factors that can help you improve your search rankings. These factors are the basis for any SEO effort; we discuss them in more depth throughout the balance of this book.

Search Note

Why is a high ranking in the search results important? Don't searchers read the entire page of search results—and then on to the next?

The answer, unfortunately, is that people *don't* read through entire web pages of results. Eye tracking studies show that searchers scan a search results page from top to bottom and from left to right as they look for relevant results. (They also seldom click to the second page of results.) With this in mind, a place at or near the top of the rankings increases the number of people who see and thus click through to your site.

Number One: Know Your Customer

This is the blatantly obvious one that far too many webmasters overlook. Search engine optimization (SEO) isn't really about HTML coding and keyword placement; it's about knowing about the people who visit your website. Or, more accurately, it's about knowing the people you *want* to visit your website.

You see, the more you know about your potential visitors, the better you can optimize your site to (1) be of value to them and (2) rank high when they search for topics of interest. Of course, these two factors are interrelated; the more valuable your site is, the higher it should rank. That's the theory, anyway.

Bottom line, you have to get inside your customers' heads; you have to learn how to *think like the customer.* When you know how the customer thinks, you know what he's interested in and what he's searching for. Just as important, you know *how* he will be searching—what keywords he's likely to use. And when you know the keywords, it's a few short steps to optimizing your site to emphasize those keywords.

So if you don't know your customer—or, more likely, if you think you know your customer but really don't—now's the time to get connected. Don't assume you know how your customers think; get out there and ask them. That's right, we're talking market research here. Do a survey, distribute some questionnaires, conduct a focus group, do whatever you have to do—including literally talking face-to-face with actual customers—to find out what your customers are looking for and how they're looking for it. Then, and only then, can you proceed to the technical business of search engine optimization.

Number Two: Improve Your Content

Once you know what your customers are thinking, you can construct your site to meet their needs. That's a simple statement, but one that involves a lot of hard work. Still, you have to do it.

Of all the methods for SEO, the one that has the biggest impact (after knowing your customer, of course) is improving the content of your website. It's simple: the better your site is, content wise, the higher it will rank.

That's right, when it comes to search rank, content is king. Ultimately, the better search engines find some way to figure out what your site is all about; the higher quality and more relevant your site's content is to a particular search, the more likely it is that a search engine will rank your site higher in its results.

So forget all about keywords and **<META>** tags for the time being, and focus on what your site does and says. If your site is about quilting, work to make it the most content-rich site about quilting you can. Don't skimp on the content; the more and better content you have, the better.

If you remember nothing else from this book, remember this: SEO isn't about technological tricks. It's about making your site more useful to visitors—and that means providing the best possible content you can. Everything else follows from this.

> **Search Note**
>
> Learn more about improving your site's content in Chapter 4, "Optimizing Your Site's Content."

Number Three: Create a Clear Organization and Hierarchy

Here's an important fact: web crawlers can find more content on a web page and more web pages on a website if that content and those pages have a clear hierarchical organization.

Let's look at page organization first. You want to think of each web page as a mini outline. The most important information should be in major headings, with lesser information in subheadings beneath the major headings. One way to do this is via standard HTML heading tags, like this:

```
<H1>Most important information
 <H2>Less important information
  <H3>Least important information
```

> **Search Note**
>
> Learn more about organizing your site's content in Chapter 7, "Optimizing Your Site's Design."

This approach is also appropriate for your entire site layout. Your home page should contain the most important information, with subsidiary pages branching out from that containing less important information—and even more subpages branching out from those. The most important info should be visible when a site is first accessed via the home page; additional info should be no more than a click or two away.

Number Four: Fine-Tune Your Keywords

Just as important as a page's layout is the page's content, in terms of keywords. We've already discussed why keywords are important—they're what potential visitors search for and, thus, are a key factor in how search engines rank your site.

> **Search Note**
>
> Learn more about using keywords in Chapter 5, "Optimizing Your Site's Keywords."

For this reason, you want to make sure that each and every page on your site contains the keywords that users might use to search for your pages. If your site is all about drums, make sure your pages include words like *drums*, *percussion*, *sticks*, *heads*, *cymbals*, *snare*, and the like. Try to think through how *you* would search for this information, and work those keywords into your content.

Number Five: Put the Most Important Information First

Think about hierarchy and think about keywords, then think about how these two concepts work together. That's right, you want to place the most important keywords higher up on your page. A web crawler will crawl only so far, and you don't want it to give up before it finds key information. In addition, search ranking is partially determined by content; the more important the content looks to be on a page (as determined by placement on the page), the higher the page's ranking will be.

Number Six: Tweak Your ‹META› Tags

When calculating search ranking, most search engines not only consider the visible content on a page; they also evaluate the content of key HTML tags—in particular, your site's **‹META›** tag. You want to make sure that you use the **‹META›** tag in your page's code and assign important keywords to this tag.

The **‹META›** tag, which (along with the **‹TITLE›** tag) is placed in the head of your HTML document, can be used to supply all sorts of information about your document. You can insert multiple **‹META›** tags into the head of your document, and each tag can contain a number of different attributes. For example, you can assign attributes for your page's name, description, and keywords to the **‹META›** tag.

SEO Tip

Most search engines also look to highlighted text to determine what's important on a page. It follows, then, that you should make an effort to format keywords on your page as bold or italic, when appropriate.

You use separate **‹META›** tags to define different attributes, using the following format:

```
<META NAME="attribute" CONTENT="items">
```

Replace *attribute* with the name of the particular attribute, and *items* with the keywords or description of that attribute.

For example, to include a description of your web page, you'd enter this line of code:

```
<META NAME="DESCRIPTION" CONTENT="All about stamp collecting">
```

Number Seven: Solicit Inbound Links

When it comes to increasing your rankings at Google, the biggest and most important search engine, you can get a big impact by increasing the number of sites that link to the pages on your site. It's simple: as far as Google is concerned, the more sites that link to your site—and the higher the corresponding PageRank of those linking sites—the higher your site's ranking will be.

Search Note

Learn more about soliciting inbound links in Chapter 8, "Optimizing Links to Your Site."

To increase your ranking, then, you want to get more higher-quality sites to link back to your site. There are a number of ways to do this, from just waiting for the links to roll in, to actively soliciting links from other sites. You can even pay other sites to link back to your site; when it comes to increasing your site's search ranking, little is out of bounds.

Number Eight: Submit Your Site

While you could wait for each search engine's crawler to find your site on the web, a more proactive approach is to manually submit your site for inclusion in each engine's web index. It's an easy process—and one that every webmaster should master.

Number Nine: Create a Sitemap

Here's something else that you can submit to increase your site's ranking—a *sitemap*. A sitemap is a map of all the URLs in your entire website, listed in hierarchical order. Search engines can use this sitemap to determine what's where on your site, find otherwise-hidden URLs on deeply buried pages, and speed up their indexing process. In addition, whenever you update the pages on your website, submitting an updated sitemap helps keep the search engines up-to-date.

Search Note

Learn more about sitemaps in Chapter 11, "Mapping Your Site for Best Results."

Note that submitting a sitemap supplements, rather than replaces, the usual methods of adding pages to a search engine's index. If you don't submit a sitemap, the search engines' crawlers may still discover your pages, and you may still manually submit your site for inclusion in each site's index.

Number Ten: Use Text Instead of Images

Finally, remember that search engines today parse only text content; they can't figure out what a picture or graphic is about, unless you describe it in the text. So if you use graphic buttons or banners (instead of plain text) to convey important information, the search engines simply won't see it. You need to put every piece of important information somewhere in the *text* of the page—even if it's duplicated in a banner or graphic.

So if you use images on your site, which you probably do, make sure you use the **<ALT>** tag for each image—and assign meaningful keywords to the image via this tag. A searchbot will read the **<ALT>** tag text; it can't figure out what an image is without it.

You should also make sure that you link from one page to another on your site via text links, not via graphics or fancy JavaScript menus. A searchbot will find and use the text links to crawl other pages on your site; if the links are nontext, the searchbot might not be able to find the rest of your site.

Stop!

Similarly, don't hide important information in Flash animations, JavaScript applets, video files, and the like. Remember, searchbots can find only text on your page—all those nontext elements are invisible to a search engine.

SEO Tip

Here's a bonus tip for anyone performing search engine optimization: update your site's content often. Since most searchbots crawl the web with some frequency, looking for pages that have changed or updated content, your ranking can be affected if your site hasn't changed in awhile. So you'll want to make sure you change your content on a regular basis; in particular, changing the content of your heading tags can have a big impact on how "fresh" the search engine thinks your site is.

Who Should Optimize Your Site?

Now we come to an important question: given all the various staff involved with creating and maintaining a website, who should do the actual search engine optimization?

Let's start by looking at who *could* do the optimization:

- ◆ **Technical staff.** The same people who built your website certainly have the technical ability to optimize it for search. When it comes to working with HTML code, these folks are more capable than any other staff.

- ◆ **Design staff.** Since site design is a factor in SEO, the people who designed your website could also be involved. I'm not talking the coders; I'm talking the graphic designers who decide what element goes where on the page.

- ◆ **Marketing staff.** Interestingly, many companies don't even think about getting their marketing staff involved with their websites—but this is a big mistake. Of all the people in your company, the marketing folks are closest to the customer; they're the ones who can best determine the keywords that potential visitors are searching for.

So which of these groups should perform your SEO? The answer, of course, is *all of them*. That's right, each department has its own strengths that contribute to the SEO effort; leaving any member off the team would only compromise what you're trying to achieve.

Here's the deal. Your SEO efforts should start with your marketing staff. They will determine what customers you're trying to attract and what those customers are looking for. This, in turn, drives the choosing of the keywords your site will focus on—and, as you've learned, keywords mean everything when it comes to SEO.

With the keywords chosen, the design staff now steps into play and decides the best placement of keywords on the site—probably in conjunction with a web copywriter, who is probably part of the marketing department. The designers, operating under the guidance of the marketing staff, focus on a site and page organization that places the chosen keywords in prominent positions. At this point, it's less about making the site look good than making it read well, in terms of keywords.

Finally, the technical staff comes in and does all the necessary coding, as directed by the design and marketing staff. The technical folks also add the chosen keywords to the site's **<META>, <TITLE>,** and heading tags.

And that's the way to optimize your site—by letting each department play to their strengths, driven first and foremost by what the customer wants. Remember, SEO isn't driven by the technical staff or by the design guys; it's not really about HTML coding or design. The best-optimized sites get that way because their marketing people get inside the heads of their potential customers and then let that drive the entire SEO process.

It's all about thinking like the customer—and letting that drive the optimization techniques you perform.

When Are You Done?

Okay, you've followed the advice in this chapter and throughout the book, and optimized your site as best you can for the customers you hope to attract. Now it's time to put your feet up, have a refreshing beverage, and congratulate yourself on a job well done. Right?

Wrong.

SEO isn't a one-time thing. As soon as you finish one round of optimization, it's time to start planning the next. The Internet is an ever-changing battlefield, requiring constant maintenance on your part to keep up with the changes. In addition, your customers subtly change over time, and you need to adapt your message to their changing wants and needs.

In other words, you're never done with SEO. It's a constant process, one that you must remain diligent about. Let down your guard for even a day, and your competitors will out-optimize you. You can't let that happen; you have to keep your site up-to-date and constantly optimized, or you'll soon find your site slipping in the search rankings.

A site that's never updated won't remain number one for long.

The Least You Need to Know

- ◆ Search engines base their rankings on how relevant your site is to a particular user's search query.

- ◆ The relevancy of your site's content is determined by your use of keywords and HTML tags, as well as the number and quality of other sites that link back to your site.

- ◆ The most important factor for optimizing your site is to know what your customer wants and is searching for.

- ◆ If you improve the content of your site, you'll attract more visitors and more links—and increase your search rankings.

- ◆ Search engine optimization should be driven by the marketing department and utilize the expertise of your company's technical and design staff.

- ◆ Search engine optimization is never done; your site has to be constantly reoptimized for changes on the Internet and in the marketplace.

Google, Yahoo!, or Microsoft: Which Search Engines Should You Target?

In This Chapter

- ◆ Understanding the Big Three search engines: Google, Yahoo!, and Microsoft Live Search
- ◆ Discovering other search engines
- ◆ Learning which search engines you should target
- ◆ Optimizing for different sites

There's no denying that the foremost search engine today is Google. In fact, more than half the web searches on any given day are done through the Google site.

But Google isn't the only search engine out there; Yahoo!, Microsoft, and, to a lesser extent, Ask.com are also important players. With all of these search engines to deal with, should you choose one over another when you're optimizing your site? For that matter, what's different about the various search engines—what do you have to do differently in terms of SEO when targeting one search engine or another?

This chapter turns the spotlight on each of the major search engines and tells you what you need to know about how each search engine works and how to optimize your site for each one. It's not as straightforward as you might think.

Getting to Know Google

The number-one search engine, in terms of searches and users, is Google (www. google.com). In any given month, depending on who's doing the counting, Google is responsible for 55 to 65 percent of all the web searches made in the United States; its market share is even higher in most other countries (approaching 90 percent in the UK, for example). That makes Google an extremely dominant player; no other search engine has half its market share.

Google's audience is as broad a cross-section of web users as you're likely to find. Where some other engines might attract less-technical users of various sorts, Google attracts technophiles and technophobes alike. And given Google's ubiquity, you're likely to find it as the default search engine on most new PCs and many web browsers.

In other words, you can't ignore Google. In fact, your search engine optimization should probably take place with Google first and foremost in your mind.

One of Google's chief appeals to searchers is its uncluttered interface, shown in Figure 3.1. Also appealing is its large search index (more than 20 billion pages and always growing) and reputation for accurate results.

> **Search Note**
>
> Translating percentages into raw numbers, in an average month Google's market share of about 60 percent equals a little over 5 billion discrete searches. In contrast, Yahoo! generates almost 1.5 billion searches per month, and Live Search gets about 800,000 searches per month.

That reputation comes from Google's superior ranking algorithm. Google is simply much better than other search engines in determining the quality and relevance of content on a web page, as well as determining whether a link to a site is real or artificial. As a result, Google's search results are heavily biased toward true informational pages, as opposed to commercial pages.

Recognizing that the key to search traffic is the quality of its search results, Google is constantly trying to improve its users' search experience. One recent improvement is what Google calls *universal search*. In the past, Google's default search results linked solely to websites; if you wanted to find other types of content, such as video or images, you had to perform separate searches. With universal search, however, Google mixes all types of content into its search results pages, as you can see in Figure 3.2; you may do a search and see a row of images at the top of the search results page, or have a video-viewing window pop up in the middle of the search results. It's all because Google is trying to give people more variety in their search results—to more accurately predict and display the different types of content a user might actually be wanting to see.

Figure 3.1

Google's uncluttered search page.

Figure 3.2

Google's universal search results—more than just web pages.

Ranking Google's Results

As I just mentioned, Google is known for its highly relevant search results. This is due in part to Google's proprietary PageRank algorithm, which heavily factors in the quantity and quality of sites linking back to your site—in addition to your site's keywords, **<META>** tags, and the like, of course.

The result is that Google does a better job than its competitors in pointing toward real information on the web; Google typically ranks informational sites higher than commercial ones in its results. That's because Google is better than its competitors in determining the true content of both queries and web pages. It doesn't just do an exact text match to the keywords in a query; instead, Google tries to figure out the idea behind the query and match results to that.

Google also does a good job of filtering out sites that have less useful content—those sites that have been assembled purely with SEO in mind. To do this, Google actively looks for multiple exact instances of a phrase in various locations (page title, headers, internal links, inbound links, and so on); if it finds too much of this internal "phrase spam," Google may exclude this page from the search results for that phrase. Google's goal, of course, is to look for organic editorial content rather than artificial SEO-focused content. For this reason, it's not unusual to see a page with only a single instance of a keyword or phrase rank higher than a similar page with multiple instances of that keyword.

Evaluating Crawling and Link Quality

It's well known that Google's PageRank algorithm heavily weights inbound links to your site. What is less known is that PageRank looks not just at the number of links, but also at the quality of those links—what Google calls *link reputation.*

To determine link reputation, Google looks at link age, your site's rate of link acquisition, the diversity of the anchor text for incoming links, the ratio of so-called deep links to normal links, the quality of the link source (who links to the linking site), and whether anyone actually clicks on those links. Google also weights higher links from the .edu and .gov domains, as they're typically more difficult to influence than the average .com site.

Inbound links to your site also determine how many pages on your site the Googlebot will crawl. And it's not just the quantity of these links, but also their quality. If your site has a high number of low-quality sites linking to it, your site will be less likely to be crawled deeply—or even included in the Google index.

The same goes for outbound links from your site to other sites. If a large number of your outbound links are of poor quality (to off-topic sites), Google may slow down the crawling of your site. This is known as a *crawl penalty*, and it results when you have an excessive number of your inbound and outbound links pointing to low-quality parts of the web.

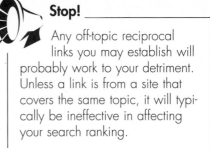

Stop!

Any off-topic reciprocal links you may establish will probably work to your detriment. Unless a link is from a site that covers the same topic, it will typically be ineffective in affecting your search ranking.

Evaluating Other Factors

Here's something else that's interesting. Google's ranking algorithm tends to favor established sites over newer ones. That means, in some instances, that older sites will rank higher than they might otherwise deserve to, based on other factors. In other words, Google tends to trust old sites a little too much.

Google also trusts other pages on a site when it likes the main page. That is, pages buried beneath the site's home page can rank much higher than they might otherwise, based on the ranking earned by the site's main pages. If a key page on a site is ranked highly due to link-tos, age, or other factors, Google assumes that other pages on the site are equally trustworthy.

That said, don't assume you can put up a lot of similar content on multiple pages and have each page show up high in Google's search results. That's not the case, because Google employs technology that aggressively filters out pages with similar content on a site. These duplicative content filters look across an entire site (or section of a site) to see how similar different pages on the site are. If Google determines that your site has a lot of similar pages, it may be less willing to crawl those pages and instead throw them into a supplemental index; pages in Google's supplemental index rarely rank highly, as they're assigned a lower trust rating in Google's ranking algorithm.

Optimizing for Google Search

When it comes to optimizing for Google search, the most important thing is your site's content. Since Google is better than other search engines at filtering out obviously SEO'ed content, your pages need to include genuinely informational copy. You need to write naturally and make your page's copy look more like a news article than a collection of random phrases. Make sure you write grammatically, and don't use sentence fragments. In some instances, using fewer occurrences of a key phrase may result in higher rankings than repeating the phrase more often.

Bottom line: if you have a better organic site than your competitors, you'll rank higher than if you try to force your way into Google's search index.

When soliciting inbound links to your site, avoid link farms and other sites that have obvious artificial links. Instead, solicit sites that have related content, where a link is more relevant. It's better to look for sites that don't link to a lot of other sites; Google ranks these "virgin" sites as higher quality than sites that give out a lot of links. It's better to focus on getting a few links from high-quality related sites than it is to solicit multiple links from less relevant sites.

> **Search Note**
>
> A link farm is a group of typically uninformative web pages that all link to one another, with the sole purpose of increasing the number of links to a given site.

When considering having other types of media appear in Google's universal search results, it's important to know that the videos shown on Google's search results pages come exclusively from YouTube, Google's wholly owned subsidiary. So if your site includes videos, you should submit them separately to YouTube (www.youtube.com), or else Google won't include them in its search index.

Using Google's SEO Tools

Google offers a variety of tools that webmasters can use to optimize their sites for Google search:

- Google Webmaster Tools (www.google.com/webmasters/tools/), which detail how well Google is crawling your site—and helps you improve Google's indexing

- Google AdWords Keyword Tool (http://adwords.google.com/select/KeywordToolExternal), which generates related keywords for any entered keyword, web page, or website

- Google Suggest (http://labs.google.com), which automatically completes search queries based on the most common searches starting with the characters or words you enter

- Google Sets (http://labs.google.com/sets), which generates semantically related keyword sets based on keyword(s) you enter

- Google Trends (www.google.com/trends), which visually depicts long-term search trends

In addition, you can use Google's related sites tool, which displays a list of sites that Google thinks are related to your site. Just enter the following query into any Google search box: **related:www.*site*.com**.

Understanding Yahoo!

Yahoo! (www.yahoo.com) has been around quite a bit longer than Google but long ago lost the number-one position to its chief competitor. Today Yahoo!'s search market share is in the 20 percent range, which makes it a steady number two to the Google juggernaut.

Unlike Google, Yahoo! has a fairly busy search page. As you can see in Figure 3.3, Yahoo!'s home page is more of a portal than pure search; while Google's strategy has been minimalist (at least in terms of search page clarity and design), Yahoo! has opted to show off much of their other content and services—a mistake, in my opinion, but their strategy nonetheless.

Figure 3.3

The Yahoo! search/content portal.

Because Yahoo!'s search page is actually a portal page, it attracts a lot of users who want to do more than search. In addition, the My Yahoo! custom start page is extremely popular, which drives even more users to the Yahoo! search engine. In reality, this translates to a user base slightly less technical than Google's core audience; because of the additional content, many nontechnical users are simply more comfortable with Yahoo! than they are with other search engines.

Ranking Yahoo!'s Results

As you can see in Figure 3.4, Yahoo!'s search results pages look much like those of Google and are universal in nature. This means that if a query generates images or videos in the results, those items will be displayed alongside traditional web page results.

Figure 3.4

A Yahoo! universal search results page.

In terms of results quality, Yahoo! is considered not quite as good as Google but better than Microsoft, befitting its traffic ranking between the two. It's not nearly as good as Google at determining the actual content of a page or the relevancy of links back to a page. This skews Yahoo!'s search results somewhat in favor of commercial results—including pages hosted on Yahoo!'s other sites.

That said, Yahoo! tends to put a higher emphasis on page content than does Google. As far as Yahoo! is concerned, the actual text on your web page is slightly more important than your HTML tags or inbound links.

Evaluating Crawling and Link Quality

Like Google, Yahoo! should do a good job of deeply crawling your site, as long as you have sufficient link popularity to get all your pages indexed. If a page doesn't have a lot of inbound links, it won't show up in the index and probably won't get crawled.

That said, the quality of inbound links is less important to Yahoo! than it is to Google. This makes Yahoo! fairly easy to manipulate by soliciting less relevant or lower-quality links from other sites. Yahoo! also doesn't discriminate if many of your inbound links share similar anchor text.

Evaluating Other Factors

While Google is more about concept matching, Yahoo! still relies on cruder text-matching technology. In addition, Yahoo! doesn't place near as much weight on site age as Google does, which lets newer sites rise higher in search results.

Optimizing for Yahoo! Search

Because Yahoo! weights the page content higher than other factors, using descriptive page titles and text goes a long way to improving your search results. It pays to put your effort into copywriting, making sure to include exact keywords and phrases within your text.

You also need to focus on building links back to your site, although you sometimes get away with lower-quality links better than you can with Google.

Using Yahoo!'s SEO Tools

Like Google, Yahoo! offers two useful SEO tools to webmasters:

◆ Yahoo! Site Explorer (http://siteexplorer.search.yahoo.com), which shows the pages Yahoo! has indexed from a site, as well as which pages they know of that link to pages on that site

◆ Yahoo! Buzz (http://buzz.yahoo.com), which shows current popular searches on the Yahoo! site

Introducing Microsoft Live Search

So far, Microsoft has been unable to unseat either Google or Yahoo! in the search marketplace. Despite various technological upgrades, site redesigns, and even name changes, Microsoft's market share remains just under 10 percent.

The current iteration of Microsoft's search product is called Live Search (www.live. com). It sports a spartan Google-like interface, as you can see in Figure 3.5.

Figure 3.5

Live Search's austere search interface.

Microsoft has tried to take advantage of its position in the operating system market to make Live Search the default search in Windows and Internet Explorer, but that hasn't worked out so well. Forgetting the lawsuits that have forced Microsoft to open up access to the IE7 default search box, it's simply too easy to switch the defaults from Live Search to Google or some other engine for Microsoft to retain any sort of home court advantage. The result is that there may be a slight bias toward newer, nontechnical users among Live Search's database, simply because these are the only folks who find it difficult to switch from Live Search to another search engine.

> **Search Note**
>
> Live Search was formerly known as Windows Live Search and, before that, MSN Search.

Ranking Microsoft's Results

Live Search results are of the universal type. As you can see in Figure 3.6, images, news headlines, and other types of results are placed alongside the traditional web page results.

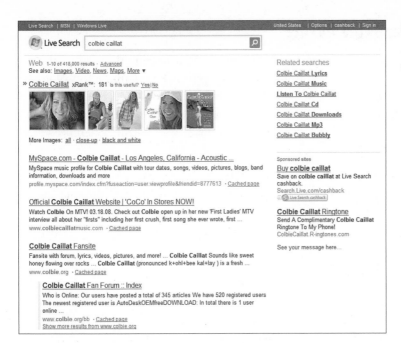

Figure 3.6
Live Search's universal search results.

It can't be denied that, of all the major players, Microsoft is still the newbie in the search engine game. That doesn't have to be a bad thing, but one can't help but feel that it informs the quality of Live Search results—which are notably less relevant than the results from either Google or Yahoo!. Live Search tends to return more commercial than informational pages, and is prone to displaying spam sites in its results. For what it's worth, search experts feel that Live Search is more easily "gamed" by savvy webmasters looking to improve the results of less-deserving sites.

In a nutshell, Live Search is less adept than either Google or Yahoo! in determining the true, contextual content of a web page. Live Search places more emphasis on page copy than HTML tags and does a poor job of analyzing the quality of inbound links. The site puts more trust in newer pages, even if those pages are less authoritative than more established ones.

Search Note

One unique thing about Live Search is that Microsoft appears to be buying an audience. Microsoft's CashBack program rewards users by giving cash rebates to those who purchase products while searching with Live Search. While some view this as an innovative marketing ploy, others see it as a desperation-fueled grab for users.

Evaluating Crawling and Link Quality

Let's talk about link quality for a moment. By not overly inspecting the quality of links to a page, Live Search lets you influence search results by obtaining lots of less relevant or even purchased links; Live Search simply isn't as good as the other major search engines in determining the difference between true organic citations and low-quality links. When it comes to link building with Live Search, quantity definitely matters more than quality.

That said, Live Search also reacts more quickly than its competitors when you get a batch of new links to your site—even if those links are low quality. For this reason, you can improve your rankings on Live Search faster than you can with any other major search engine.

Optimizing for Microsoft Search

All this means, fortunately or unfortunately, that you don't have to do a really good job with SEO to improve your rankings with Live Search. It's a two-pronged approach: obtain a bunch of links from other sites to your site, and then tweak your page content to include a large number of descriptive phrases and keywords. (You should also make sure the keywords or phrases are in the **<META>** and **<TITLE>** tags, of course.)

It's not that important that you use your keywords and phrases in an organic manner, nor is it as important that you strive for high-quality, authoritative content. It's the words and phrases themselves that matter to Live Search, which means that a poor-quality site with good SEO might rank higher than a more authoritative site that hasn't been well optimized. In other words, Live Search is an SEO specialist's dream; enact textbook SEO practices, and you'll get good results.

Using Microsoft's SEO Tools

Microsoft provides some useful and unusual SEO tools for webmasters to use:

- ◆ Live Search Webmaster Center (http://webmaster.live.com), which details the web-crawling status of your website and helps you manage how your site is crawled

- ◆ Live Search Local Listing Center (http://ssl.search.live.com/listings/ BusinessSearch.aspx), which lets local businesses add their listings to Live Search Local

◆ Live Product Upload (http://productupload.live.com), which enables merchants to upload product information to Live Product Search

◆ Search Funnel Tool (http://adlab.msn.com/SearchFunnel/), which shows terms that people search for before or after they search for a particular keyword

◆ Demographics Prediction Tool (http://adlab.msn.com/Demographics-Prediction/), which predicts the demographics of searchers by keyword—or site visitors by website

These last two tools are quite interesting and are part of Microsoft's adCenter Labs. You can find more of these targeted tools at http://adlab.msn.com.

Evaluating Other Search Engines

Even though there are dozens of other search engines out there, only two additional engines bear close examination here: AOL Search and Ask.com. AOL Search typically has about a 4 percent market share, while Ask.com has about a 2 percent share—not enough to challenge Google or Yahoo!, but still enough to be statistically significant. The other smaller players in this space combined, unfortunately for them, don't match Ask.com's 2 percent share.

Looking at AOL Search

AOL Search (http://search.aol.com) is a weak number four in the search engine market, with less than half the users of number-three Live Search. The AOL Search engine is basically the Google search engine (they have a business partnership) with a few enhancements and AOL-specific content thrown into the results. As you can see in Figure 3.7, AOL Search even looks a little like the Google search page; the results generated are also very Google-like.

As such, optimizing your site for Google search also does a good job of optimizing it for AOL Search. You don't need to do anything more than what you would otherwise do for Google.

Know, however, that users of AOL Search tend to be either younger or older than average, and definitely less technical than those you find using Google or Yahoo!. That's because AOL Search users are, more often than not, users of the America Online service—people who, these days, are not among the technological cutting edge.

Figure 3.7

The home page for AOL Search, powered by Google.

Asking About Ask.com

Ask.com (www.ask.com), however, is a different beast. As the number-five player in the search market, Ask.com doesn't command a lot of attention, although it has always been a bit of an innovator in how it approaches the search function.

The site started out as Ask Jeeves, with the conceit that you were asking a butler named Jeeves your search queries; it purported to accept natural language queries that other sites couldn't recognize. That conceit didn't win them many users, so the site eventually reverted to its current Ask.com branding and more traditional search approach, as shown in Figure 3.8.

Figure 3.8

The home page for Ask.com.

That said, Ask.com differs from the other sites, in that it looks heavily at topical communities on the web and uses links from within those communities to determine page relevance. As such, it's slower at increasing the rankings of new or changed sites; Ask.com waits until the relevant community recognizes the site (via page links) and then adjusts its search results accordingly.

The practical purpose of this is that, while Ask.com isn't nearly the size of Google or Yahoo!, the site is important if you're in a vertical market or your site is about a narrowly defined topic. For example, if you run a hobbyist site about model airplanes, Ask.com is likely to rank your site higher than Google or Yahoo! might—after you win the support of (and links from) the model airplane community, of course.

Optimizing for Ask.com is thus a bit different than optimizing for the traditional search engines. Don't bother so much with keywords and HTML tags; instead, focus on getting links from trusted sites in the relevant topical community.

Which Search Engines Should You Target?

When it comes to targeting specific search engines for your search optimization, which ones are worth your time?

Obviously, you have to optimize your site for Google. Google is the big dog in search, for good reason, and if you ignore it, you'll kiss off more than half your potential site traffic. You simply can't do that; you have to optimize your site with Google in mind.

Beyond Google, both Yahoo! and Microsoft's Live Search probably deserve your attention, if only because their demographics differ a bit from Google's. While Google attracts a more general demographic, Yahoo! and Live Search both skew a little older and a little less techno-savvy. The same with AOL Search, which benefits from AOL's somewhat captive audience of oldsters and youngsters.

So it helps if you know who your audience is. If your audience is female and over 50, you might not get a lot of traffic from Google; you might find that you get more queries from Yahoo! and Live Search users. Look at your site metrics and see where your current traffic is coming from. If you're already getting a lot of non-Google traffic, there's probably a reason for that—and a good reason for including Yahoo! and Live Search in your SEO plans.

Optimizing for Different Search Sites

So when we're talking about search engine optimization, which is what this entire book is about, do you do things differently when you're optimizing for different search engines?

The short answer is, no. Even though each search engine has slightly different algorithms for ranking their search results, all major search sites consider the same general factors. They may apply a slightly different weighting to one factor or another, but if you're paying attention to basics, you'll get results no matter which search engine we're talking about.

That's the bottom line. If you adhere to core SEO principles—starting with your site's content and working through keywords and inbound links and all the rest—you'll improve your rankings at all major search engines. There's little value in tweaking your results for one site or another; stick to the basics and you'll be rewarded everywhere.

The Least You Need to Know

- Google is the most important search engine today, with approximately 60 percent of the total search market; it rewards those sites that have the most authoritative content and relevant inbound links.

- Yahoo! is the number-two player, with about a 20 percent share, while Microsoft's Live Search brings up the number-three position with less than a 10 percent share; they tend to be more easily manipulated by textbook SEO techniques.

- Each of the search engines considers the same basic factors when ranking a page, although they may weight those factors differently.

- If you pay attention to SEO basics, you'll improve your rankings at all the major search engines; there's no need to tweak your optimization for one site over another.

Part 2

Optimizing Your Website for Search Engines

Here's the meat of the thing—everything you need to know about implementing SEO on your website. Learn about optimizing your site's content, keywords, HTML tags, design and navigation, images and videos, and inbound links. You'll also learn how to submit your site to the major search engines and create a sitemap.

Chapter 4

Optimizing Your Site's Content

In This Chapter

◆ Understanding why content is important

◆ Discovering how great content affects your search ranking

◆ Learning how to improve your site's content

◆ Providing unique content to "noncontent" sites

When it comes to search engine optimization, the most important tool you can wield is your website itself—in particular, your site's content. This is the dirty little secret of SEO: all the tech and keyword gimmicks you can employ are secondary to creating relevant, high-quality content for your website.

Why is content so important in optimizing your site's search engine results? And how do you add the right kind of content that will increase your site's ranking? That's what we cover in this chapter, so read on to learn more.

Why Content Matters

It's been said before but it's worth saying again:

When it comes to SEO, content is king.

Why is the content of your site so important? After all, a lot of so-called SEO special-ists tell you to focus on cramming as many keywords as possible into each page, or to target your site's **<TITLE>** and **<META>** tags. Are these tricks totally without merit?

The reality is, all the other SEO strategies (which we cover throughout the balance of this book) can improve your search ranking at most major search engine sites. But none of them will improve your ranking as much or as fast as when you create useful, informative, authoritative content for your site. The better your site's content, the higher your site will rank. It's that simple.

What Is Quality Content?

Before we answer the question of why quality content is important, let's address the issue of what quality content is—and what it isn't.

Let's go with the negative first. Quality content is not spam content. It's not a list of keywords and phrases repeatedly inserted into your text, almost at random. It's not self-congratulatory promotional blathering. It's not text lifted verbatim from another site—or even lifted content that's been slightly rewritten. It's not irrelevant blathering. It's not mindless drivel.

Quality content, in contrast, is useful content. It's informative or educational or even entertaining. It's grammatically correct, it's punctuated properly, it reads well. It's orig-inal, it's lean and mean, and it's on point. It's relevant to the topic at hand and, most important, it's authoritative.

Quality content, in most cases, is not promotional or even commercial content. It's content that informs the reader without being self-serving. It answers important ques-tions without leaving more questions unanswered. It serves a useful and practical pur-pose.

In short, quality content distinguishes your site from competing sites. When a visitor says, "I learned something important there," you know you have quality content. If a visitor instead says, "I'm not sure why I bothered visiting that site," you know that your content is lacking on the quality front.

SEO Tip

The quality of your content is also somewhat dependant on the quantity of your content. To some extent, the more text you have about a given topic, the more likely it is that your site will cover a particular aspect of a given topic. In addition, some search engines place an emphasis on text length; they assume that a large website has had more effort put into its development, and thus is more likely to be of higher quality.

Quality content is something you yourself would want to read. If you find your site shallow or uninformative, you know you have some work to do.

Why Does Quality Content Matter?

Now we come to the issue of why quality content matters. The answer, of course, has to do with the types of results that the major search engines want to serve to their users. Even the worst search engine site today wants to provide searchers with sites that best answer their users' queries; they don't want to serve up sites that leave their users still asking the same questions.

Of course, some search engines are better than others at determining useful and relevant content on a website. Some search engines still rely on crude keyword or phrase matching, which doesn't provide a true picture of the actual content of a website; it only tells you how many times a particular keyword or phrase is found on the site. Other search engines rely too heavily on the words contained in a site's **<TITLE>** or **<META>** tags; this is also an inferior approach, as the site's designer can stuff all manner of keywords and phrases into these tags, regardless of what the actual content of the site is.

The best search engines today (and, in this regard, Google is *the* best) employ numerous techniques to determine the true content on a web page. This process isn't perfect, unfortunately, if only because technologies do not yet exist for a search engine to effectively parse the words on a page into coherent thoughts and ideas—although that's the goal of Google and other search engines, and that goal will certainly someday be achieved. No, today we have to rely on cruder methods to determine authority and relevancy, methods that actually do a pretty good job of determining quality content.

That said, Google especially values quality content when ranking a web page in its index. The more authoritative your site's content, the more likely it is that Google will rank it higher in its results. You can't fool Google with keyword or **<META>** tag stuffing; Google, as best as it can, will shift out those obviously gamed pages in favor of pages with legitimate and original content.

Other sites do this less well. With Yahoo! and Live Search, for example, it's still possible to game the system by the judicious use of keywords and HTML tags. These search engines are less capable of ignoring SEO tricks and focusing on the true content underneath. That doesn't mean, however, that you should ignore content when optimizing for these search engines; it simply means that your content efforts are likely to be more highly rewarded by Google than by its competitors. It doesn't matter which search engine you're optimizing for; you still need to focus on the content first and other factors second.

There are other reasons for improving your site's content, of course. First and foremost, the better your site's content, the more satisfied users you'll have. There's little point in attracting visitors to your site by some means, only to disappoint them with the content you offer. You should want to create the most useful, authoritative site possible on the topic at hand; you should not be willing to settle for offering second-rate content to visitors who can quickly and easily click away from your site to one that offers better content.

In addition, the better the content on your site, the more likely it is that other sites will link to your site—and you know how important links are to your site's search ranking. If your site's content disappoints, other sites won't link to you; if your content excels, you'll get a lot of links without having to ask for them.

Quality content matters no matter what type of site you have. It's obvious that if you're providing encyclopedic information, you want that information to be as complete as possible. It's less obvious but equally important that if you run a product-oriented commercial site, for example, you also must provide a wealth of useful information to users. It's not enough to post a small photograph, a short blurb, and a price on a product page. Instead, you have to provide a thorough description of your product, including all manner of physical and technical details—enough information to make the customer comfortable in purchasing your product sight unseen. For a product page, this is what we mean by quality content; the definition varies, of course, for different types of web pages.

How Content Affects Your Search Ranking

Some might view focusing on content as a purist's approach to SEO. I agree and argue that there's nothing wrong with being a purist. If creating quality content is a virtue, it's a virtue that the major search engines are increasingly rewarding. (And isn't it good to know that, at least in the search engine world, virtue trumps the dirty little tricks of keyword and tag manipulation?)

How does quality content affect your search ranking? It's a bit of an involved process, I admit.

The theory is simple: over time, quality content attracts the attention of other sites focusing on the same or similar topics. This results in those sites linking to your site, and the more quality inbound links your site has, the more a search engine will trust your site's authority and relevance—which, of course, results in higher rankings in that search engine's search results.

> **Search Note**
>
> Experts dub content that attracts links from other quality sites as "linkworthy." If your site is just like all the others out there, it's not linkworthy—that is, there's no reason for other sites to link to yours.

In addition, the best search engines today do a pretty good job of weeding out fake content in favor of real information on a web page. Using a variety of heuristic filters and such, these sites (Google, in particular) do their best to determine what you're really talking about and how relevant that is to what their users are searching for. For Google, at least, it's not just about which keywords appear where on your page; it's about how those keywords and phrases are used in context. And that context, of course, reflects the actual content that your site offers.

That said, while improving the content of your site will likely result in improved search rankings, that improvement might be slow in coming. It's true that, on some search engines, cramming in more keywords might provide more immediate results. But those results are likely to be short-lived; in the long run, the site with the better content rises to the top—and stays there.

How to Improve Your Site's Content

All this talk about creating quality content is fine, but just how do you go about doing it? It's all about including authoritative information, crafting that information into engaging copy, and then massaging other SEO techniques into that copy.

Providing Authoritative Information

Let's start with the notion of authoritative information. Providing authoritative content is both a simple and complex undertaking.

It's simple to say that you want your site to have content so complete that users won't have to visit any other site to find out more about the topic at hand. Include every piece of information that's relevant and be sure to answer any questions your user base might pose; you then establish your site as the leading authority on the topic.

Unfortunately, all of that is easier said than done—especially when you're competing in a crowded subject area. If your site is the only site on the web covering the gray eastern tree frog, any information you provide will be welcome and rewarded. On the other hand, if you're trying to cover everything there is to know about the Apple iPhone, you have a lot of competition from some really informative sites; it will be tough to do a better job than the other sites out there.

Then there's the matter of *relevant* content; the longest web page isn't necessarily the most authoritative. If you do a good job figuring out what particular information your target audience is looking for, your page can be more concise than a competing page that throws in everything but the kitchen sink. In other words, offering targeted information is often a better approach than being unnecessarily comprehensive.

So at the core of providing authoritative information is knowing what that information should be—which is a function of knowing what your target visitor is looking for. It all gets back to the concept I mentioned back in Chapter 2, developing the ability to *think like the customer*. You have to know what the customer wants to know—what information he's looking for and how he's looking for it. When you can provide exactly the right information, you become the authority.

Writing Engaging Copy

Now we come to the softer side of authority—how you present your information. While you could present everything you know in a series of short bullet points, that isn't very engaging to the reader; in fact, some search engines (such as Google) might see the lack of complete sentences as a form of keyword stuffing and actually lower your site in their search results. So there's a lot to be said for presenting your information in a grammatically correct, properly punctuated, engaging fashion.

> **Search Note**
>
> Learn more about copywriting for the web in Chapter 5, "Optimizing Your Site's Keywords."

What does this mean? Well, to be frank, for many website developers, it means learning how to write— or, if you can't write well, hiring someone else to do it. There's a whole category of web-friendly copywriters out there, and they know how to put a half-dozen words together into a compelling sentence—as well as how to fine-tune their copy for the particular needs of a web audience. It's just like traditional marketing copywriting, except different.

Bottom line: facts alone don't make for quality content. You have to present your facts in a way that is readable and easy to follow. If you don't know how to do this, hire someone who does.

Crafting SEO-Friendly Content

Your site's content not only has to be authoritative and engaging, but it also has to be presented in such a fashion that search engines notice it. This means making your content SEO-friendly—which is a skill unto itself.

Just what is SEO-friendly content? Here's a list of things that can make or break the way search engines interpret your site's content:

- **Use words, not pictures.** It bears repeating as many times as necessary, but today's search engines look only at the text on a web page, not at a page's images, videos, Flash animations, and the like. If you have important content to present, present it in the body text on your page.

- **Include keywords and phrases.** When you're presenting your core concepts, make sure you work in those keywords and phrases that your potential visitors will be searching for. If a keyword doesn't exist on a page, most search engines won't return that page as part of the relevant search results.

- **Repeat keywords and phrases—naturally.** It's not enough to include your most important keywords and phrases once on a page. You need to repeat those keywords and phrases—but in a natural manner. It can't look as if you're keyword stuffing; the words have to flow organically in your text. If you're looking for a guide, try to use keywords twice in every 400 words of copy.

- **Make the important stuff more prominent.** Whether we're talking keywords or core concepts, the most important information on your web page should be placed in more prominent positions on the page; the more prominent the information, the more likely searchbots will find it. This may mean placing the information in one of the first two or three paragraphs on your page; it may also mean placing key concepts in your page's headings and subheadings.

- **Break up the copy.** To that last point, it's not a bad idea to modularize the content on your page. Instead of presenting a long train-of-thought block of text, break up that block into short chunks, each chunk introduced by its own prominent heading or subheading. Make it easy for readers—and searchbots—to find the information they want on your page.

- ◆ **Length matters.** While I'm an admirer of concise copy, some search engines actually reward those sites that have more words per page. On average, today's top search engines seem to have a preference for pages with content in the 1,000-word range. But that's just an average. For Google's top ten search results, the average number of words per page is about 950; for Yahoo!, it's closer to 1,300 words per page.

Remember, though, that the way you present your content is secondary to the content itself. You have to start with authoritative content and then work from there.

Adding Content to "Noncontent" Sites

I can already hear some webmasters complaining that their sites aren't "content-based" and that they're not trying to or can't provide authoritative content to site visitors. This complaint is common among business sites: "I'm just trying to sell some-thing here, not be a Wikipedia," is the frequent response. "I'm not selling anything unique; how can I be authoritative?" is another. These webmasters think they can forgo the content thing and focus instead on other elements of SEO.

While other forms of optimization are always important, it's pure bunk that content isn't important for any particular website. If you're not providing content to your site's visitors, just what are you providing? Pretty pictures? Almost every site on the web provides some sort of content to its visitors; the type of content differs, of course, but it's always content.

A business site, for example, provides information about the company itself or the products it sells. If you think this is generic information, you have no business being on the web—or even being in business. You need to discuss your company or products in as much detail and with as much enthusiasm as you can muster. And the information you provide doesn't stop at simple company or product facts; you can talk about how your company benefits your community or customer base, or how customers can make better use out of your products.

In short, every site can present unique content. You may need to be creative, and you definitely need to know what your customer is looking for, but then it's a simple mat-ter of Copywriting 101.

The Least You Need to Know

◆ The most important SEO tool is your site's content.

◆ Quality content not only attracts more quality inbound links, but it also ranks higher with search engines that do a better job in determining useful and relevant web pages—such as Google.

◆ Authoritative content needn't be exhaustive; concise content that precisely targets a specific topic may be better than a comprehensive listing of facts. (That said, pages in the 1,000-word range tend to rank higher than shorter—or longer—pages.)

◆ Your page shouldn't just be a listing of facts; the information you present should be presented in full, grammatically correct, properly punctuated sentences and paragraphs.

◆ The three keys to improving a site's content are to provide authoritative information, write engaging copy, and craft the content in an SEO-friendly fashion.

Optimizing Your Site's Keywords

In This Chapter

- ◆ Understanding why keywords are important
- ◆ Choosing your keywords
- ◆ Using keywords in anchor text and HTML tags
- ◆ Incorporating keywords into your site's body text

By now you should be aware that keywords are an important factor in SEO. But what exactly is a keyword—and how do you use them in your site's code and content?

It could be said that all search optimization revolves around the use of keywords. Whether you're talking the content on a page or the code that underlies that content, you use keywords to give your content and code more impact. It's vital, then, that you learn how to create a list of keywords relevant to your site—and how to include them in your site's coding and content.

That's what this chapter is about.

What Is a Keyword—and Why Is It Important?

A keyword is a word that someone includes in a search query. Similarly, a key phrase is a group of words that someone includes in a query. In other words, keywords and phrases are what people search for—and how they ultimately find your page on the web.

If someone is searching for the word *tennis*, only sites that somewhere include the keyword *tennis* in their content or underlying HTML code will be a match for that query. If your site doesn't mention the word *tennis* at all, it won't be a match and won't show up in the search results. So if you want to target your site to people who search for "tennis," you'd better include the keyword *tennis* somewhere on your site.

Similarly, if someone is searching for the phrase "tennis racket," only sites that include that phrase will register as a match. If your site includes the word *tennis* but not *racket*, it won't be a match. You need to include the entire key phrase somewhere on your site.

In short, keywords are important because they're what people are searching for. If your site includes the keywords that people are searching for, it will show up higher in any search engine's results than sites that don't include those keywords; in fact, a site that doesn't include the relevant keywords probably won't show up in those searches at all.

Choosing the Best Keywords

How, then, do you determine which keywords people are searching for? As I've said before in this book, it's a matter of learning how to *think like the customer*. In other words, you need to get inside searchers' heads to determine which words they're using in their queries.

Performing Keyword Research

The art of determining which keywords to use is called *keyword research*, and it's a key part of SEO. When you know which keywords and phrases your target customers are likely to use, you can optimize your site for those words and phrases; if you don't know how they're searching, you don't know what to optimize.

While you can conduct extensive (and expensive) market research to determine how your target audience is searching, or even guess what the top searches are, there are simpler and more effective ways to get smart about this. Several companies offer keyword research tools, which are software utilities or web-based services that compile and analyze keyword search statistics from all the major search engines. You can use the results from these keyword research tools to determine which are the most powerful keywords to include on your site.

 Stop!

Don't guess at what keywords searchers are using or assume that the way you search is the way everyone else searches. Instead, use keyword research tools or traditional market research to determine the real keywords used.

How Keyword Research Tools Work

Most keyword research tools work by matching the thrust or content of your website with keywords relevant to your content; they've already searched through hundreds of thousands of possible keywords and phrases on the most popular search engines and mapped the results to their own database. You enter a word or phrase that describes what your site has to offer, and the research tool returns a list of words or phrases related to that description, in descending order of search popularity.

For example, if you run a web-hosting company, you might describe your site with the phrase "web hosting." The keyword research tool, then, would return a list of keywords and phrases like the one in Figure 5.1; those words and phrases at the top of the list are the ones that show up most often in search results and, thus, will best improve the ranking of your site on those search engines.

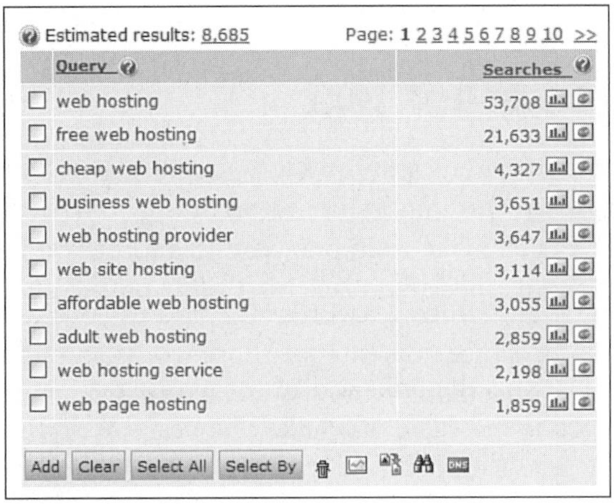

Estimated results: 8,685	Page: 1 2 3 4 5 6 7 8 9 10 >>
Query	**Searches**
☐ web hosting	53,708
☐ free web hosting	21,633
☐ cheap web hosting	4,327
☐ business web hosting	3,651
☐ web hosting provider	3,647
☐ web site hosting	3,114
☐ affordable web hosting	3,055
☐ adult web hosting	2,859
☐ web hosting service	2,198
☐ web page hosting	1,859

Add | Clear | Select All | Select By

Figure 5.1

Sample results from the KeywordDiscovery keyword research tool.

In this example, the top-ranking phrases are "web hosting" (no surprise), with 53,708 hits, and "free web hosting," with 21,633 hits. All the other phrases fell well short of these top phrases, none rising above the 5,000-hit level. Given these results, you'd choose to focus your efforts on the key phrases "web hosting" and "free web hosting," and ignore the other, less-searched-for phrases.

Choosing a Keyword Research Tool

When it comes to choosing a keyword research tool, the most popular among SEO professionals is Trellian's KeywordDiscovery (www.keyworddiscovery.com). KeywordDiscovery is available on a subscription basis; a standard subscription costs $69.95 per month.

Also popular with professionals is Wordtracker (www.wordtracker.com). Like KeywordDiscovery, Wordtracker is available on a subscription basis, with a $59.95 per month cost.

Finally, WordZe (www.wordze.com) is an up-and-coming keyword research tool. It's priced a little lower than KeywordDiscovery or Wordtracker, at just $35 per month.

The best of these tools provide more than just raw keyword research data. They may also include features such as industry keyword tracking (the top keywords that drive traffic to sites in specific industries), spelling mistake research (common misspellings in user queries), related keywords, seasonal trends, and the like.

Once you use a keyword research tool to generate a list of top-ranking keywords and phrases, you can work on optimizing your pages to include these words and phrases. We examine how in the next few sections.

Using Keywords in Anchor Text

Let's start by recalling the importance of links to your site's search ranking. Not only are inbound links from other sites important, but so are the outbound links you make to other sites and the links you make from one page to another on your own site. Most search engines (Google especially) place high value on the quantity and quality of such links.

That said, the text that contains the link—called the *anchor text*—is one of the ways the search engines determine the value of a link. The best way to increase the value of an outbound or intrasite link is to include keywords in the anchor text. This lets the searchbots know that the site you're linking to is related to the keyword—and is thus a more relevant link.

For example, if one of your top keywords is *pastrami* and you're linking to the Carnegie Deli website, the anchor text that links to the website should include the word *pastrami*. In this instance, you might write and link from the following sentence:

> Some of the best pastrami sandwiches in New York can be found at the world-famous Carnegie Deli.

While you could limit the link to the phrase "Carnegie Deli," the anchor text would not include your keyword *pastrami*. Better, then, to format the entire sentence—including the word "pastrami" as the anchor text for the link.

Obviously, you create the link for the anchor text using basic HTML codes. This sort of linking is done automatically by most HTML editing or web page–creation programs, or you can code the text manually, like this:

```
<a href="http://www.carnegiedeli.com">Some of the best pastrami sandwiches
in New York can be found at the world-famous Carnegie Deli.</a>
```

SEO Tip _____

It's also important that the anchor text accompanying links to your site from other sites include the keywords you want to be ranked for. Make sure you communicate with linking sites so they know the best anchor text to use for their links to your site.

The takeaway here is to always include one or more keywords in the anchor text you use to link to related sites. Don't link without anchoring the link with keywords!

Using Keywords in HTML Tags

The linking tag isn't the only HTML tag in which you can or should make use of your chosen keywords. You should also use keywords in your site's **<TITLE>**, **<META>**, and heading tags, as discussed next.

Using Keywords in the ‹TITLE› Tag

One of the most important things that a search-bot looks at to determine the content of your site is your site's title—as determined by the **<TITLE>** tag. For this reason, you want to include the most important keyword or phrase as your site's title—but in an organic fashion.

Search Note

Learn more about use of HTML tags for SEO in Chapter 6, "Optimizing Your Site's HTML Tags."

You don't want to force the keyword into the title, yet it's important that you use the keyword to describe your site.

For example, if your site is about various types of fruit, and your top three keywords are *apples*, *oranges*, and *peaches*, you want to try to get all three of these keywords into the title. Assuming that the name of your site is The Fruit Site, here's one way to do so:

```
<TITLE>The Fruit Site: All About Apples, Oranges, and Peaches</TITLE>
```

See how this little trick works? You essentially create a title (the official name of your site) and a subtitle (after the colon), with the subtitle being used to hold the descriptive keywords.

Alternately, you may want to rename your site to include one or more relevant keywords. But this option is good only as long as the keyword stays relevant; since the keywords users search for can change over time, you want to make sure your site name doesn't become outmoded, at least in SEO terms.

Using Keywords in ‹META› Tags

We discuss **<META>** tags in more depth in Chapter 6. Suffice it to say that **<META>** tags can be used to force-feed keyword information to searchbots; these are tags that only search engine crawlers see, not your site's visitors.

For example, the **<META> KEYWORDS** tag provides searchbots with the keywords you choose to highlight on your site. Continuing the fruit example, if your keywords are *apples*, *oranges*, and *peaches*, you might enter a **<META>** tag like this one:

```
<META NAME="keywords" CONTENT="apples, oranges, peaches">
```

Note that this tag works by defining the **NAME** attribute as *keywords*, and then by defining the content of the attribute as your three keywords—listed one after another, separated by commas. A searchbot will read this tag, register the keywords, and—perhaps—use those keywords to help index the page.

 Stop! _____

Due to abuse by overzealous site spammers, many search engines now discount or even ignore the **<META> KEYWORDS** tag. While there's little harm in using this tag as described, it doesn't have the impact that it used to have.

Using Keywords in Heading Tags

More important than **<META>** tags are those tags used to create headings within your page's body text. That's because most searchbots assume (rightly so, in most instances) that a topic given its own major heading is an important topic on your site.

For that reason, you want to break up your copy into two or more major sections, announce each section with a heading or subheading, and include one or more keywords in each heading. When coding in HTML, headings are created using tags **<H1>** through **<H6>,** with **<H1>** being the highest-level heading and **<H6>** being the lowest level. You might create a first-level heading with code like this:

SEO Tip

Many search experts now believe that lower-level tags (<H2> through <H6>) have slightly more influence on search rankings than the first-level <H1> tag. This argues for the creation of a hierarchical heading structure on your page.

```
<H1>The Truth About Apples</H1>
```

Using Keywords in Other Tags

Keywords can also be used in other HTML tags for positive effect. For example, surrounding keywords with bold (**<B>**), emphasized (**<EM>**), or strong (**<STRONG>**) tells searchbots that this particular word or phrase is important and, thus, more relevant—and, since searchbots are all about relevancy, this is a good thing.

SEO Tip

It also helps if the keyword is somehow incorporated into the file name of the image.

You should also use keywords, when appropriate, in the **<IMG>** tag's **ALT** attribute. This attribute provides alternate text in case an image can't be displayed, and is used to describe the image to searchbots, which can't otherwise determine the content of an image. For example, a picture of an apple might utilize the following **<IMG> ALT** tag:

```
<IMG SRC="apple.jpg" ALT="picture of an apple">
```

Using Keywords in Your Site's Body Text

While it's important to use keywords with selected HTML tags, it's more important to incorporate keywords and phrases within the real content of your site—that is, within the body text itself. Of course, keywords shouldn't just be thrown into the text randomly; they must flow organically, as part of the underlying content itself.

Let's look at how to do this.

Determining the Right Keyword Density

First, know that the more often you use a keyword in your body text, the more likely it is that searchbots will register the keyword—to a point. If you include a keyword too many times, searchbots will think you're artificially "stuffing" the keyword into your phrase, with no regard for the actual content. If you're suspected of keyword stuffing in this fashion, don't be surprised to see your search ranking actually decrease—or your page disappear completely from that search engine's search results. (Search engines don't like keyword stuffing ….)

Thus, you need to determine the correct keyword density when you're optimizing the content of a web page. What is an optimal keyword density? That depends. If you have a lot of different keywords on a long page, you could have a density of 20 percent or more and still rank fine. If you have only a handful of keywords on a short page, a 5 percent keyword density might be too much. The key is to make sure your page is readable; if it sounds stilted or awkward due to unnecessary keyword repetition, chances are, a searchbot will also think that you're overusing your keywords.

> ### Search Note
>
> Keyword density is the number of times a keyword or phrase appears compared to the total number of words on a page.

Keyword-Oriented Copywriting for the Web

So what's the best way to incorporate keywords into your site's content? It definitely takes skill, which is something a professional copywriter has. Assuming you're not a professional copywriter, however, let's look at a few things to keep in mind as you're crafting your site's copy.

First, know that web copywriting is very similar to direct response copywriting. You have to describe what you're providing in words, not pictures—and, if you're selling something, provide a strong "why to buy" message. The big difference between direct response copywriting and web copywriting is that, with web copywriting, you have two different audiences: the site's visitors and the search engines.

Search Note

Learn more about keyword stuffing and other bad practices in Chapter 18, "Avoiding the Most Common Search Engine Mistakes."

This means you have to provide readable, compelling copy for your visitors, while at the same time incorporating all the necessary keywords and phrases that matter to the search engines—and in the fashion that influences how the search engines rank a page. You don't want to sacrifice one for the other; never make your page less readable just to cram in another keyword. Go for readability first, and then incorporate the keywords as you can.

One way to improve both readability and search optimization is to break your copy into small sections or chunks of text, and then introduce each section with a heading or subheading. As we discussed previously, searchbots look for keywords in your heading tags; headings also help readers identify important sections on your page. So chunking up your text benefits both your audiences.

Two other good places to include keywords are in your page's first and last paragraphs. Not only do searchbots look more closely at the beginning and end of your page and tend to skip the middle parts, but readers look to the first and last paragraphs to introduce key ideas and then summarize your page's content. It's just like in writing a newspaper article; the first and last graphs are most important.

When you incorporate keywords and phrases into your text, you have to do so in a natural fashion—while using the word or phrase verbatim. So if your key phrase is "budget European travel," you have to use that exact phrase—in a way that doesn't sound forced. This is a definite copywriting challenge, but one that can be met.

At the end of the day, you have to create compelling copy that includes all the important keywords and phrases you've previously identified. It's not enough to just include those key phrases, repeated as often as possible; doing so results in copy that sounds artificial. Imagine a site that is selling iPod accessories and the resulting key phrase–stuffed copy:

> Our iPod accessories are the best iPod accessories because our store sells iPod accessories.

Not very compelling or informative—even though you do get the point that the website sells iPod accessories.

So that's not the way to do it; not only will visitors be turned off by the repetitive and ultimately uninformative copy, but many search engines will penalize you for keyword stuffing. Instead, you have to get across the point that you sell iPod accessories (using that exact phrase) within the natural flow of your page's copy. Write for your visitors first and for the search engines second.

One last thing: on the web, there's little benefit to short copy. Not only do readers want as much information as possible, but longer copy provides more opportunity for you to place your keywords and phrases without overly increasing keyword density. Let's face it, if you have 10 keywords to include, it's easier to do so on a 1,000-word page than on one that only includes 100 words total. (Put another way, a shorter page is more likely to sound keyword stuffed than a longer one.)

So write more copy, if you need to. In fact, some studies say that pages in the 1,000-word range rank best with most search engines; certainly, anything less than 250 words is too little. Use the extra words to add more keywords and phrases to your page—and to provide more useful information to your site's visitors.

The Least You Need to Know

- ◆ Keywords and key phrases are words and phrases that users use in their search queries.

- ◆ To be seen as relevant by the search engines, you must include keywords and phrases on your web pages.

- ◆ To determine the best keywords for your site, get to know how your customers are searching—and use a keyword research tool.

- ◆ Once you determine what keywords to use, incorporate those keywords in your site's anchor text and appropriate HTML tags.

- ◆ You should also work your keywords and phrases into your site's body text—in a natural fashion and without "keyword stuffing."

Chapter 6

Optimizing Your Site's HTML Tags

In This Chapter

◆ Understanding how to optimize the **<TITLE>** tag

◆ Learning how best to use **<META>** tags

◆ Creating the most effective header tags

In Chapter 5, we discussed why keywords are important to SEO and how to choose the right keywords for your web pages. Well, one of the primary uses of keywords is within your site's HTML code; most searchbots scan specific HTML tags for information they use in indexing a page. Insert your keywords and phrases into these tags, and you'll improve your site's results for that search engine.

Which HTML tags do you need to focus on? There are a few, but they're relatively easy to work with—assuming you know a little HTML, of course. Read on to learn more.

Working with the ‹TITLE› Tag

Let's start at the very top of your web page, at the page's title. The title is the text that appears in the title bar of a web browser, as shown in Figure 6.1; the title should reflect your page's official name (if it has one) and content. It's also an effective place to use your chosen keywords.

Figure 6.1

The title bar in Internet Explorer—displaying the name and content of a web page.

Why Your Page's Title Is Important

Your page's title is important because it's one of the first places that searchbots look to determine the content of your page. Searchbots figure, hopefully rightly so, that the title accurately reflects what the page is about; for example, if you have a page titled "The Dutch Apple Pie Page," that page is about Dutch apple pies. Unless you mistakenly or purposefully mistitle your page, the searchbot will skim off keywords and phrases from the title to use in its search engine index.

In addition, when your page appears on a search engine's results page, the title is what the search engine uses as the listing name. Using the *New York Times* example, you can see in Figure 6.2 that the page's Google listing is identical to the text displayed in a web browser for that page.

Figure 6.2

Title text displayed in Google's search results.

> The **New York Times** - Breaking News, World News & Multimedia
> Online edition of the newspaper's news and commentary. [Registration required]
> www.nytimes.com/ - Similar pages - Note this

Search Note
The title also appears in the favorites list when a visitor adds your site as a favorite.

For all these reasons, you need to get your most important keywords and phrases into your page's title—which you do via the HTML **<TITLE>** tag.

Creating the ‹TITLE› Tag

The **<TITLE>** tag appears in the head of your document, before the body text. It's a simple tag, really, that looks something like this:

```
<TITLE>Insert your title here</TITLE>
```

Just insert your chosen title text between the **<TITLE>** and **</TITLE>** tags. Whatever is between the tags is your page's official title, and this is what appears in the web browser's title bar.

The length of your title cannot exceed 64 characters. If you include more text than this, your title will be truncated.

What's the ideal length of a title? Keeping the 64-character limit in mind, you should probably pace your title to include from 3 to 10 words total. This makes the title both readable for users (short enough to scan) and useful for search engines (long enough to include a handful of keywords).

What to Put in Your Title

Now we come to the crux of the matter: what exactly should you include in your title?

First and foremost, you should include the official name of your page or site (unless, that is, the name exceeds 64 characters—in this instance, consider abbreviating). Since the title is what users see in search results and when they make your page a favorite, you want them to know what page they're going to visit. Give your page a descriptive and distinctive name, something better than "Page 3," and then make sure everybody sees it.

Next, you want to tell people and searchbots what the page is about. That means including your most important keywords and phrases—as many as you have space for. Of course, your page name may include a keyword or two, and that's great. But if you need to attach more descriptive words, do so immediately after the page name, following some sort of divider character—perhaps a colon (:), a semicolon (;), a vertical line (|), a dash (-), or even a simple comma (,).

For example, if your site is named "Used Car Parts" and you sell parts for Fords, Chevys, and the like, you might enter the following **<TITLE>** tag:

```
<TITLE>Used Car Parts: Ford, Chevy, Dodge,
Toyota, Honda, Nissan, Audi</TITLE>
```

That's 63 characters and 10 words, both of which fit within our guidelines. Users will see the name of the site in their title bar and in the search results, and searchbots will link this page to queries regarding all major car brands.

What NOT to Put in Your Title

Given how important your page's title is to your ultimate search ranking, should you avoid putting certain things in the **<TITLE>** tag? You bet—they include the following:

- **Nothing.** Probably the least useful title is the one that isn't there at all. If you happen to leave your **<TITLE>** tag blank, the file name for that page will appear as the page's title. So if you leave the **<TITLE>** tag for your home page blank, you'll see the text "index.htm" in the browser's title bar—and that's how Google and other search engines will display your page info.

- **The site's URL.** Similarly, using your site's URL as the page's title has little value. Searchbots and users already know the URL; why waste valuable title space for that?

- **Internal navigation.** Too many webmasters think in terms of the project and, thus, use title pages (quite logically) with internal names, such as "Page 3." That's not very informative for either searchbots or real people, and it should be avoided.

- **Too much text.** Remember the 64-character limit? Well, if you use 65 or more characters, know that anything past the 64th character will simply be omitted in the title bar and on search result page descriptions.

- **Repeated keywords.** Here's another big no-no, for many different reasons. When you repeat a keyword two or more times, many searchbots will view this as intentional keyword stuffing and penalize you for that. The penalty may be a lower search ranking, or it may be a full deletion from that search engine's index. So if you run a site for a coffee house, don't use the following title code:

```
<TITLE>Mike's Coffeehouse: Coffee Coffee Coffee and More Coffee</TITLE>
```

Working with ‹META› Tags

Next up on our list of important HTML tags is the **<META>** tag, which is used to convey so-called metadata to searchbots. The **<META>** tag is actually several tags, each with its own specific attribute. You can insert multiple **<META>** tags (one for each attribute) into the head of your document, like this:

```
<HEAD>
<TITLE>Mike's Coffee Pages</TITLE>
<META NAME="DESCRIPTION" CONTENT="Everything you need to know about coffee
drinks!">
<META NAME="KEYWORDS" CONTENT="coffee, drink, beverage, java, joe,
cappuccino, latte">
</HEAD>
```

As you can see, there are two primary **<META>** attributes—**DESCRIPTION** and **KEYWORDS.** Each attribute is defined by the **NAME** attribute, as in **NAME="ATTRIBUTE".** Then the **CONTENT** attribute is used to define the content for the description or keywords. It's all fairly straightforward.

The only problem with **<META>** tags is that they've been so overused that many searchbots now ignore them. Back in the early days of the web, SEO experts realized that they could use the **<META> KEYWORDS** attribute to convey a large list of keywords for a page; the result was that some pages stuffed 500 or 1,000 keywords into the tag. While that may have worked 10 years ago, it doesn't today.

That said, you can't ignore **<META>** tags because they do feed information to some search engines. While some search engines have devalued the tag, others still look at it—and, in some instances, the information in the tag helps users determine what a page is about.

> **Search Note**
>
> There are more **<META>** attributes than the ones listed here (such as **CHANNEL, DATE,** and so on), but they either aren't read by searchbots or don't affect your search ranking.

Working with the DESCRIPTION Attribute

We'll start by looking at the **DESCRIPTION** attribute. Some search engines use the text assigned to this attribute as the description for your web page in their search results. This means you want to think of the **DESCRIPTION** text as a short promotional blurb that describes what your page is about.

The tag works like this:

```
<META NAME="DESCRIPTION" CONTENT="Insert your description here">
```

The variable text is the bit between the quotation marks. It's read as a complete text string—a block of text, as it were. (And it's okay to include commas in the **DESCRIPTION** text; they're treated as is.) Within this descriptive text, be sure to include as many keywords or phrases that fit naturally; avoid keyword stuffing.

Your descriptions should be different for different pages on your site; you shouldn't use the same generic site description for each page. You also shouldn't duplicate your page's title in the description; use the **DESCRIPTION** tag to provide additional information not possible in the title. For length, try to limit your description to about 160 characters; anything longer will be truncated in most search results pages. And, once again, don't use keyword stuffing!

Working with the KEYWORDS Attribute

The second important **<META>** tag uses the **KEYWORDS** attribute. As you might suspect, this attribute is your opportunity to tell searchbots which keywords your page is targeting.

The problem with the **KEYWORDS** attribute is that spammers quickly learned to abuse it, using it to stuff hundreds or thousands of keywords into a single page—sometimes stuffing the same keyword dozens of times, trying to improve the page's rank. Well, that sort of artificial SEO is easy to catch and soon backfired; many search engines today simply ignore the **<META> KEYWORDS** tag.

Which search engines still pay attention to this tag? Yahoo! and Ask.com do; Google and Microsoft Live Search don't.

So half of the major search engines support the **KEYWORDS** tag, and half (including Google) don't. While you might get no value (positive or negative) from a **KEYWORDS** tag with Google or Live Search, it still will help your ranking with Ask.com and Yahoo!—which makes it worth using.

It's easy to add this tag to your page's HTML code. Just use the following template:

```
<META NAME="KEYWORDS" CONTENT="keyword 1, keyword 2, keyword 3">
```

Separate each keyword or phrase with a comma. You can include as many keywords or phrases as you like; capitalization doesn't matter. And—this is important—the keywords you include in this tag *don't* actually have to appear on the web page.

So, for example, if you run a sports site and want to include sports teams as key phrases, you might use the following code:

```
<META NAME="KEYWORDS" CONTENT="Indianapolis Colts, Denver Broncos,
Pittsburgh Steelers, Green Bay Packers">
```

One good use of the **KEYWORDS** tag is to include common misspellings of legitimate keywords used on your site. For example, if you use the keyword *Spider-Man*, you might use the **KEYWORDS** tag to include the misspellings *Spiderman*, *Spyderman*, *Spidderman*, and *Spidermann*. Similarly, you can use the tag to list synonyms for your actual keywords.

Bottom line: because it may help you with Yahoo! and Ask.com (and won't hurt you with Google and Live Search), it's worth inserting your keywords into the **<META> KEYWORDS** tag. Insert as many keywords as you like—including common misspellings, synonyms, and other related words and phrases.

> **SEO Tip** _____
>
> If you don't want your page listed in search indexes for some reason, you can use the **<META>** ROBOTS attribute, like this: **<META name="ROBOTS" content="NOINDEX">**.

Working with Header Tags

One last class of HTML tag has a significant impact on your search ranking, and that's the header tags. A header is a heading or subheading within your body text, kind of like a newspaper headline or the headings between sections in this book. The HTML standard lets you use six different levels of headings, from **<H1>** to **<H6>,** in descending order.

Headers are important because most searchbots look in these tags for content information. They figure that if a topic or keyword is important enough to be included in the header, it probably describes your page's content—and it's important enough to index.

So, first of all, you have to organize the information on your page into short chunks of text, and then introduce each text block with its own header. In the header, include text that describes the following text and uses, in an organic fashion, as many keywords and phrases as you can.

The form of this HTML code is simple:

```
<H1>This is the header text.</H1>
```

Obviously, insert your own text between the "on" and "off" tags. And use the other header tags (**<H2>**, **<H3>**, **<H4>**, and so on) for lower-level headers.

Stop!

Know that most cutting-edge web designers have switched from the older **<H1>**-style heading tags to Cascading Style Sheet (CSS) **<DIV>** and **<SPAN>** codes. That's unfortunate, as most search engines look for the traditional heading tags to determine the content of a page. If you want to optimize your ranking in most search indexes, you'll have to dump the CSS coding and switch back to the **<H1>** and **<H2>** tags instead.

The Least You Need to Know

- Most searchbots read particular lines of HTML code to determine a page's content and indexibility; this HTML is a perfect place to insert relevant keywords and phrases that describe your site.

- The **<TITLE>** tag is perhaps the most important tag, as all search engines use it and your title text appears in the title bar when the page is viewed in a web browser.

- The **<META> DESCRIPTION** tag is supported by most search engines—and is used to provide the description shown on search results pages.

- The **<META> KEYWORDS** tag is used by Yahoo! and Ask.com (but not Google and Live Search); it's a good place to list misspellings, synonyms, and alternate words and phrases to your actual keywords.

- Most search engines look to a page's header tags for indications of the page's most important content.

Optimizing Your Site's Design

In This Chapter

- ◆ Understanding how to optimize your page design
- ◆ Learning how to assign keywords to pages
- ◆ Discovering how to organize your site

As you've learned, the content of your site is important to optimizing your search results. But the actual design of your site is also important, if for no other reason than that a bad design can negatively affect where your site ranks with the major search engines.

That's right, you can do certain things with your site that will actually lower your search results—or, in some instances, make your site invisible to searchbots. Assuming that you want your site seen and indexed, that means you need to pay attention to a few design basics.

SEO Tips for Page Design

Let's start with some tips you can use to optimize individual pages on your website. These are universal tips that work on any type of page on any type of website.

Use Text, Not Pictures (or Videos or Flash ...)

If you remember nothing else from this chapter, remember this: search engine crawlers read text and nothing but text. They don't read images, they don't read Flash animations, they don't read videos. Every element on your page other than text is essentially invisible to searchbots. It's only the text that matters.

Why is this important? Well, many sites put a fair amount of content in nontext elements. In fact, many overdesigned sites use nothing but Flash animation on their introductory pages, which not only annoys many users, but also causes most searchbots to skip completely over those pages—and perhaps the rest of the site.

That's right, a complete Flash page is basically a blank page, as far as the major search engines are concerned. If the page is completely in Flash, the search engines have no idea what the page is about. They can get some idea of the content from the page's **<TITLE>** and **<META>** tags, or even from the anchor text of inbound links to that page, but that's not nearly as good as reading the site's actual content—which they can't do because there's no text to read.

The same thing goes with pages that rely on images or videos for the bulk of their content. A searchbot can't look at an image or view a video; it has no way (short of the file's **ALT** tags) to determine what the image or video is about. Again, the page appears blank to the searchbots.

So the first thing you need to do is throw out those designers who want to Flash up your site, and take a back-to-basics, text-based approach. You probably don't need to get rid of all images, animations, and videos, but they need to be downplayed on the page—and supplemented by well-written, descriptive text.

Put the Most Important Stuff First on the Page

Searchbots start at the top of a page and then read downward. Like human readers, they may not read the entire page. So it's essential to put the most important elements at the top of your page, in the main headings and initial paragraphs. A searchbot will see your leading content and register it as important; content lower on the page will be registered as subsidiary, if it's noted at all.

Use Headings and Subheadings

Another way to tell a searchbot that something is important is to include it in a heading or subheading on the page. As you learned in Chapter 6, most searchbots single out your page's heading tags, assuming that they highlight the most important content of your site. So you need to use headings to separate and highlight content on your page, and to highlight your most important keywords and phrases.

For example, you might construct a page in this fashion:

```
<BODY>
<H1>This is the First Level-One Heading</H1>
 <H2>This is a level-two heading</H2>
 <P>This is a paragraph of body text.</P>
 <H2>This is another level-two heading</H2>
 <P>This is another paragraph of body text.</P>
<H1>This is Another Level-One Heading</H1>
 <H2>This is a new level-two heading</H2>
 <P>This is a new paragraph of body text.</P>
 <H2>This is another level-two heading</H2>
 <P>This is another paragraph of body text.</P>
</BODY>
```

Of course, you don't have to be as symmetrical as this example; that is, you don't have to always have two **<H2>** heads after each **<H1>** head, nor do you need two **<H1>** heads. The point, however, is to break out your information in a logical hierarchy, and use the heading tags to direct attention to the following text and display appropriate keywords and phrases.

Simplify Long URLs

We discuss dynamically generated web pages later in this chapter, but one bad thing about this type of page is that the URL is typically long and complex—which is not ideal for either users or searchbots.

Here's the deal. Searchbots like URLs that are short and simple. (For that matter, so do human beings; ever try to type one of those URLs—typically from a news site or online retailer—that goes on and on and on for several lines? Next to impossible!) Searchbots have trouble deciphering overly long URLs, especially those that have values after a "?" character. The longer your URL, the less likely it is that it will be indexed by the major search engines.

For that reason, you need to create search engine–friendly URLs. Use short file names for each page, and keep the navigation as flat as possible to shorten the file path.

This is an example of a URL that is longer than it needs to be:

```
http://www.mysite.com/folder1/folder2/folder3/folder4/
thisisthelongnameformypage.htm
```

And here's a URL that is shorter and friendlier:

```
http://www.mysite.com/mainfolder/ashortfilename.htm
```

Which would you rather type? Well, that's the one that searchbots prefer, too.

For those dynamically generated pages with lots of "?" values, consider performing a URL rewrite. This essentially creates a URL lookup table for your site; when a server query is generated, it checks the lookup table for the appropriate page and returns a virtual path to the file instead of using dynamically generated values.

For example, this might be the way the dynamically generated URL looks in its original form:

```
http://www.mysite.com/Article?Id=52&Page=5
```

And this is what it might look like after the URL rewrite:

```
http://www.mysite.com/Article/ID/52/Page/5/
```

Not the simplest of URLs, but at least it's readable by most searchbots.

To perform a URL rewrite, use a tool such as ISAPI_Rewrite (www.isapirewrite.com) on the Windows side, or mod-rewrite (httpd.apache.org/docs/1.3/mod/mod_rewrite.html) for Apache servers.

SEO Tips for Keyword Assignment

Now we look at some tips that involve thoughtful placement of keywords and phrases throughout your site. That's right—not every keyword belongs on every page of your site.

Determine Which Keywords Go on Which Pages

Not every keyword you've targeted belongs on every page of your website. You have to figure out which pages of your site which keywords belong on.

It's not a simple matter of stuffing all your keywords onto every page; that's bad form and could result in keyword-stuffing penalties. Besides, that typically results in some fairly unreadable pages.

Instead, look at the pages of your website and see where your keywords and phrases fit in, where they make the most sense. Don't force a keyword on a page; make sure it's a natural fit, not an artificial one.

Then, to ensure that all your keywords are used somewhere on your site, make a list of your keywords and phrases and another list of your website pages. Make sure that each keyword or phrase is used at least once on your site and that each page includes at least one keyword or phrase. No page should lack keywords, and no keyword should go unused.

Make Every Page a Gateway Page

As much as you might wish or plan otherwise, not every visitor to your site is going to get there via your home page. Some people click links from other sites that take them to subsidiary pages; some search engines index pages deep into your site's navigation. So it's likely that a good amount of your site's traffic will find your site through some subsidiary page.

This means, of course, that every page on your site can and should be a gateway page. It's not just the home page that deserves your SEO efforts; every page needs to be optimized. And here's the good news—every page can be optimized in a different way.

This is the takeaway from this little piece of information: each page of your site can be a *different* gateway page. That is, you may optimize one page for a particular keyword and another page for a different keyword. This way, both pages can appear in search results pages—but for different queries. Not all pages have to or should match the same query; use all the pages on your site to multiply the number of search results pages that your site matches.

Use Keywords in Your File and Folder Names

Per our file-naming discussion previously in this chapter, you want to keep your page file names as short as possible. However, you also benefit from including keywords in your file names—and in your folder names. That's because searchbots will look at the list of files and folders on your site; if the searchbot finds a matching keyword there, you'll score big points.

So, for example, instead of naming a page something like **page32.htm,** you might name it **horses.htm** (assuming it's about horses, that is). If you're inserting a phrase instead of a single keyword, separate the words of the phrase with hyphens (not underlines). So if your key phrase is "Ford auto parts," you might name the page file **ford-auto-parts.htm.** You get the idea.

Tips for Site Organization

Let's conclude by moving beyond the page to address the organization of your entire site. Are there ways to organize your site's pages that deliver higher search rankings? You bet there are ....

Be Shallow

When it comes to the files and folders of your website, you need to be organized. While it's tempting to organize with a deep hierarchy, full of subfolders inside of subfolders inside of subfolders, that makes it harder for searchbots to find pages buried deep in your site. (It also makes for overly long URLs, which we now know are not good things.) It's better to keep your site hierarchy relatively shallow, with more pages on the same level.

For example, Figure 7.1 shows a deep hierarchy with multiple folder/directory levels. This is not the best organization; the URLs for the deepest pages look like this:

```
http://www.mysite.com/homepagelevel/products/productcategory/productline/
product.htm
```

Figure 7.1

A website with a deep hierarchy—not good.

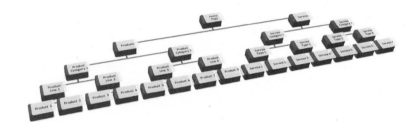

Figure 7.2 shows a reorganization of the same web pages into a shallower folder/directory structure. The distance from the home page to the deepest page is only two levels, as opposed to the five levels in the first organization. Much easier to navigate; the URLs for the deepest levels look like this:

```
http://www.mysite.com/homepagelevel/products/product.htm
```

Figure 7.2

A website with a narrow hierarchy—it takes fewer clicks to get from top to bottom.

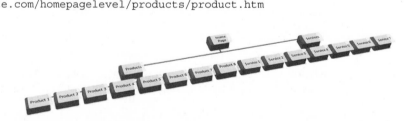

Here's the reality. The more clicks it takes for a visitor to get from your home page to the deepest page on your site, the lower that page's ranking will be with most search engines. You get a higher ranking by minimizing the number of clicks.

That said, there's no reason to limit your website to just a single level. Being too shallow is also difficult to navigate and makes for messier folders. It's okay to go two or three levels deep, really.

SEO Tip _____

After you map out your site's organization, you should create a *sitemap* of the structure and then submit the sitemap to the major search engines; this helps them index all the pages on your site. Learn more about sitemaps in Chapter 11, "Mapping Your Site for Best Results."

Avoid Duplicate Content

Whatever your hierarchy, one of the problems with larger websites is that you might have different navigational paths to the same information. Imagine, for example, that you sell 20 types of widgets in 20 different colors in 20 different cities. Users might want to navigate by widget > color > city, or by city > widget > color, or by color > widget > city, and so on. In any case, the final content page is the same whether they go by product or location—which means you could end up with the same content on multiple pages. And, as you're starting to learn, many search engines don't like duplicate content; they think you're trying to spam, and they introduce a penalty or even a blackout.

Stop! _____

It goes without saying that you shouldn't deliberately introduce duplicative content to your site. This is deliberate content spamming and will be noticed by the major search engines.

In short, you need to provide the specific content your users are asking for, while also trying to optimize your site for the search engines. The solution is to use a single page for multiple navigational paths—and thus avoid the duplicative content that can penalize you with the search engines. This is done via what is called *dynamic drill-down navigation* or *faceted navigation*, where the pages in your site are all essentially on your same level, but accessed through different virtual paths; there are no predefined paths or hierarchy, just what a user chooses dynamically.

Figure 7.3 shows an example of faceted navigation, from Best Buy's website; users can drill down through the results by selecting various facets, such as TV type, screen size, and price range. To add this type of dynamic drill-down navigation to your site, turn to a tool such as Dieselpoint's Search (www.dieselpoint.com) or the Endeca Information Access Platform (www.endeca.com).

Figure 7.3

Dynamic drill-down naviga-tion on the Best Buy website.

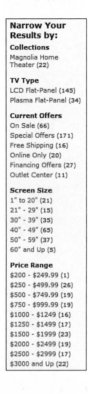

Narrow Your Results by:

Collections
Magnolia Home Theater (22)

TV Type
LCD Flat-Panel (145)
Plasma Flat-Panel (34)

Current Offers
On Sale (66)
Special Offers (171)
Free Shipping (16)
Online Only (20)
Financing Offers (27)
Outlet Center (11)

Screen Size
1" to 20" (21)
21" - 29" (15)
30" - 39" (35)
40" - 49" (65)
50" - 59" (37)
60" and Up (5)

Price Range
$200 - $249.99 (1)
$250 - $499.99 (26)
$500 - $749.99 (19)
$750 - $999.99 (19)
$1000 - $1249 (16)
$1250 - $1499 (17)
$1500 - $1999 (23)
$2000 - $2499 (19)
$2500 - $2999 (17)
$3000 and Up (22)

Link to All Important Pages in Your Main Navigation

If a page is important to your site and you want it to show up in search engine indexes, then you can't hide it. For this reason, all important pages should be linked from your site's home page and should appear on your master menu system.

You see, most searchbots start on your home page and follow links from there. If a page is linked from your home page, the searchbot will find it; if a page isn't linked from the home page, the searchbot may not be able to index it.

When a page is listed in your site's main navigation, you're telling the search engines that this is one of the most important pages on your site. It will be indexed accord-ingly.

Avoid Dynamic Content

Dynamic web pages are those that don't exist until someone searches for them on your site. For example, you may dynamically generate a page based on information a user enters into a web form; it's becoming quite common.

The problem with this type of dynamic content is that search engines can't find it. The generated web page doesn't exist until someone enters information into the web form, and searchbots don't know how to enter information. They'll see the web form but go no further than that. (And, as you recall, those dynamically generated URLs are particularly difficult for searchbots to decipher.)

Now, some search engines (such as Google) are working on searchbots that can enter some common terms when they encounter certain types of web forms, but you still have a problem if you rely heavily on dynamic web pages. While it may be impossible to move to a completely static site, you need to know that the more content you generate dynamically, the fewer pages on your site the major search engines will index. The more static pages you have, the higher your site will rank.

Test Your Site Structure

One final tip that applies to sites small or large: before you finalize your site design or redesign, test it. You can use numerous programs to determine how easily your site can be crawled; if you get a low ranking, you know you have to go back and make some changes.

Search Note
Learn more about tools for testing your site in Chapter 17, "Using Third-Party SEO Tools."

There's no reason whatsoever to design a site in the dark. Don't wait until your site goes live to determine how well it ranks; make testing a key part of your site development process.

The Least You Need to Know

- ◆ Design your pages with key information in text form; don't rely on images, videos, or Flash animations.

- ◆ Put the most information near the top of your page, and use headings and subheadings to point out important topics and keywords.

◆ Simplify long URLs and avoid dynamic content and dynamically generated URLs.

◆ Assign keywords and phrases to the most appropriate pages on your site; make every page on your site a gateway page.

◆ Organize your site with a shallow hierarchy, and link to all important pages in your main navigation.

◆ Before you launch your site, test it!

Chapter 8

Optimizing Links to Your Site

In This Chapter

- ◆ Understanding the importance of inbound links
- ◆ Learning how to increase the number of sites linking to your pages
- ◆ Discovering how to improve the quality of inbound links
- ◆ Learning how to optimize internal links on your site

While content and keywords are important to increasing your site's search ranking, they're not the only indication of how relevant a page might be to a given search query. Google (and, presumably, other sites) also looks at how many and what kinds of sites link to your page, assuming that the more authoritative and relevant your content, the more inbound links you'll have.

It's imperative, then, to work on increasing the inbound links to your site. You need to work on not just the quantity of these links, but also their quality; the more relevant and authoritative the sites are that link to yours, the more importance search engines will assign to those links.

Why Inbound Links Are Important

Links are a key part of the web. That's how most users find other sites; they follow the links from one page to another.

In fact, links (properly termed *hyperlinks*) form the background of the web. The Hypertext Transfer Protocol (HTTP) is built on the concept of linking one document to another, originally so that researchers, academics, and scientists could find documents more easily. That's the "web" of the World Wide Web—a web of links where anybody can link to anything.

Links are important to search rankings because Google says they are. Before Google, search rankings were determined primarily by keyword matching; with its proprietary PageRank algorithm, Google changed that and put the focus on inbound links.

Google's PageRank determines a page's importance by counting the number of other pages that link to that page. The more pages that link to a page, the higher that page's PageRank—and the higher it will appear in Google's search results. The PageRank is a numerical ranking from 0 to 10, expressed as PR0, PR1, PR2, and so forth—the higher, the better.

Google doesn't give out detailed information about how it calculates PageRank (the information is highly proprietary), but experts believe that Google takes into account some combination of quantity and quality of links that point to a web page. Inbound links from pages with a higher PageRank are assumed to be more important than links from pages with a lower PageRank; it's an assumption that makes a lot of sense. The result, of course, is that a page with a lot of inbound links could rank lower than one with just a few higher-quality links.

A page can also get a lower PageRank when it's linked to by a page that has a ton of outbound links. Google assumes that a page with only a few outbound links has paid more attention to those links than a similar page with many more outbound links. For example, a page with 100 outbound links has less credibility than one with just 10 outbound links. Too much quantity is assumed to adversely affect the link quality.

Google's PageRank shook up the world of search, primarily because it worked. From the beginning, it was apparent that Google's search results were consistently more relevant than those of its competitors, and that was and continues to be due to the PageRank algorithm. Naturally, Google's competitors took notice, and all major search engines today factor inbound links to some degree into their ranking of web pages.

For this reason, you need to incorporate inbound links as part of your SEO strategy. The goal is to increase the number of high-quality sites linking to your web pages—by whatever means possible.

How to Increase the Number of Sites Linking to Your Pages

You can build links to your site in a number of ways. These range from the completely "white hat" approach of building quality content and waiting for other sites to notice that and link to you, to the "black hat" approaches of buying links or building phony websites to link back to your main site. Naturally, I'm a fan of the organic white hat method—although there's no harm in asking for links, if you want.

Creating Linkworthy Content

The most important part of attracting inbound links is having site content that other sites want to link to. It's a matter of building a "linkworthy" site; put another way, no legitimate site will link to yours if it doesn't include quality content.

The keys to creating linkworthy content are to be authoritative, to be creative, and to add value not found in competing sites. Your site needs to fully address the chosen topic and offer unique content. If related sites find your content to be both valuable and unique, they'll link to you.

SEO Tip _____

Many webmasters look at link building as an afterthought. That's not an effective way to do it. Instead, prepare to spend at least as much time building your inbound links as you did building your site. Remember, your website is effectively invisible until other sites link to it!

Getting the Word Out

Of course, for a site to link to you, it has to know about you. The old adage of "if you build it, they will come" is viable only if they actually hear about what you're doing.

You can get the word out about your site in many ways. The most white hat of these methods is traditional publicity. Issue a press release (paper or electronic), hire a public relations firm, fire off some e-mails to relevant blogs and forums—anything you

SEO Tip

When you attract links organically, you should experience a trickle-down effect—that is, other sites will link to your site when they see the link on other respected sites. It's a truism; quality links beget more links.

have to do to create a buzz about your site. Once other sites and blogs start talking about your site, you'll attract interested visitors, some of whom will find it worthwhile to link to your site.

The nice thing about generating links in this fashion is that they're truly organic. The links come from sites that are interested in your content and are thus highly relevant. They link because they want to, not because they're asked to or paid to. They're quality links—just what Google and the other engines tend to rank highly.

Making Link Requests

That's not to say that you can't ask other sites to link to yours. In fact, making link requests is an important part of any SEO strategy; sometimes you have to be a little aggressive in creating new inbound links.

How do you ask another site to link to yours? It's as simple as identifying the site (based on its relevance and quality) and then sending an e-mail to the site's webmaster or owner.

Let's start with how you identify a relevant site. Here's where you rely on the quality of the search engines. Query Google or Yahoo! for your site topic, and see which sites appear at the top of the rankings. If you filter out any commercial results, you should have a short list of those sites that might be interested in what your site has to offer.

Now you want to spend a little time on each of these sites. Get to know what the site does and also who does it. It's best if you can identify the webmaster or content provider by name; a personal e-mail works a lot better than one addressed to "Dear Webmaster." If it's a site with a thriving community, make your presence known on the message boards or via blog comments. You'll get a better response to your request if you're a known friend of the site than if you're a random stranger.

The actual request process requires some hands-on work. Compose an e-mail, addressed to the correct person, that describes your site, tells why it's relevant to his site, and then asks that person to create a link to your site. Make sure you include the URL of the page to which you want them to link; you should also include some suggested text to include as the anchor text for the link. (Remember, the anchor text should include one or more keywords or phrases important to your site.)

At that point, the targeted site either will or won't make a link to your site. If the answer is yes, you're good to go. If the answer is no (or, more likely, if you don't receive an answer), there's no harm in asking again.

Automating Link Requests—or Not

If the entire link request process sounds too tedious to you, you can always send out bulk (and impersonal) e-mails or engage the service of a link request specialist. The former is easy enough to do, although it smacks of spam; as to the latter, you can find plenty of firms that do this via a simple Google search.

That said, I'm not a big fan of automating the link request process. As some experts have noted, the quality of any link you get from a "Dear webmaster, please link to our site" request is, in all probability, quite low. You'll almost always generate higher-quality links from personal requests; this is not a process that should be automated.

You probably know this yourself. How do you respond when you get one of these generic requests? Me, I delete them—and I assume that's what most webmasters do. Ultimately, the process of link building is a very human process, requiring hands-on interaction. You'll get better results when you send your e-mail to "Dear Bob" than to "Dear webmaster"; take the time to find out the name of the person who runs the site—and to learn more about what the site offers.

Engaging in Link Trading

Then there's the issue of link trading. There are two ways to do this, one of which generates higher-quality results than the other.

The best way to trade links is directly with another site. That is, you identify a site that you'd like to have linked to yours, and e-mail that site. In your e-mail, you offer to link from your site to theirs if they reciprocate with a link back to your site. You both benefit from the link exchange.

The more suspect way to trade links is via a link exchange service or program. These services, such as GotLinks (www.gotlinks.com) and Link Exchanged (www.linkexchanged.com), can provide hundreds of sites to link to your site, in exchange for links from your site to theirs. The only problem with these link exchanges is that the linking sites are not necessarily high-quality sites; they're often not even sites relevant to your site's topic. In some instances, the links you get are from obvious link farms—not sites that help you increase your search ranking.

I'm obviously not a big fan of automated link exchanges. I am, however, a fan of active link trading. There's no harm at all in exchanging a link on your site to a link from a relevant website. One good turn deservers another, as the saying goes; sometimes it takes a link to get a link.

Purchasing Links

Finally, we come to the topic of link purchasing—paying for links back to your site. This could involve sending the other site a one-time check or perhaps agreeing to share some portion of your site's ad revenue.

Some view link purchasing as a black hat technique, somehow less pure than trading links or generating links organically. But there are some good reasons to consider this approach.

For example, if the only way you can get a link from a relevant, high-quality site is to pay for it, that may be better than not getting the link at all. And some high-volume sites only sell their links, which means you have to pay to play.

Bottom line? Paying for links shouldn't be your first approach, but you shouldn't rule it out, either. Sometimes it's the only way to get the inbound links you need.

Beyond Quantity: Increasing the Quality of Your Inbound Links

As noted previously, Google looks at more than just the quantity of your page's inbound links. It also looks at the quality of those links.

Google determines link quality by the topical relevance of the linking site and by the number of links it gives out. A site that includes links to 100 other sites will be considered lower quality than one that includes only a handful of links. In this instance, it pays to be a member of an exclusive club.

The quality issue is one compelling reason not to engage in automated link requests or link exchanges. If you garner links via spam or black hat techniques, the links you receive will not be of the highest quality. The only way to ensure high-quality inbound links is to hand-pick them—which argues for good old manual link building. There's no better way to do it.

And how do you determine the highest-quality sites to solicit links from? Searching Google for topically related sites is always good, making sure to take the top sites on the search results page. Another approach is to use Google's **related** operator to find sites that Google thinks are related to yours. Enter **related:www.*yoursite*.com** and then contact the top 10 or 20 related sites. (You might point out that you're contacting them because Google lists your two sites as related; that's bound to have a little influence.)

It's also a good idea to browse or search the main web directories, such as the Open Directory (www.dmoz.org). Directories theoretically have higher-quality results because human editors hand-pick the sites listed there—which means other sites listed in the same category as yours should be topically related.

Whichever approach (or approaches) you use, make sure you check out any site personally before you make a request. A little hands-on evaluation goes a long way in determining relevance and quality.

Optimizing the Other Links—Between Pages on Your Site

There's one last type of link to deal with, and it's not one coming from another website. The internal links between pages on your site are also important because they help alert searchbots to the various pages on your site, build the relevancy of a page to a keyword or phrase, and increase the ranking of a given internal page.

First, and perhaps most important, internal links help the individual pages on your site get spidered by the various searchbots. Searchbots look for internal links; they use these links to identify further pages on your site. For this reason, you need to include links to all your important pages on your site's home page, as well as in your site's menu and navigation system.

Second, using a keyword or phrase in the anchor text accompanying an internal link helps to build the relevancy of the linked-to page. It's a simple thing; searchbots look to

Stop!

This doesn't mean that you should link to every one of your pages from your home page; this will diffuse the importance of each individual link and prove unattractive and unwieldy to your site's human visitors. Instead, carefully choose which internal pages you link to from your home page, based on the importance of each page.

the anchor text for targeted keywords. The more anchor text you create, via internal links, the more keywords get noticed.

This also increases the ranking of your site's internal pages with that search engine. The closer a page is from your site's home page, in terms of number of clicks, the higher that page will rank with the search engine. Include a direct link from your site's home page to ensure a higher ranking for the linked-to internal page.

For all these reasons, you need to pay as much attention to your site's internal links as you do to building inbound links from external sites. There's no getting around it—every link is important, whether it's inbound or internal!

The Least You Need to Know

- Inbound links to your site are important because Google and other search engines use these links to gauge your site's popularity and relevance; the more high-quality links you have, the higher your page will rank.

- To attract inbound links, you first have to create linkworthy content on your site—content that other sites want to link to.

- The best way to solicit relevant links is to manually ask for a link, via a personal e-mail.

- You can also request a link exchange; you put a link to their site on your site in exchange for a link to yours on theirs.

- Link quality is as important as link quantity; Google looks at the relevance of the linking site, as well as the number of links on that site (fewer is better).

- You also need to optimize the internal links between pages on your site, which help identify pages to searchbots and increase the ranking of your internal pages.

Optimizing Images and Videos

In This Chapter

◆ Discovering how searchbots can index your images

◆ Learning how to get your videos into the Google and Yahoo! search indexes

Throughout this book, I've stressed that searchbots pretty much ignore images, videos, and other media files. They crawl your site's text and look at certain HTML tags, but that's about it. This means, of course, that any content on your site that isn't text is essentially invisible to the search engines.

So what do you do if you use a lot of images and videos on your web pages? Well, there are ways around the crawlers' limitations, as you'll learn in this chapter.

Making Images Visible to Search Engines

It's true: searchbots can't view images. When a crawler comes across a JPEG file on your website, it doesn't know whether it's a picture of a tree or a picture of a pretty girl; it's just an undecipherable collection of digital bits.

How, then, do you tell a searchbot what you're showing on your site? There is a way, believe it or not—and, not surprisingly, it involves text.

Using the ALT Attribute

Images are inserted into a web page via the following bit of HTML code:

```
<IMG SRC="image.jpg" WIDTH="XXX" HEIGHT="XXX" ALT="description"
TITLE="title" >
```

Decoding the code, the **<IMG>** tag says that there's an image to insert, the **SRC** attribute defines the location of the image file, and the **WIDTH** and **HEIGHT** attributes define the size of the image (in pixels)—all pretty standard stuff. The **ALT** and **TITLE** attributes, however, deserve closer inspection.

The **ALT** attribute defines what a web browser should display if, for some reason, the image file isn't available or doesn't display on a page. Instead of seeing the chosen image, the user would see the text entered between the quotation marks in the **ALT** attribute.

The unfortunate thing is, many web page creators neglect the **ALT** attribute. Maybe they figure their images will always display, or maybe they're just lazy, but the attribute is more often honored in the breech—that is, the **<IMG>** tag is most often entered with the **ALT** attribute missing.

That's a bad idea, for two reasons. First, what happens if the image doesn't display? Second, and more important, the **ALT** attribute is what a searchbot reads to determine the content of an image file.

That's right, searchbots do crawl your site's **<IMG>** tags. Since they can't view the content of an image file itself, they rely on the text description in the **ALT** attribute to tell them what the image is about. It's an inexact science, of course; not only are most **ALT** attributes missing (meaning there's no description of the image), but there's no guarantee that the **ALT** text entered will adequately describe the image shown. There's no law, after all, prohibiting a site designer from describing an image of a wrinkled old man as a "hot babe."

Limitations noted, the **ALT** attribute is how you trick the search engines into recognizing your page's images as valid content. This means you need to enter descriptive text into the **ALT** attributes for each and every image on your website. Make sure the attribute text not only describes the image, but also includes (you guessed it!) important keywords and phrases. In other words, use the **ALT** tag to reinforce your site's keyword scheme—while still describing how an image looks.

Using the TITLE Attribute

The final attribute for the **<IMG>** tag is the **TITLE** attribute. This attribute assigns a title to the image, which is what displays if a user hovers his cursor over an image, as demonstrated in Figure 9.1.

Figure 9.1

The TITLE text displayed when the cursor is hovered over an image.

Photo by Sherry Elliott

While the **TITLE** attribute isn't crawled as often as the **ALT** attribute, it still represents an opportunity to describe your image in words. Follow the same approach as you do with the **ALT** attribute; use the **TITLE** attribute to hold a description of the image, along with important keywords and phrases.

Search Note
If no **TITLE** text is entered, nothing is displayed if a user hovers his cursor over an image.

Optimizing for Image Search

A surprisingly large number of Google and Yahoo! users search not for text, but for images. For these reasons, the major search engines have specific algorithms they use to ascertain the content of the images found on the pages in their index, and to rank those images for relevance.

Knowing this, there are ways you can optimize your images for an image search ranking. Employ these techniques:

◆ Add the **ALT** and **TITLE** attributes to all your image tags, and use them to embed keywords and phrases—as well as text that describes the image.

◆ For the image file itself, create a file name that both describes the image and includes one or more keywords. Use hyphens in the file name to isolate the keywords.

◆ Add a descriptive caption for each image in the body text of your web page, as shown in Figure 9.2. Don't leave any image standing alone without mention in the text; searchbots can derive the content of an image by the text that surrounds it.

Figure 9.2

A descriptive caption added in the page text below an image.

Violet-crowned Hummingbird, adult feeding

◆ Include the **WIDTH** and **HEIGHT** attributes in the **<IMG>** tag so that Google Image Search can bucket your image in the right-size bracket.

Getting Search Engines to Notice Your Videos

Videos are even harder for searchbots to index than are images. When a video is embedded in a web page, via the **<EMBED>** tag, there are no **ALT** or **TITLE** attributes to the tag, nothing to tell a searchbot what kind of video content is included.

You can, of course, describe the video in the surrounding text; a caption is always good. But that's often not good enough to get your videos into the Google and Yahoo! search indexes.

Using YouTube

The best way to get a video into both of these search indexes, believe it or not, is to post it on YouTube—in addition to your own site, of course. That's because Google automatically includes all YouTube videos in its main search index (Google owns YouTube, after all); Yahoo! also crawls YouTube to add videos to its index.

So if you have a video on your site, upload a copy of it to YouTube (www.youtube.com), shown in Figure 9.3. YouTube is one of the hottest sites on the web, consistently rating in the top five of all websites, with close to 80 million visitors per month. And those visitors watch a lot of videos—more than 3 billion videos a month, or a third of all the videos viewed on the web.

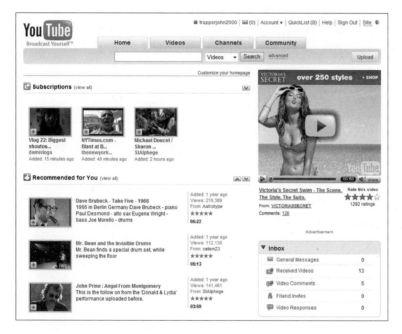

Figure 9.3

YouTube, the biggest video-sharing site on the web.

Uploading videos to YouTube is easy; you first have to create an account (free), then it's a matter of clicking the Upload link found at the top of any YouTube page. Follow the onsite instructions, and your video will be made available to YouTube's millions of viewers—which itself can draw increased traffic to your site.

YouTube knows what your video is about via the title, description, and tags you supply for that video when it is first uploaded. (Figure 9.4 shows all three of these elements on a typical video-viewing page.) Optimize YouTube's title and description the same way you would the **<TITLE>** tag and body text on your own website, being sure to liberally sprinkle keywords throughout. Your keywords should also be used to create the tags that accompany the video; this is how users search for videos on the YouTube site and how Google and Yahoo! index the video.

Figure 9.4

A typical YouTube video-viewing page, complete with title, description, and tags.

Many businesses are using YouTube to market their products and services online. Learn more in my companion book, *YouTube for Business* (Que, 2008).

You also should include the URL for your website in your YouTube video description. If you do your job right, Google and Yahoo! will pick up information about your video from its placement on YouTube. This will help your video get placement in these search engines' search results; when users click through to view the video, they'll see the link to your website and hopefully visit there.

Optimizing for Video

Of course, you still need to optimize your site for your videos. While you can't do much with the standard **<EMBED>** tag, you can still tweak your site a little to help the searchbots deal with any videos on your pages.

Here's what you should do:

◆ For the video file itself, create a file name that both describes the video and includes one or more keywords. Use hyphens in the file name to isolate the keywords.

◆ If the video format you employ allows the use of metadata, use this feature to include title, keywords, length, and other pertinent information about the video.

◆ Add a descriptive caption below or beside the video, in the body text of your web page. Don't leave any video standing alone without mention in the text; searchbots can often derive the content of a video by the text that surrounds it.

 Stop! _____

When at all possible, present your videos in a common video format, such as WMV, AVI, or MOV. Do not embed your videos in Flash animation; searchbots have no method for reading the contents of Flash files.

While it's still difficult to get searchbots to recognize videos on your site, these methods can sometimes convey the content of your videos to the search engines.

The Least You Need to Know

◆ While searchbots don't crawl image or video files, there are ways to get the content of your images and videos indexed.

◆ For images, use the **ALT** and **TITLE** attributes in the **<IMG>** tag to convey keywords and a description of the image.

◆ For videos, the best way to get them indexed is to post them on YouTube—in addition to your own website.

◆ For both images and videos, place a descriptive caption under the image on your web page, or in the surrounding text.

Submitting Your Site to Search Engines and Directories

In This Chapter

◆ Submitting your site to Google, Yahoo!, and Windows Live Search

◆ Generating traffic through other search engines and directories

◆ Understanding website submittal services

◆ Removing your site from a search engine index

While all search engines employ crawler or searchbot software to crawl the web, indexing pages and sites as they go, you also have the option of supplementing the crawl. That's right, instead of waiting for a searchbot to find your site on the web, you can take a more proactive approach—by manually submitting your site for submission in a search engine's index.

Manually submitting your site to the major search engines offers a few advantages. First, it ensures that they'll crawl your site; you don't have to worry about whether their searchbots will stumble over your site in the course of their normal web-crawling process. Second, it can help your site get into an index faster than otherwise; think of it, with some search engines, as moving your site to the front of the line.

Fortunately, submitting your site to a search engine is an easy process. In fact, it's probably the easiest part of the SEO process. Read on to learn the details.

Submitting Your Site to Google

When I say that manual site submittal is an easy process, I mean it. That's particularly the case with Google, as you'll soon discover.

To submit your site to the Google index, all you have to do is go to www.google.com/addurl/, shown in Figure 10.1. Enter the URL for your home page into the appropriate box (including the **http://**), add any comments you might have about your site, and then click the Add URL button. That's it; Google will now add your site to the Googlebot crawl list, and your site will appear in appropriate search results.

Figure 10.1

Submitting your site to the Google index.

Note that you have to add only the top-level URL for your site; you don't have to add URLs for any subsidiary pages. For example, if your home page is **http://www.homepage.com/index.html,** enter only **http://www.homepage.com.** Googlebot will crawl the rest of your site once it finds the main URL.

Submitting Your Site to Yahoo!

Submitting your website to Yahoo! is an equally simple process. Point your web browser to http://siteexplorer.search.yahoo.com/submit/. You'll see the page shown in Figure 10.2. Here you have the option of submitting the URL for a website or for a blog or website feed. You'll probably use the former, although if your site has an RSS feed, you can achieve better ongoing results by submitting the URL of the feed instead.

Figure 10.2

Submitting your site to Yahoo!.

Search Note

An RSS feed automatically keeps interested users—and search engines—informed of changes to your site or blog. You can also use Yahoo!'s RSS feed option to submit a sitemap for your site; learn more about sitemaps in Chapter 11, "Mapping Your Site for Best Results."

Taking the simple approach, all you have to do is enter your website's URL into the Submit a Website or Webpage box; make sure you include the **http://** prefix. After entering your URL, click the Submit URL button, and you're done.

Submitting Your Site to Windows Live Search

Google and Yahoo! are just two of the big three search engines; you should also submit your site to Windows Live Search. When you go to http://search.msn.com. sg/docs/submit.aspx, you'll see the page shown in Figure 10.3; enter your entire site URL into the box (including the **http://**) and then click the Submit URL button. As with the Google and Yahoo! submission services, Live Search's MSNBot crawler will be instructed to crawl your site and index all the internal pages linked from your home page.

Figure 10.3

Submitting your site to Windows Live Search.

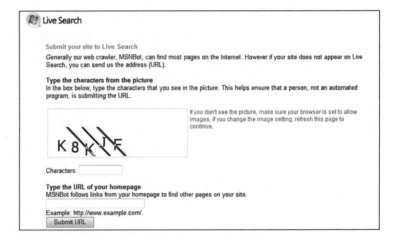

Submitting to Other Search Engines and Directories

Why stop at the big three? The web has a lot of other search engines and directories; even though none has the reach of Google, Yahoo!, or Live Search, they can still generate traffic to your site.

With that in mind, Table 10.1 details 10 additional search engines and directories, along with instructions on how to submit your site.

Table 10.1 Search Engine/Directory Submissions

Search Engine/ Directory	Main URL	How to Submit
AlltheWeb	www.alltheweb.com	Submit at www.alltheweb.com/ help/webmaster/submit_site.
AltaVista	www.altavista.com	Submit at www.altavista.com/ addurl/.
AOL Search	http://search.aol.com	Submit via Google (www.google. com/addurl/).
Ask.com	www.ask.com	Does not accept site submissions.
Best of the Web	www.botw.org	Paid submittal at www.botw.org/ helpcenter/submitcommercial. aspx.
Gigablast	www.gigablast.com	Submit at www.gigablast.com/ indexphp?subPage=addUrl&page= about&.
JoeAnt	www.joeant.com	Submit at www.joeant.com/ suggest.html.
Open Directory	www.dmoz.org	Go to appropriate category page and click Suggest URL.
Starting Point	www.stpt.com	Paid submittal at www.stpt.com/ directory/addsite.htm.
Wikia Search	http://search.wikia.com	Click the Add button on any relevant search results page.

Using Website Submittal Services

As easy as this site submittal process is, some webmasters prefer to offload the task to a site submittal service. These services let you enter your URL once and then submit your site to multiple search engines and directories; they handle all the details required by each search engine. Given that many of these services are free, it's not a bad way to go.

Some of the more popular site submittal services include these:

◆ 1 2 3 Submit Pro (websitesubmit.hypermart.net)

◆ AddMe! (www.addme.com)

◆ AddPro.com (www.addpro.com)

◆ SubmitExpress (www.submitexpress.com)

Stop! _____

Beware those services that charge a high fee for search engine submission—they don't do anything that you can't do yourself, for free.

How to Remove Your Site from a Search Engine Index

If you want to remove your website from a search engine's index for some reason, you can do so—although the process is slightly more involved than what is required to add your site in the first place. You need to place a special text file in the root directory of your website's server. This file should be named **robots.txt** and should include the following text:

```
User-agent: *
Disallow: /
```

The **robots.txt** file is read by all the search engine's crawlers and conveys specific instructions to the crawlers. The first line tells the crawler that the following instructions apply to all search engines; the second line tells the crawler not to crawl the entire website.

If you want to remove your site from only a specific search engine index, enter the name of that search engine's crawler into the first line instead of the asterisk. For example, to remove your site from the Google index, know that Google's crawler is called Googlebot and enter the following text:

```
User-agent: Googlebot
Disallow: /
```

You can also change the second line of text for specific purposes. For example, if you want to remove only certain pages on your site from indexes, insert the following text into the **robots.txt** file, replacing *page.html* with the file name of the specific page:

```
User-agent: *
Disallow: /page.html
```

You can also use the **robots.txt** file to exclude all pages within a specific directory. To do this, insert the following text, replacing *directory* with the name of the directory:

```
User-agent: *
Disallow: /directory
```

Note, however, that it can take six to eight weeks for your site to be removed from all indexes. That's because you have to wait for all the crawlers to recrawl your site, and then for the search engine to reindex its listings. Once everything washes through the system, however, your site (or designated page) should disappear from the results, as requested.

The Least You Need to Know

- ◆ If you don't want to wait for the search engine crawlers to find and index your site, you can manually submit your site to most search engines for indexing.

- ◆ To submit your site to Google, go to www.google.com/addurl/; to submit your site to Yahoo!, go to http://siteexplorer.search.yahoo.com/submit/; and to submit your site to Live Search, go to http://search.msn.com.sg/docs/submit.aspx.

- ◆ If you prefer to submit your site once and have that submittal sent to multiple search engines and directories, use a website submittal service.

- ◆ You can also instruct searchbots to remove your site from the various search engine indexes, using the **robots.txt** file.

Chapter 11

Mapping Your Site for Best Results

In This Chapter

◆ Understanding how sitemaps work

◆ Discovering why a sitemap is important

◆ Creating your sitemap

◆ Letting crawlers know where your sitemap is

◆ Learning how to submit sitemaps to the major search engines

When you submit your site to a search engine, as discussed in Chapter 10, you basically submit the URL for your home page only. This instructs the search engine's crawler to visit your home page and crawl any internal links you have from your home page to other pages on your site.

However, not all the pages on your site are linked to from your home page. When you want all the pages on your site submitted for indexing, you have to use a different approach.

The key is to create something called a *sitemap*—literally, a map of your entire website. You then submit this sitemap to the major search engines, and they use the sitemap to index all the relevant pages on your site.

How do you create a sitemap and then submit that map to the major search engines? It's not as simple as traditional site submittal, but it's definitely worth the effort. Read on to learn more.

How Sitemaps Work

A sitemap is, quite simply, a method of submitting the pages of your site to search engines, using site feeds that list all the pages on your site. The big three search engines (Google, Yahoo!, and Live Search), along with Ask.com, all support a single sitemap standard, which means you can create just one sitemap that all the search engines can use; you don't have to worry about different formats for different engines.

Your sitemap is created in a separate sitemaps file. This file contains the distinct URLs of all the pages on your website. When a searchbot reads the sitemap file, it learns about all the pages on your website—and can then crawl all those pages for submittal to the search engine's index.

By the way, the new unified sitemap format also allows for autodiscovery of your site's sitemap file. Previously, you had to notify each search engine separately of where on your site the file was located. Now you can do this universally by specifying the file's location in your site's **robots.txt** file.

Search Note

As you learned in Chapter 10, the **robots.txt** file is a small text file that all search engine crawlers automatically read; it contains commands that tell the crawler what to (or what not to) crawl on your site.

Learn more about sitemaps and the unified sitemap protocol at www.sitemaps.org.

The sitemap file itself is an XML page that lists the pages of your site in simple hierarchical order, along with important information about each page. The included code looks something like this:

```
<URLSET xmlns="http://www.sitemaps.org/schemas/sitemap/0.9">
 <URL>
 <LOC>http://www.yoursite.com/</LOC>
 <PRIORITY>1.0</PRIORITY>
 <LASTMOD>2008-04-24T16:33:07+00:00</LASTMOD>
 <CHANGEFREQ>daily</CHANGEFREQ>
```

```
</URL>

<URL>
<LOC>http://www.yoursite.com/page01.htm</LOC>
<PRIORITY>0.5</PRIORITY>
<LASTMOD>2008-04-24T16:33:07+00:00</LASTMOD>
<CHANGEFREQ>daily</CHANGEFREQ>
</URL>

<URL>
<LOC>http://www.yoursite.com/page02.htm</LOC>
<PRIORITY>0.5</PRIORITY>
<LASTMOD>2008-04-24T16:33:07+00:00</LASTMOD>
<CHANGEFREQ>daily</CHANGEFREQ>
</URL>
</URLSET>
```

The initial **<URLSET>** tag contains the obligatory information about the sitemap format used and serves as a container for all the URLs on your site. Following this tag is a succession of **<URL>** tags, one for each page on your site. Within each **<URL>** tag are several other tags, including these:

- ◆ **<LOC>** The exact URL of the page.

- ◆ **<PRIORITY>** The relative importance of the page on your site. For example, your home page might have a relative importance of 1.0, while subsidiary pages might have an importance of 0.5 (half as important as the home page).

- ◆ **<LASTMOD>** The date and time the page was last modified.

- ◆ **<CHANGEFREQ>** How often the page changes—daily, weekly, monthly, and so on.

SEO Tip

Some search engines let you create specialized search engines for specific types of content. For example, Google lets you submit news, video, mobile, code search (application development), and geo (Google Maps) sitemaps. See each individual site for more details.

Why a Sitemap Is Important for SEO

Given that searchbots are supposed to crawl all the links on your site, and that you can always manually submit your site for crawling, why bother creating a sitemap? It involves more work to do, after all.

SEO Tip

Sitemaps are especially useful if your site has dynamically generated content. That's because search engine crawlers typically don't discover dynamic pages; the fact that you can point the search engines to all your dynamic pages makes them visible when they otherwise might not be.

Search Note

Sitemaps supplement instead of replace the usual methods of adding pages to the search engines' indexes. If you don't utilize a sitemap, the search engines' crawlers may still discover your pages, and you may still manually submit your site for inclusion in the search engines' indexes.

Here's the simple reason sitemaps are important: they work. Searchbots might crawl all your pages, especially if you have a larger site or one in which your home page doesn't link to all your pages. That's not a problem when you have a sitemap; all the pages on your site, no matter how well buried, are listed for the searchbot to index.

In addition, your sitemap contains additional useful information about each page on your site. You can use your sitemap to tell the search engines how important each page is on your site, as well as the freshness of each page. That's very useful when the search engines compile their rankings.

Finally, since the sitemap includes the date when each page on your site was last updated, it's also an excellent way to inform the major search engines of all the new and updated pages on your site. This is a benefit both to you and to each search engine; you get your newer content indexed faster, and they get to provide more up-to-date pages in their search results—that is, to improve the freshness of their indexes.

In other words, creating a sitemap has nothing but upside potential. It's a little more work, yes, but that's well worth the potential improvement in the rankings of all the pages on your website.

Creating a Map of Your Site

I assume you're now sold on the idea of creating a sitemap for your website. Just how do you do this?

While you can create a sitemap file by hand, following the example listed earlier (and naming the file **sitemap.xls**), it's far easier to generate that sitemap automatically. To that end, many third-party sitemap-generator tools exist for just that purpose.

For most of these tools, generating a sitemap is as simple as entering your home page URL and then pressing a button. The tool now crawls your website and automatically generates a sitemap file; this typically takes just a few minutes. Once the sitemap file is generated, you can upload it to the root directory of your website, reference it in your **robots.txt** file, and, if you like, submit it directly to each of the major search engines.

Some of these tools are web based, some are software programs, and most are free. The most popular of these tools include the following:

◆ AutoMapIt (www.automapit.com)

◆ AutoSitemap (www.autositemap.com)

◆ G-Mapper (www.dbnetsolutions.co.uk/gmapper/)

◆ GSiteCrawler (www.gsitecrawler.com)

◆ Gsitemap (www.vigos.com/products/gsitemap/)

◆ Site Magellan (www.sitemagellan.com)

◆ SitemapsPal (www.sitemapspal.com)

◆ SitemapDoc (www.sitemapdoc.com)

◆ XML-Sitemaps.com (www.xml-sitemaps. com)

In most instances, you should name your sitemaps file **sitemaps.xml** and place it in the uppermost (root) directory of your website—although you can name and locate it differently, if you like.

> **Search Note**
>
> Google also offers its own free sitemap generator (www.google. com/webmasters/tools/docs/ en/sitemap-generator.html)— although, to be honest, it's not quite as user-friendly as some of the third-party tools available.

Referencing Your Sitemap from the robots.txt File

Once you've create your sitemaps file, you have to let crawlers know where it is. You do this via a reference in the **robots.txt** file, which should be located in the root directory of your website.

Add the following line to your **robots.txt** file:

```
SITEMAP: www.sitename.com/sitemaps.xml
```

Naturally, you need to include the actual location of your sitemaps file. The previous example works only if you have the file in your site's root directory; if it's in another directory, include that full path. Also, if you've named your sitemaps file something other than **sitemaps.xml,** use the actual name instead.

The next time a searchbot crawls your site, it will read your **robots.txt** file, learn the location of your sitemaps file, and then read the information in that file. It will then crawl all the pages listed in the file and submit information about each page to the search engine for indexing.

Submitting Sitemaps Directly to the Major Search Engines

Most of the major search engines also let you manually submit your sitemaps files. While you don't have to do this (the **robots.txt** method works just fine), there are advantages to submitting your sitemap directly.

The primary advantage to going direct to Google, Yahoo!, and the rest is that most search engines then give you access to specialized monitoring and reporting tools.

Stop!

If you don't reference your sitemaps file in the **robots. txt** file, it may not be discovered by some search engines' search-bots. Don't rely solely on formal sitemap submission; use the **robots.txt** as well, even if it's only for a backstop.

For example, Google's Webmaster Tools Dashboard (www.google.com/webmasters/tools/dashboard) provides a variety of summary, diagnostic, and statistical information about your site. The Overview page, shown in Figure 11.1, tells you what it found in your sitemap—how many errors, unreachable URLs, and the like; the Diagnostics page analyzes your site's metadata and displays problems the Googlebot crawler encountered; and the Statistics page shows you how the Googlebot views your site, in detail.

Submitting Your Sitemap to Google

To submit your site directly to Google, start by going to www.google.com/webmasters/tools/dashboard. If your site is not yet added to your Dashboard, do so now; then click the Add link in the Sitemap column beside your site.

This displays the Add Sitemap page. Pull down the list and select Add General Web Sitemap; this expands the page as shown in Figure 11.2. Enter the URL for your sitemap file, then click the Add General Web Sitemap button.

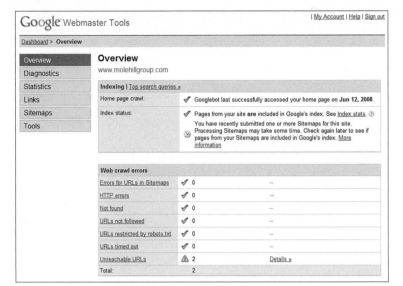

Figure 11.1

The Google Webmaster Tools Dashboard Overview page.

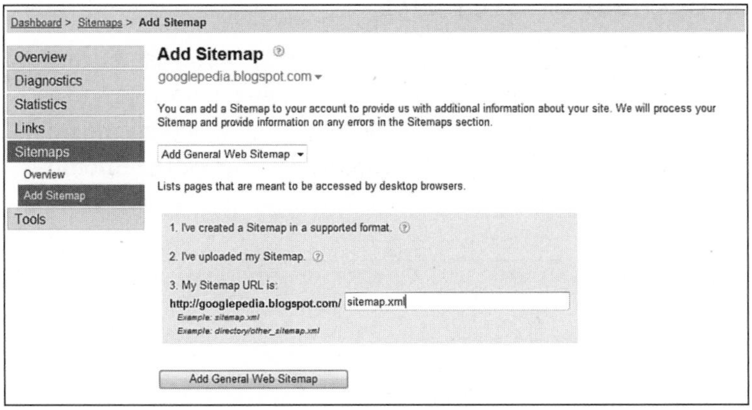

Figure 11.2

Submitting a sitemap to Google.

Submitting Your Sitemap to Yahoo!

To submit your site directly to Yahoo!, go to http://siteexplorer.search.yahoo.com/ submit/, shown in Figure 11.3. Enter the path and file name of your sitemaps file into the Submit Site Feed box, and then click Submit Feed.

Figure 11.3

Submitting a sitemap to Yahoo!

Submitting Your Sitemap to Windows Live Search

To submit your site directly to Windows Live Search, go to http://webmaster.live.com and click the Sign In to Use These Tools button. On the next page, click the Add a Site button. This displays the Add a Site page, shown in Figure 11.4; add all the information requested, including the location of your sitemap file, then click the Submit button.

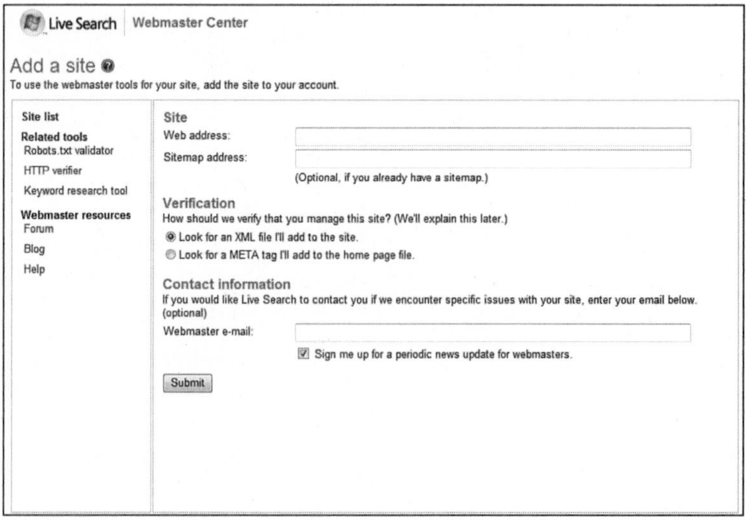

Figure 11.4

Submitting a sitemap to Windows Live Search.

Search Note

Even when you submit a complete sitemap, Google and the other search engines don't guarantee that they will crawl or index all the URLs on your website. However, since the search engines use the data in your sitemap to learn more about your site's structure, this should improve the crawler schedule for your site and ultimately improve the inclusion of your site's page in the search results.

The Least You Need to Know

◆ A sitemap is a complete listing of all the pages on your website, accompanied by pertinent details about each page.

◆ Search engines use sitemaps to learn about which pages on your site to crawl—and to find out which pages have recently changed.

◆ You can use a free sitemap-generator service to create the **sitemap.xml** file for your website, and then reference that file in your site's **robots.txt** file.

◆ Alternately, you can submit your sitemap directly to Google and Yahoo!, which provides access to their detailed site-analysis tools.

Part 3

Other Types of Optimization

SEO isn't just for regular websites and the big three search engines. This part shows you how to optimize your site for local and mobile search, as well as social media. You'll also learn how to optimize your blog for search.

12

Optimizing Your Site for Local Search

In This Chapter

- ◆ Understanding why local search is important
- ◆ Discovering how to submit your site for local search
- ◆ Learning how to optimize for local search

Most websites aim for a very general, almost global audience. But broader is not necessarily better if you run a local or regional business. What you want is to attract visitors and customers from your trading region, not from another coast or hemisphere.

The problem, of course, is that if you do a great job optimizing your site for Google, Yahoo!, and the like, you will attract a lot of visitors that you don't necessarily want. What you need to do, instead, is optimize your site for local search—to show up in the results of people searching in your area.

What Is Local Search—and Why Is It Important?

The concept of local search is an interesting one. When a person is looking for a local business, product, or service, just where do they look?

Well, many people continue to use the major search engines for their local searches. That's a challenge to Google, Yahoo!, and Microsoft—how do they determine whether someone is looking for local sites, and then how do they serve up locally relevant results to those searchers?

Local Search with the Major Search Engines

For local search to work on a global search engine, the searcher needs to include some local information in his query—a city or state name, maybe a zip code, something like that. The smarter the search engine (and Google is probably best at this today), the more likely it will parse the query to provide local results to the searcher.

For example, a person living in Chicago and looking for a pizza joint might enter the query **pizza chicago,** or perhaps go the zip code route and enter **pizza 60614.** The search engine would hopefully understand the query and return a list of nearby pizza restaurants.

Localized Search and Mapping Sites

Even better, the big three search engines all offer localized search services. These services are designed to steer users to nearby businesses that offer what users are looking for.

Let's start with Google's local search service. Originally called Google Local, the local service is now part of Google Maps (http://maps.google.com), shown in Figure 12.1. Users enter a location into Google Maps and can then search for businesses within that location.

Microsoft takes a similar approach with its Live Search Maps offering (http://maps.live.com), shown in Figure 12.2. Similar to Google Maps, users can enter a separate location and then search for a business, or combine their queries into a single search for a business within a particular area. Different from Google Maps, Live Search Maps obtains its business listings from the Superpages directory.

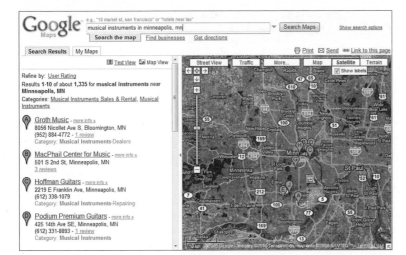

Figure 12.1

Local search results from Google Maps.

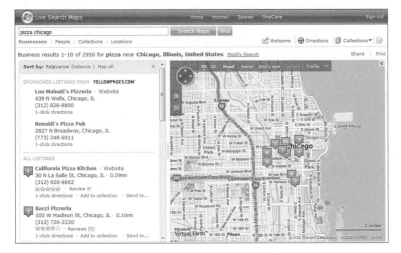

Figure 12.2

Searching for local businesses with Live Search Maps.

Finally, Yahoo! offers its dedicated Yahoo! Local site (http://local.yahoo.com), shown in Figure 12.3. Yahoo! Local combines local information (such as restaurant reviews and upcoming events) with a searchable directory of local businesses.

Search Note
The search results listings for most of these local sites typically include only a business name, address, and phone number, and perhaps a link to that business's website. Some search results listings also include links to reviews of that business.

Figure 12.3

Local search and information via Yahoo! Local.

Local Directories

Many local searchers are passing up the big search engines entirely to use more targeted local directories. There are a number of these directories, such as Local.com (www.local.com) and TrueLocal (www.truelocal.com), shown in Figure 12.4. These sites build a database of local business listings and attach some sort of front end (typically a search box) to help users find specific types of local businesses.

Figure 12.4

TrueLocal's local directory.

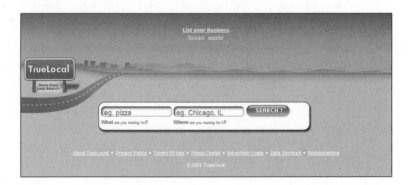

Yellow Pages Directories

Similar to local web directories are the online versions of traditional Yellow Pages directories. These sites, such as AT&T's YellowPages.com (www.yellowpages.com), shown in Figure 12.5, also use a database of local businesses, typically the same database used to create the corresponding print Yellow Pages.

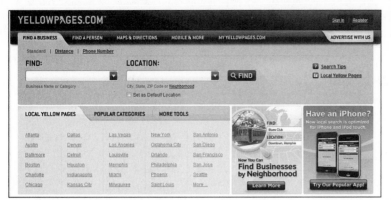

Figure 12.5

The online YellowPages.com directory.

Where Should You Submit Your Site for Local Search?

The point is, people looking for local businesses, products, and services will attempt to conduct some sort of local search, whether that's at Google or a more specialized site. They're looking for something down the road, not across the country, and they want their queries to deliver local results.

For that reason, if you're a local business trying to attract local customers, you need to let the search engines know that. Optimizing for local search requires putting information onto your site that identifies your locality and your desire for local customers—which we discuss later in this chapter.

Equally important, when you're optimizing for local search, you need to submit your site to more and different sites than you normally do. Yes, Google and Live Search and Yahoo! are still of the utmost importance, but now you have to consider a handful of local search engines and directories as well.

Submitting to Local Directories and Search Engines

When you're optimizing a site for traditional search, directories aren't an important consideration; the big three search engines are so big that web directories simply don't hit the radar screen. For local search, however, directories are critical, as are the various web Yellow Pages. It's important for you to be listed with any site where people look for local businesses—even if it's just their phone numbers and addresses.

Here's the thing: these directories aren't just a destination for users searching for local businesses. They're also a source of information for the big search engines. That makes them doubly important in the local search space.

So which are the most important local directories for you to target? Table 12.1 provides a short list, along with information on how to submit your site to each.

Table 12.1 Local Search Directories

Local Directory	Home Page URL	How to Submit Your Site
AskCity	http://city.ask.com	Send e-mail to askcitybusiness@ help.ask.com with the subject line "Ask City Feedback—Business." Include the following information in your e-mail: business name, address, phone number, business category, website URL, and e-mail contact address.
Dex	www.dexknows.com	Submit at www.advertisewithdex. com.
Google Maps	http://maps.google.com	Submit at www.google.com/local/ add/.
Local.com	www.local.com	Submit at advertise.local.com.
Superpages	www.superpages.com	Submit at advertising.superpages. com.
TrueLocal	www.truelocal.com	Submit at www.truelocal.com/ BusinessSuggest.aspx.
Windows Live Search Maps	http://maps.live.com	Listings provided by Superpages; submit at advertising.superpages. com.
Yahoo! Local	http://local.yahoo.com	Submit at listings.local.yahoo.com/ csubmit/.
YellowPages.com	www.yellowpages.com	Submit at http://store.yellowpages. com/post/.

SEO Tip

For more information on how to submit to each of these sites, consult the site's help files.

Submitting to General Web Directories

In addition, most of the major web directories have local and regional categories (Figure 12.6 shows a local category in the Open Directory). You should definitely submit your site to these directories if you want to be noticed locally.

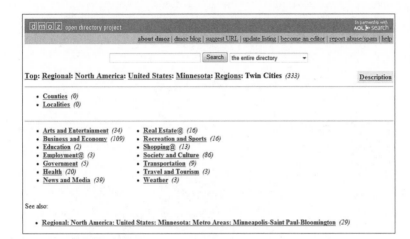

Figure 12.6

Browsing for local businesses with the Open Directory.

Table 12.2 details how to list your local site with the most important general web directories.

Table 12.2   General Web Directories

Directory	Home Page URL	How to Submit Your Site
Best of the Web	www.botw.org	Paid submittal at www.botw.org/helpcenter/submitcommercial.aspx.
JoeAnt	www.joeant.com	Submit at www.joeant.com/suggest.html.
Open Directory	www.dmoz.org	Go to appropriate category page and click Suggest URL.
Starting Point	www.stpt.com	Paid submittal at www.stpt.com/directory/addsite.htm.

Submitting to Local Websites

Many cities and localities have their own local websites and directories, often run by local newspapers or television stations. For example, the Boston.com site (www. boston.com), shown in Figure 12.7, provides local information as well as news from the *Boston Globe*. In addition, many local governments, chambers of commerce, and city convention bureaus host their own local sites; Figure 12.8 shows the Meet Minneapolis site, run by the city's Convention & Visitors Association.

Figure 12.7

The local Boston.com website.

Figure 12.8

Meet Minneapolis—courtesy of the city's Convention and Visitors Association.

These websites often include directories of local merchants and are great places to list your business. You should search for any local sites or directories for your area and do what you need to get listed on these sites.

Submitting to Business Information Providers

Finally, you should list your site information with the three major providers of business information:

◆ Acxiom (www.acxiom.com)

◆ Amacai (www.amacai.com)

◆ InfoUSA (www.infousa.com)

These companies consolidate business data (names and addresses) and then sell that information to other companies. Making sure these services have your location and website information ensures that your business will appear in lots of other places, both online and off. Visit their sites and look for the links that let you add or update your business data.

How Do You Optimize for Local Search?

Optimizing your site for local search requires a new angle on established techniques. That is, you do many of the same things as you do for general SEO, while emphasizing local information.

You have to include explicit local information on your site—local addresses, city and state names, store locators, local events and calendars, and the like. You then have to expose this information to the search engines by treating the most important local information as you would traditional keywords and phrases.

It's important that this information, especially store addresses, be in text format. Including a map of each of your locations is no good if you don't also include each location's address in text format. Remember, a map is an image file, and searchbots can't read or index image files. Maps are good for your human visitors, but they have to be supplemented by text information.

Remember, customers will be searching for businesses or products that are local to them. Their keywords will include things like a city name, state name, zip code, even street name or address. It's important, then, for you to add your local information as keywords and phrases to your site. These keywords can include any or all of the following:

◆ Street address

◆ City

◆ State

◆ Zip code

◆ Region

◆ Native nicknames ("Hoosier," "Gopher," and so on)

You should include these keywords—especially your street name, city, and state—in your site's **<META>** tags. If you have multiple locations, create a page for each one and include that location's address in each page's **<TITLE>** tag. Work the address and other local locators into the first paragraph of text on each page. You also shouldn't assume that your visitors know where you're located; even if they do, the searchbots won't.

And when you're defining your location, think the way your customers are likely to think. People do search within their city, but they may also search by larger metropolitan area or region. For example, if your business is in San Jose, California, you should definitely include "San Jose" as a key phrase—but you should also use phrases such as "Silicon Valley," "Bay Area," "South Bay," and the like. You want to reach as many potential customers as possible; as I continue to stress, you need to *think like the customer* and describe your location the way your customers are likely to.

So optimizing your site for local search is really just a matter of broadening your keyword set. Take into account your location(s), different ways of referring to that location, abbreviations for your region, local nomenclature, and the like. That means more keywords in more places on your site—a little more work, but worth it when you start attracting more of the local customer base.

Then, after you've optimized your site with local keywords, take the time to list your site with all the important local search engines, directories, and Yellow Pages sites. Most of these sites let you list your business for free; take advantage of this opportunity to put your site in front of as many users as possible.

The Least You Need to Know

◆ It's important to optimize your site for local search if you're trying to attract customers from a specific geographic area.

◆ When it comes to local search, local directories and search sites are as important as the major search engines—if not more so.

◆ Optimizing your site for local search involves placing your location and other local information in your site's content and using that information as keywords and phrases throughout your site.

◆ When you define your business's location, broaden your thinking to include the entire geographic region.

Chapter 13

Optimizing Your Site for Mobile Search

In This Chapter

◆ Defining mobile search

◆ Building a separate site for mobile users

◆ Optimizing your site for mobile search

In Chapter 12, we discussed the issue of local search and how to optimize your site for customers looking for local businesses and products. One growing subset of local search is *mobile search*—people using their mobile phones to search for places to go and things to buy. By some accounts, mobile search is *the* next big thing in search.

Is your site ready for the mobile search revolution? How do you optimize your site for mobile searches and for proper display on mobile phones—including Apple's popular iPhone?

Mobile search is similar to traditional search, but it definitely has its own set of challenges. Read on to learn more about mobile search—and mobile SEO techniques.

What Is Mobile Search—and Why Is It Important?

Mobile search is, quite simply, search optimized for and performed on a mobile device of some sort, typically an Internet-enabled mobile phone. There are many such phones on the market today, most notably Apple's iPhone.

Searching from a Mobile Phone

The iPhone makes searching the web surprisingly easy, thanks to the search application that Google provides as a free download from the iPhone Apps Store. That said, you can also use the iPhone's web browser to query any search engine optimized for mobile use, not just Google.

Figure 13.1 shows the Google search page on an Apple iPhone; you can use the iPhone's touch keyboard to enter a query. When the search results page appears, tap the link for any result to be taken directly to that page on the iPhone screen.

Figure 13.1

Searching Google on an iPhone.

Of course, the iPhone isn't the only smartphone on the market that lets you search the Internet. Figure 13.2 shows how the Google search page looks on a typical cellular phone; since the screen isn't quite as big as that of the iPhone, there's a bit more scrolling involved.

Figure 13.2

Google search on a more traditional mobile phone.

Users aren't limited to searching Google Mobile. People can point their phones' web browsers to any search site. Most notably, both Yahoo! and Live Search have pages optimized for mobile phone use. (Figure 13.3 shows Yahoo!'s mobile search service, Yahoo! oneSearch.)

Figure 13.3

Yahoo! oneSearch on a mobile phone.

Mobile Search Is Big—and Getting Bigger

Why should you concern yourself with mobile search? It's a matter of size; the market for mobile search is already big—and is going to get much bigger.

According to eMarketer (www.emarketer.com), there are already an estimated 28.8 million mobile searchers in the United States (as of 2008). This number is projected to grow to 55.8 million users by 2011. That's about 75 percent of all mobile Internet users, or 22 percent of all mobile phone users—a big chunk of the cellular market.

And here's the thing: most of these mobile searchers are looking for businesses. They use their phones when they're out and about and need to find something—a restaurant, a gas station, a bookstore, whatever. So if you work for a business with a local presence, you don't want to miss out on these millions of mobile searchers. If you're not appearing in mobile search results, you're missing out on all those customers.

That said, SEO for mobile search is arguably more important than for traditional web-based search. That's because of the small size of most mobile phone screens. Where it's okay to be number 20 in traditional search results, because most search engines display 20 results per page, most mobile search engines return just a half-dozen or so results per screen. If you're not in the top five or so, you're on page two (or three or four)—and, as we all know, results on the first page perform significantly stronger than those on subsequent pages.

Which Search Engines Are Important for Mobile Search?

Even though a lot of startups are targeting the mobile search market, things appear to be shaking out in favor of the big three, each of which has a mobile-specific search offering. These include the following:

> **Search Note**
>
> Some of the more interesting newcomers in the online search space allow you to find businesses via voice commands or text messages. These services include ASKbyText (www.askbytext.com) and ChaCha (www.chacha.com).

- Google Mobile (www.google.com/mobile)
- Live Search Mobile (www.livesearchmobile.com)
- Yahoo! Mobile oneSearch (http://mobile.yahoo.com/onesearch)

So when you're optimizing your site for mobile search, these are the sites to keep in mind—and submit to.

What Does Your Site Look Like on a Mobile Phone?

Before we get to the issue of mobile SEO, let's talk a little about what your site looks like on a mobile phone. The reality is, most websites don't look good on a mobile's smaller screen; you may also run into a problem of slow load times, as most mobile networks aren't as fast as most home Internet connections.

Bottom line: you can't rely on your current site to work well on mobile phones, which can frustrate any customers you attract via mobile search engines. Instead, you need to create a separate version of your site for mobile users.

Your mobile website should be smaller and less graphic-intensive than your normal site. Pages should be shorter and contain primarily text; avoid all Flash animations and videos, and keep images small and to a minimum. This new mobile site will exist side-by-side with your normal website, typically with a URL that looks like this: **m.yoursite.com** instead of the normal **www.yoursite.com.**

When coding for mobile devices, you should code to the XHTML 1.0 standard. Your code needs to be really tight; any coding errors will play havoc with the way your pages display on many devices. In addition, bad mobile code will really trip up most searchbots. So make sure you validate your code—and test it on various types of mobile phones.

> **Search Note**
>
> You can also use Cascading Style Sheets to offer an alternate version of your site for mobile devices. With the right CSS coding, mobile devices will trigger a different display of your pages, using more appropriate fonts and layouts.

You see, it's likely that your site will look different on different devices, and you need to account for that. If nothing else, there are four different screen sizes used for various types of phones, as you can see in Figure 13.4: 138×160 pixels, 176×220, 320×240, and 320×480 (used on the iPhone). You want to make sure your site looks good on all these different screens, which can be a bit of a challenge.

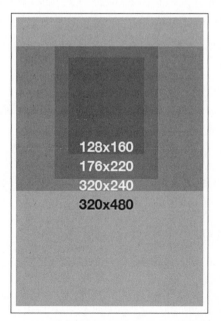

Figure 13.4

The four common mobile phone screen sizes.

Much more is involved in developing a mobile site than we have space for here. What's important, for now, is that you know you must develop a version of your site for mobile phones and other devices. For more information on how to do so, I suggest you check out *Microsoft Mobile Development Handbook* (Microsoft Press, 2007), by Andrew Wigley, Daniel Moth, and Peter Foot. This book contains just about everything you need to know to develop a first-class mobile website.

How Do You Optimize for Mobile Search?

Here's the most important thing to know about mobile SEO:

> Mobile search = local search

Most people searching on their mobile phones are looking for local information. They're looking for local businesses and services—in fact, they're looking for places close to their current location. (That makes the addition of GPS to Apple's iPhone an interesting development for the search engines.) In fact, you can think of mobile search as the "last mile" in SEO.

Performing Mobile Search Optimization

So what are the best practices for mobile SEO? They're primarily what you do to optimize your site for local search, including this:

Stop!

Don't forget to include your phone number on each mobile page. Many mobile users will want to phone you once they see your site in their search results.

- Add your address, city, state, zip code, and other location identifiers to your keyword list.

- Include your local keywords in each page's <TITLE>, <META>, and heading tags.

- Fold your local keywords into the body text of each page, as appropriate.

It's pretty straightforward stuff.

Creating Mobile Sitemaps

Just as creating a sitemap is important to getting all the pages on your traditional website noticed, you need to create a sitemap for your mobile site. In fact, both Google and Yahoo! have separate mobile sitemap submittal services for just that purpose.

Assuming that you have a separate mobile site, you need to create a distinct sitemap for that site. You can then submit your mobile sitemap to the major search engines.

To submit your mobile sitemap to Google, go to www.google.com/webmasters/tools/dashboard, enter the URL of your mobile site, and then click the Add Site button. On the next page, click the Add a Sitemap link beside your site. When the Add Sitemap page appears, as shown in Figure 13.5, pull down the drop-down list and select Mobile Sitemap; enter the full URL (including file name and path) for your sitemap; select the markup language you use for your site (XHTML, WML, or cHTML); and then click the Add Mobile Sitemap button.

SEO Tip _____

You can use the same sitemap-generation tools you use for your regular site to create your mobile sitemap.

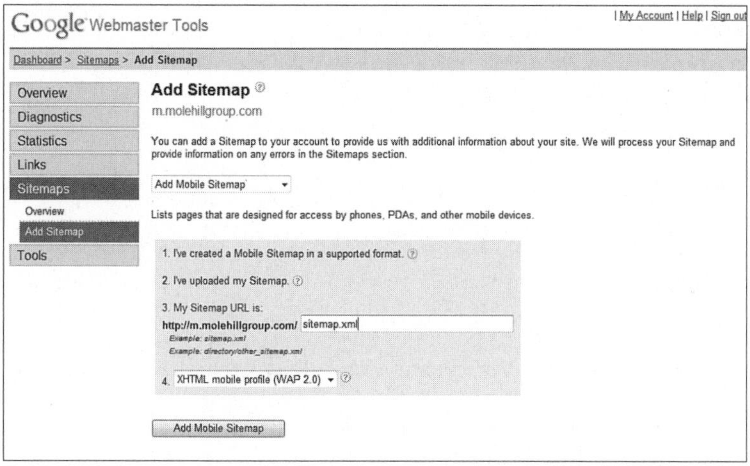

Figure 13.5

Adding a mobile sitemap to Google.

To submit your mobile sitemap to Yahoo!, go to http://siteexplorer.search.yahoo.com/mobilesubmit, shown in Figure 13.6. Enter the full URL (including file name and path) for your sitemap into the Submit Site Feed box, and then click the Submit Feed button.

Figure 13.6

Adding a mobile sitemap to Yahoo!.

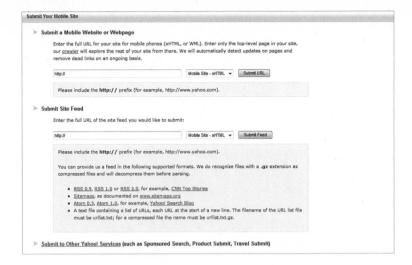

Unfortunately, there's no way to submit mobile sitemaps directly to Windows Live Search. Instead, insert a pointer to your sitemap in your mobile site's **robots.txt** file, as described in Chapter 11.

The Least You Need to Know

◆ The huge growth in Internet-enabled mobile phones, such as the Apple iPhone, has created an equally huge growth in mobile search—people using their cell phones to search for local businesses and places.

◆ If you have a local presence, you need to create a mobile website and optimize that site for mobile search.

◆ Mobile SEO is similar to local SEO—include keywords for all local identifiers, and place them in prominent positions on your site.

◆ You should also create a sitemap for your mobile site and submit it to both Google and Yahoo!.

14

Optimizing Your Site for Social Media

In This Chapter

- ◆ Defining social media
- ◆ Understanding why social media is important
- ◆ Optimizing for social media

Social media is the hottest new thing on the Internet. We're talking social networking sites, social bookmarking and news sites, blogs, and other forms of online communities. These are all sites that enable social interaction between users—and, in some instances, create new virtual communities around user interests.

Optimizing your site for social media involves a lot of the same techniques you use for search engine optimization, along with some new tricks and techniques. If you want these social media sites to link to your site, you need to learn more about how social media ticks—and how to become part of these social communities.

What Is Social Media?

"Social media" is a big buzzword among online marketers today, and for good reason. Social media sites are generating huge traffic numbers; if you can siphon off a portion of those visitors, you can increase your own site's traffic.

But what, exactly, is social media? Put as simply as possible, social media are those websites, services, and platforms that people use to share experiences and opinions with each other. That covers everything from social bookmarking services (users share the sites and articles they like) to social networks (users share the details of their own lives), and includes blogs and other forms of online communities.

The thing is, all of these sites and services are places you can put your marketing messages—which, of course, can and should include links back to your website. In this fashion, social media function as kind of an ad hoc search network; instead of querying a single search index, users search for information in their favorite online social communities.

In case you're new to this whole social media thing, let's take a quick look at each type of social media—and the big players to target.

Social Networking Sites

Social networking is perhaps the most visible social medium today. Chances are, you've at least heard of the two leading social networks, Facebook and MySpace— especially if you have a teenager in the household. The young people today like their social networks! In fact, my wife's teenaged kids can't spend more than five minutes or so without checking in or posting something new to their social network profiles; it's addictive.

A social network is a large website that aims to create a community of users. Each user posts his or her own personal profile on the site, like the one shown in Figure 14.1. There's enough personal information in each profile to enable other users with similar interests to connect as "friends"; one's growing collection of friends helps to build a succession of personal communities.

Most profile pages include some form of blog, discussion forum, or chat space so that friends can communicate with the person profiled. In many instances, individual users also post a running list of their current activities so that their friends always know what they're up to.

Figure 14.1

The author's Facebook profile page.

If you're targeting social networks, the two biggest in the United States are Facebook (www.facebook.com) and MySpace (www.myspace.com). Of the two, Facebook is more of a site for older youngsters, typically high school and college aged and older. MySpace is more of a site for younger teenagers and preteens.

You can make it easy for social networking users to add content from and to your site to their profile pages. All you have to do is insert a "quick add" button on your web page; for example, Figure 14.2 shows a "quick add" button for Facebook. Users who click this button are prompted to add this page to their social network profile page. The selected content now appears, typically in summarized form with accompanying link, in the "feed" section of that user's profile page, as shown in Figure 14.3.

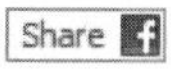

Figure 14.2

A Facebook "quick add" button.

Figure 14.3

Web page content added to a Facebook profile page.

Social Bookmarking Services

A social bookmarking or news service lets users share their favorite websites with friends and colleagues over the web. Here's how it works: a user visits a website or page or even news article that he likes, then clicks a button or link to bookmark that site. (Figure 14.4 shows a typical bookmarking button, from Digg.) This bookmark then appears in his master list of bookmarks on the social news site; the user can share all or specific bookmarks with anyone he designates.

Figure 14.4

Click the button to bookmark the site with Digg.

Most social bookmarking sites use tags to help users find bookmarked sites. When users bookmark a site, they add a few tags or keywords to describe the site. Other users can then search by keywords to find the most popular matching bookmarked sites—just as they search Google and the other traditional search engines.

The top social bookmarking services include these:

- BlinkList (www.blinklist.com)
- ClipClip (www.clipclip.org)
- Clipmarks (www.clipmarks.com)
- del.icio.us (http://del.icio.us), shown in Figure 14.5
- Digg (www.digg.com)
- Feedmarker (www.feedmarker.com)
- Furl (www.furl.net)
- Google Bookmarks (www.google.com/bookmarks/)
- Ma.gnolia.com (ma.gnolia.com)
- Mixx (www.mixx.com)
- Reddit (www.reddit.com)
- StumbleUpon (www.stumbleupon.com)
- Tagseasy (www.tagseasy.com)
- Yahoo! MyWeb (http://myweb.yahoo.com)

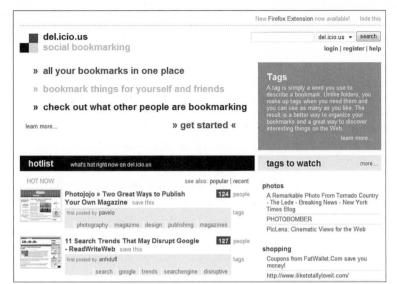

Figure 14.5

The del.icio.us social book-marking site.

Social bookmark services are great ways to spread timely and interesting content. The most notable bookmarks on these sites quickly turn viral, as one user after another shares links with other users.

Blogs

Blogs can also send a lot of visitors to your website. When a blog mentions your site in a post and includes a link back to your site, you can see your traffic spike. For this reason, many online marketers view blogs as important outlets for their public relations activities, cultivating personal relationships with the top bloggers in their chosen field.

While optimizing for social networks and social bookmark services tends to result in long-term visibility, optimizing for blogs is both a long-term process and a bit of a hit-and-run affair. The long-term optimization comes from getting your site on a blog's blog roll, the list of blogs the blogmeister recommends. The hit-and-miss aspect comes from targeting individual blog posts; the resulting hit is good only as long as the post is current.

Search Note

Learn more about blogs in Chapter 15, "Optimizing Your Blog for Search Engines."

Online Communities

You can find a lot of other online communities on the web. These typically take the form of websites or groups devoted to a particular topic or hobby. The community aspect comes from the site's forum or message board, where users gather to exchange messages about the topic at hand.

For example, Google Groups (groups.google.com) hosts tens of thousands of topic-specific groups. Each group includes a message forum (for text-based messages), the ability to upload and share files, and group notices and e-mails. Similar to Google Groups is Yahoo! Groups (groups.yahoo.com), which also offers message forums (shown in Figure 14.6) and file uploading, as well as photo libraries, group calendars, and polls.

Figure 14.6

A Yahoo! Groups message forum.

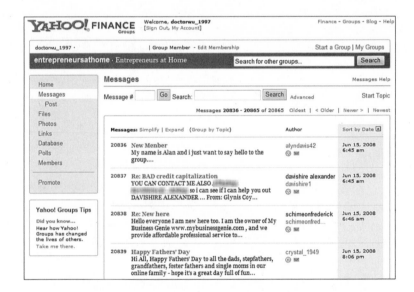

It makes sense to seek out those online groups and communities related to your site's primary topic. You can solicit links in the community's "related sites" list, as well as contribute to and encourage links from the group's message forums.

Why Is Social Media Important?

For a number of reasons, you need to include social media as part of your online marketing mix and optimize your site for social media. For some sites, social media optimization can be just as important as search engine optimization.

First, know that social media sites can drive huge amounts of traffic to your website. If your site builds a large friends list on Facebook, gets bookmarked on Digg, or gets mentioned in a post for a major blog, you can see a significant spike in traffic—as well as a lasting long-term increase in your visitor base. These social network sites have a lot of users, and getting your site in front of them can make or break your traffic goals.

An added benefit of getting mentioned on any of these social sites is that each link or bookmark creates a new link back to your site. And, as you know, your ranking in Google, Live Search, and Yahoo! search results at least partly depends on the number of inbound links your site receives. The more bookmarks, the more links—and the higher your search results.

And here's a cool thing about the links you get from social media sites—these links are organic. Individual users are making the decision to create these links; they're not being paid or otherwise induced to do so. To your benefit, search engines view these organic links as high-quality links and reward your site accordingly.

At the end of the day, think of social media as word-of-mouth marketing. Online or off, a strong word-of-mouth campaign trumps just about any form of paid advertising or promotion you can engage in. It's quality attention, which results in quality traffic.

SEO Tip

Mention from a prominent blogger or community member often carries more weight than a regular website link. That's because these people are influencers; other users look to them to help form their opinions. When you have an influencer linking to your site, you'll soon see other sites and bloggers linking to you—because they were positively influenced.

What Is Social Media Optimization—and How Does It Work?

Social media optimization (SMO) is the act of fine-tuning your website so that it is more easily linked to from social media sites, more visible in searches conducted on those sites, and more frequently included in relevant posts and messages on those sites. SMO is a lot like SEO, in that you utilize important keywords and phrases, but it has its own unique aspects.

Let's look at what you need to do.

Improve Your Linkworthiness

Before you can get bookmarked and linked to, your site has to include content that people want to share with their friends and colleagues. This is our old friend, the concept of "linkworthiness." Your content must be linkworthy, or no one will link to it or bookmark it.

This also means keeping your content fresh. Older, unchanged content may get bookmarked once, but bookmarks quickly age. It's much better to constantly add fresh content to your site so that each new item you add has the opportunity to be bookmarked anew.

Make Bookmarking Easy

This is a no-brainer that not enough sites do. If you want your site to be bookmarked with the major social bookmarking services, include a button that makes bookmarking a one-click process. That means picking the social bookmark sites you want to target, such as Digg and del.icio.us, and adding buttons to each page that users can click to automatically bookmark those pages. (Figure 14.7 shows the plethora of "quick add" buttons that the Slate website includes with each of its articles.) Add these buttons in a prominent position, typically in a sidebar along the left or right side of your page; try not to hide them at the very bottom. Preface the buttons with text along the lines of "Share this article" or "Bookmark this page."

Figure 14.7

"Quick add" buttons for a variety of social bookmarking services, attached to a Slate article.

You can even get fancy and use JavaScript to display a pop-up menu of social bookmark links when a user clicks a Share This link. For example, Figure 14.6 shows what users see when they click the Share link at the top of an article on the *Indianapolis Star* website—"quick add" links for del.icio.us, Digg, Reddit, Yahoo!, and Google.

In addition, you may want to include a list of relevant tags or keywords alongside the "quick add" buttons, like the one in Figure 14.9, so that bookmarkers will know how to tag their bookmarks. These should be a subset of your site's existing keyword list. You may also want to include suggested text that people can use when they create a link to your site.

Figure 14.8

A pop-up menu of social bookmarking links on an Indianapolis Star *article.*

Figure 14.9

Suggested tags alongside social networking buttons on CNET's News.com website.

Participate in the Communities

Finally, if you want your site to get mentioned on a blog or web community, you have to participate in those communities. Social media is a two-way street: you can't just ask for links—you have to provide something in return. In most instances, that something is your own input—commenting on blog posts, joining in on message board threads, and the like. When you become a member of a given community, the results will snowball.

The Least You Need to Know

◆ Social media include social networks (Facebook and MySpace), social bookmarking services (Digg and del.icio.us), blogs, and online communities and groups.

◆ Social media not only drives traffic to your website, but it also provides high-quality links to your site—which can improve your ranking with Google and other search engines.

◆ Optimizing your site for social media involves creating linkworthy content and inserting "quick add" buttons for all the major social bookmarking services on your web pages.

◆ To get full benefit from social media, you have to be an active participant in these online communities; social media is a two-way street.

Chapter 15

Optimizing Your Blog for Search Engines

In This Chapter

◆ Understanding how blogs differ from traditional websites

◆ Searching for blog posts

◆ Optimizing your blog for search

◆ Submitting your blog to search engines

If you don't have your own blog yet, you probably will soon. It seems as if everybody and his dog has a blog these days; some people have more than one. And blogs have become an essential part of many companies' online presence, a way to humanize the company while delivering timely information to customers and employees alike.

Traditional websites argue for traditional SEO methods. But blogs aren't traditional websites, so they require a slightly different SEO approach. How do search engines deliver blog postings in their search results? How do you get your blog posts to rank as high as possible? And what other ways are there for users to find specific posts on your blog?

All good questions—and all answered in this chapter. Read on to learn more.

How Blogs Differ from Traditional Websites

In case you've been living in a cave without Internet access for the past few years, a blog (short for "web log") is a kind of online journal that its author updates frequently with new musings and information. Blogs can be personal or professional; there are a ton of company and industry-specific blogs out there.

A blog's content consists of a series of various and sundry musings, in the form of individual blog posts. Posts can be made as frequently or infrequently as you want, although it's generally best to keep the content fresh in order to keep readers from wandering. Readers of a blog can typically comment on postings, and you can respond to their responses. In this way, a blog is an organic thing.

And although blogs reside on the web and are viewed via web browsers, they're organized much differently than normal websites. Instead of the standard home page plus subsidiary page structure, a blog typically has just a single page of entries. This main page contains the most recent posts and might require a bit of scrolling to get to the bottom. There is no introductory page; this main page serves as both introduction and primary content.

Older posts are typically stored in the blog archives. You'll typically find a link to the archives somewhere on the blog's main page; there might be one huge archive or individual archives organized by month.

The blog posts themselves are displayed in reverse chronological order. That means that the most recent post is always at the top of the page, with older posts below that. Comments to a post are typically in normal chronological order; you may have to click a link to see a separate page of comments.

Aside from the blog posts themselves, most blogs have some form of subsidiary and relatively constant content in the form of a sidebar, as shown in Figure 15.1. This is a small column running down the left or right side of the blog; a sidebar typically contains links to archived posts, access to articles via common tags or labels, and, in some cases, a search box to search the contents of the blog for specific information. (And, in case you're wondering, search engines can search the content in both blog posts and the blog sidebar.)

Beyond this basic structure, that's all the organization you're likely to find in most blogs. That's because, for many bloggers, blog entries are a stream-of-consciousness thing. Bloggers blog when they find something interesting to write about, which makes the typical personal blog a little like a public diary. Don't look for a logical flow or organization; that's not what blogs are about. Instead, post your thoughts and opinions as they occur. It's the way the blogosphere works.

Figure 15.1

A typical blog, with chrono-logical posts and a static sidebar.

This makes a blog quite different from a traditional website. Instead of the relatively static content of a traditional website, a blog's content is constantly changing. New content is added on a regular basis; newer posts kick the older posts off the main page. And loyal readers don't even bother going to the blog page—instead, they receive new posts via subscription to a syndicated feed. In this manner, a blog is more like a daily newspaper, delivered to subscribers via e-mail or a blog-reader program.

The Many Different Ways to Search for Blog Posts

Not discounting regular readers, how does someone new find out about your blog? Is there a way for the search results of Google and other major search engines to serve up the content in your blog?

Users can search for the content contained in blog posts in several ways. Not surprisingly, Google plays a big role in all these kinds of blog search.

Traditional Search Engines

The first and perhaps most common way that users can find your blog and blog posts is by searching Google, Yahoo!, and the other traditional search engines. All three of the major search engines are quite good at integrating blog posts into their universal search results; they treat blog content the same as they do content from traditional websites.

Blog Search Engines

Then there are the dedicated blog search engines, search engines devoted solely to searching blogs and blog posts. The most popular of these is Google Blog Search (blogsearch.google.com), shown in Figure 15.2. When you query Google Blog Search, the results are limited to content posted on blogs only; as you can see in Figure 15.3, matching blogs are listed at the top of the results page, while matching blog posts are displayed underneath. You can also filter the results by freshness, listing posts published in the last hour, last 12 hours, last day, past week, past month, or anytime.

Figure 15.2

Searching blog posts with Google Blog Search.

Figure 15.3

A Google Blog Search results page, with matching blogs listed above individual posts.

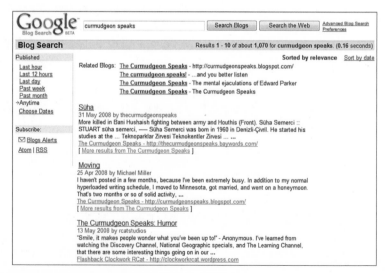

Other blog search engines include the generically named Blog Search Engine (www. blogsearchengine.com) and Ask.com's blog search tool (go to www.ask.com and click the Blogs icon).

Search Note

Several blog *directories* also exist on the web. These are listings of blogs, typically organized by category. But most users find these directories less usable than the afore-mentioned search engines, as not all blogs are listed in each directory. In addition, these directories list only blogs, not the contents of individual blog posts, making them even less usable. For that reason, we're going to ignore blog directories here—just as most users do.

How to Optimize Your Blog for Search

Now we come to what you're most interested in—how to optimize your blog for search. The good news is, blogs are structured in a way that is very easy for searchbots to crawl. Because of their natural hierarchical structure, search engines like blogs a whole lot.

You see, a blog is really a database of information (the blog postings) and a page template. The information in the database is displayed via the template, which results in the blog page readers see in their web browsers. You need to optimize the data in the database and the layout and content of the template.

Optimizing the Blog Template

The first thing to pay attention to is your blog's template, which defines how blog posts are displayed. The template also contains the content that surrounds the blog posts themselves—the blog title and description, as well as everything displayed in the blog's sidebar.

As with traditional websites, keywords are important to optimizing your blog. After you decide on the keywords and phrases that reference the main topics of your blog, you need to insert those keywords within your blog's descriptive text—which, ideally, should appear high on your blog page, probably directly underneath the name of the blog. You should also place important keywords in the template's **<TITLE>** tag, **<META>** tags, and all alternative image text. Search engines look for these keywords when they're indexing blogs; the more prominent and relevant the keywords in your blog, the higher your blog will appear in the search engine's results.

You also need to take a look at your blog template to see how it handles the display of your blog posts. In most blogs, the template determines that the title of the blog post links to the full text of the post. You need to make sure that the titles of your posts actually are links, so that search engines pick up the link from the title to the post. Not all blog templates do this by default.

Finally, look at the contents of your template's sidebar. To get your blog and blog posts noticed in social media, you want to add "quick add" buttons for major social bookmarking services (Digg, del.icio.us, and so on) and social network sites (Facebook and MySpace). If you can, configure your template so that these buttons are automatically added to the bottom of each blog post as well.

Optimizing Blog Posts

You can also optimize each post on your blog. Here you use traditional SEO techniques.

Start by including keywords and phrases in the title of each blog post. This is even more important than with traditional websites, since many content syndicators and aggregators list only the title of a post. Because only the title is seen in most news readers, this makes the title much more important than the main text of a post.

Next, focus on the content of each post. Again, it's important to weave keywords and phrases into the post text, especially in the first paragraph of longer posts. Consider the first few sentences of a blog post as important as the **<META> DESCRIPTION** tag on a traditional website; it's what you see when your post is listed on a search engine's results page.

If a post includes links to other blogs or websites, make sure you sprinkle keywords into the links' anchor text. Do the same if you include an internal link to another post on your blog.

Finally, liberally apply labels or tags to each of your posts. These tags are one of the ways that readers find content on your blog, but they're also useful to searchbots trying to determine your blog's content. Assign each keyword or phrase a separate label; since these labels are internal links to your post, that increases the number of links, which is always a good thing.

Submitting Your Blog to the Major Search Engines

Although submitting your blog to the major search engines is very similar to submitting your website, you need to take several differences into account. The most important difference involves something called a *site feed*—and you need to know how it works.

Understanding Site Feeds

One of the key ways to disseminate blog posts is to syndicate your blog content via a site feed. This feed is an automatically updated stream of a blog's contents, enabled by a special XML file format called RSS (Really Simple Syndication). When a blog has an RSS feed enabled, any updated content is automatically published as a special XML file that contains the RSS feed. The syndicated feed is then normally picked up by RSS feed reader programs and RSS aggregators for websites.

When you enable your blog for syndication, any new post you make is automatically fed to any user subscribing to your site. In effect, your new content is "pushed" to interested subscribers, without them having to revisit your site to find out what's new. The more subscribers you have, the more interested readers/viewers you have.

And here's the neat thing about RSS blog feeds: Google, Yahoo!, and Windows Live Search automatically index them. That's right, the major search engines use your RSS feed to update their search indexes.

For this reason alone, you want to enable your blog for both RSS and Atom syndication. Most blog-hosting services make this easy to do, typically when you sign up for the service. You can also enable feeds for your blog via Feedburner (www.feedburner.com), a free service (owned by Google) that automates the syndication process.

Search Note
Atom is a feed format similar to RSS, with a few extra features. You should make your blog compatible with both RSS and Atom feeds.

Submitting Your Site Feed

Site feeds are important because Google and the other major search engines have difficulty tracking frequently updated content—in particular, the type of dynamic content blogs generate. Put simply, searchbots don't crawl dynamic pages as well as they do static pages. (This has to do with how long it takes some dynamic pages to load; spiders allocate only a certain amount of time per page before they move on to the next site to index.)

The solution, as you might suspect, is to publish your blog's content as an RSS feed. The search engines do a good job digesting RSS feeds to populate their search

> **Stop!** _____
>
> The only downside to sub-mitting your blog feed to the major search engines is that your feed may include only information about your most recent posts. Older blog posts may not end up in the search indexes.

indexes. When in doubt, make sure that you generate an RSS feed for all your dynamic content.

To submit your site feed to the major search engines, you first need to know the URL of the feed. You can find this by clicking the RSS or Atom button found on your blog; the URL of the next page, like the one shown in Figure 15.4, is your site feed URL. It's typically something like www.yourblogname.com/rss.xml or www.yourblogname.com/atom.xml, although that varies from service to service.

Figure 15.4

A typical site feed page; use the URL of this page to submit your feed to search engines.

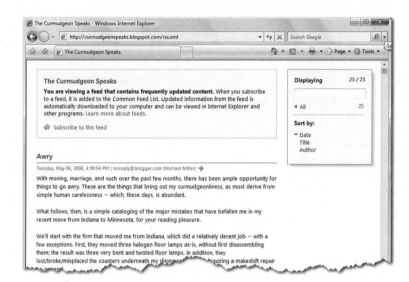

> **SEO Tip** _____
>
> Google owns Blogger, the popular blog-hosting service. If you use Blogger to host your blog, Blogger automatically submits a sitemap of your blog to the Google Search Index—there's nothing more you need to do.

With Google, you submit your site feed using Google's sitemap submission process; Google accepts RSS 2.0 and Atom 1.0 feeds. Begin by going to www.google.com/webmasters/tools/dashboard and adding your blog as a new site. Then click the Add a Sitemap link and enter the URL for your site feed.

With Yahoo!, go to http://siteexplorer.search.yahoo.com/submit/ and enter the URL of your feed into the Submit Site Feed box, shown in Figure 15.5. Yahoo! accepts RSS 0.9, 1.0, and 2.0 feeds, as well as Atom 0.3 and 1.0 feeds.

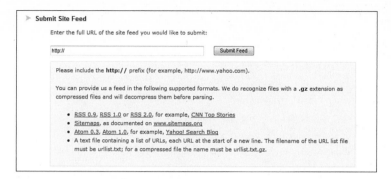

Figure 15.5

Submitting a blog site feed to Yahoo!.

To submit your feed to Windows Live Search, go to http://search.msn.com.sg/docs/submit.aspx and enter the URL of your site feed.

With your feed submitted, the search engines should be notified via the feed whenever you make a new post to your blog. There's nothing more for you to do.

The Least You Need to Know

◆ A blog is similar to a traditional website, except with a constant flow of new content (in the form of blog posts).

◆ Users can search for blog posts at Google and the other traditional search engines, or via specialized blog search engines, such as Google Blog Search.

◆ To optimize your blog for search, you must target both the blog's template and the content of each individual post.

◆ To make sure the search engines know about your blog and its newest content, submit your blog's RSS or Atom site feed to the search engines.

Part 4

Analyzing Your Site's Performance

Want to know how well your SEO is working? Then turn to this part, which addresses how to track search engine performance, use third-party tracking and analysis tools, avoid the most common SEO mistakes, and maintain your site's SEO on an ongoing basis.

Chapter 16

Tracking Search Engine Performance

In This Chapter

◆ Learn six metrics that help you determine how well your SEO is working

◆ Discover the ultimate metric

◆ Understand why it pays to improve your performance and analyze the results

◆ Find out how to track Google, Live Search, and Yahoo! performance

Okay, you've evaluated all the SEO techniques presented so far in this book and applied those that you think will work best with your site. You've revamped all your pages accordingly and submitted your site to the major search engines.

Now what?

Well, you could just wait for new traffic to arrive—or hope that it will. But that could be a long wait—if, in fact, your efforts have a positive effect. A better approach is to proactively track your rankings at the major search engines, to determine how effective your SEO efforts really were.

How do you track your site's search engine performance? Each search engine has its own tools, which we discuss in this chapter.

What Data Is Most Important?

As we review the analytical tools available from the major search engines and various third parties, you may be overwhelmed by the sheer number of statistics that can be generated. All of these tools are quite good at collecting data about the visitors to your website and then cutting that data in countless different ways. With all this data available, which should you focus on?

Every expert has his or her own opinion on this, but I've chosen six metrics that will help you determine how well your SEO is working. I'm not implying that you should ignore all the other data, of course—it's just that these metrics are good indicators of why your site ranks as it does.

Visitors

Our first key metric is a simple one—the number of visitors, either on a site-wide or page-specific basis. You want to look at the number of visitors over time instead of on a specific date; a one-time snapshot doesn't really tell you that much. But if you see that the number of visitors per day is increasing over time, you know you're doing something right.

Pageviews and Landing Pages

Next up are two related statistics. We'll start with pageviews.

A pageview is simply how many times a particular page has been viewed. The more pageviews, the more popular the page. You should look at pageviews for two reasons. The first is to see how the popularity of a page increases over time; an increasing number of pageviews means that you're doing something to attract more traffic to the page. The second reason is to determine the relative popularity of pages on your site—that is, which are your site's most popular pages, as determined by their respective number of pageviews.

A landing page is the page where a visitor enters your site. Don't assume that all visitors enter via your site's home page; that simply isn't the case. Instead, look at the most popular landing (or entrance) pages, and try to determine why these pages attract so many visitors. Is it because they're searched for or linked to? (You can use two of the other metrics—queries and inbound links, which we discuss in short order—to help answer this question.)

Visit Length

Getting visitors to your site is one thing; keeping them there is another.

To that end, examine the average length of a visit to your site. How long did the typical visitor stay on your site (in minutes), and how many pages did he view while visiting? A short visit with few pages viewed means you're not retaining users. You should always strive for longer visits, which gives you more time to sell your products, services, or brands to potential customers.

Above all, you want to be alerted to any page on your site that has a high *bounce rate*—that is, a page that visitors land on and then immediately leave for another site. These are pages that definitely aren't working!

Referring Sites

Now let's turn our attention to how visitors get to your site. I'm always interested in which sites drive the most traffic to my site; these are sites to cultivate in terms of reciprocal links or optimized keywords.

First, look for some sort of pie chart or graph that breaks out referring sites by type. These charts typically segment inbound traffic as coming from *referring sites* (sites with direct inbound links to yours), *search sites* (Google, Yahoo!, and the rest), *direct links* (users entering your site's URL directly into their web browsers), and *other*. Analyzing this data tells you how important search engines and referring sites are to your site traffic.

Next, take a look at which specific sites are driving the most traffic to your site. Chances are, Google and Yahoo! will be among the top traffic drivers, but that isn't always the case. Display this data in descending order, and make a note to pay special attention to the top-referring sites; it's also a good idea to find out *why* a lot of traffic is coming from a given site.

Stop!

If your site shows a low percentage of traffic coming from search engines, don't assume that search engines aren't important. It's just as likely that your site is ranking low with the major search engines, and you need to beef up your SEO efforts.

For example, one month I was curious why I had an unexpected spike in traffic. I analyzed the traffic and discovered that most of the extra traffic came from a single site, a popular topic-based message forum. Further analysis determined that someone on that forum had posted a positive comment about a page on my site, along with a link to that page. That single message resulted in a noticeable uptick in traffic—and it was totally unplanned and unexpected!

Queries

For the portion of traffic coming from the search engines, you want to determine which keywords are generating the most traffic. Take a look at the list of queries or keywords generated by your analytical tool; this will tell you the most important keywords for your site.

If this list matches your own internal keyword list, great. If not, you may want to either rethink which keywords are most important (based on the ranking of actual keyword queries) or rework your site's SEO to better emphasize your desired keywords.

Inbound Links

Finally, examine those sites that have the most effective inbound links to your site. You want to see not only which sites are doing the linking, but *how* they're linking—which pages on your site they link to, and the anchor text used for the links. This will tell you what content on your site is most popular with these external sites. It's a great way to judge what you're doing well, at least in the eyes of other sites on the web.

The Ultimate Metric: Search Engine Rank

Up till now, we've discussed metrics that measure your site traffic—number of visitors, where they come from, how long they stay, and so on. But when you want to see how well your SEO plan is working, there's one much more direct metric to measure. That's right, we're talking raw search engine rankings.

To be precise, you have to judge your ranking at a given site for a given keyword. That is, your site doesn't rank in and of itself; it ranks only in regard to searches conducted for a specific keyword or phrase. So to ascertain your search ranking, you have to query the search site for the keyword or phrase in question and see where your site ranks. The higher your site ranks in the results, the better you're doing.

The problem with trying to determine your site's ranking, however, is that your ranking at any given search engine depends on more than just your site; the quality of competing sites also affects how high you rank. This is why your ranking might change from day to day, or even from hour to hour. It may be nothing you're doing; it may, in fact, be the result of changes made to competing sites.

For example, let's say that you typically rank in the middle of the first page of Google's search results for a given keyword. If a new and better site comes online, you could find your ranking decrease—even if you changed nothing about your site. The performance of the new site affects your ratings, knocking you down as the new site takes your place in the rankings.

> **Search Note**
>
> Google's Webmaster Tools tells you the average PageRank of the pages on your site (in terms of High, Medium, or Low), but it doesn't tell you the absolute ranking of any of your pages. You have to find that out manually for each keyword you're optimizing for.

Remember this, then. All the analytical tools we discuss in this chapter and the next can't tell you your precise ranking. You can determine your ranking only at a given point in time by querying a search engine with a particular keyword or phrase.

Why It Pays to Improve Your Performance

So you work hard to optimize your site and use the tools discussed in this chapter to analyze your performance. Obviously, you want your SEO to improve your site's ranking on various search results pages and, thus, to increase traffic to your site. But how much of an increase can you can expect to achieve?

Oneupweb (www.oneupweb.com), a firm offering search engine optimization and marketing solutions, analyzed what a bump in Google's search rankings might mean to a website, in terms of increased traffic. The gains are impressive.

The first month a site appears on Google's first page of search results, the number of unique visitors to the site more than triples, increasing 337 percent from preresults levels. By the end of the second month, traffic doubles again, for a total increase of 627 percent from preresults levels.

That's right, if you successfully employ SEO techniques in a way that places your site in Google's top 20 matching sites, you can expect your site traffic to increase six-fold. That, my friends, is why SEO is important—and why it pays to analyze your results to maximize your site's performance.

Tracking Google Performance with Google Analytics

We start our tour of performance-tracking tools with those tools provided by the three major search engines. As you might suspect, these tools track a page's search performance at that particular search engine; for example, don't expect Google's tool to tell you how well you're doing with Yahoo! or Live Search.

That said, the search engines' tracking tools are surprisingly robust—none more than Google Analytics, Google's in-house analytical tool. Like just about everything Google, Google Analytics is free.

What Google Analytics Analyzes

Google Analytics (www.google.com/analytics/) generates a variety of detailed statistics about your website's visitors. You can use Google Analytics to determine the following:

◆ The number of visitors to your site and how much time they spend there

◆ The speed of the Internet connection used by your visitors

◆ The types of web browsers and screen resolution used by your site's visitors

◆ Which sites are sending you the most traffic

◆ Where, geographically, visitors are coming from (on a city level)

◆ What keywords your visitors searched for to find your site

◆ Which pages on your site were most popular

◆ The most popular entrance (landing) and exit pages on your site

◆ Visitor trending over time

> **SEO Tip**
>
> If you use Google's AdWords pay-per-click advertising program, Google Analytics helps you optimize your AdWords campaigns. The tool lets you define and track various goals, including sales, lead generation, page views, and file downloads.

Activating Google Analytics

You access Google Analytics from www.google.com/analytics/. After you first sign in with your Google account, you're prompted to sign up for the GA program; it's free to do so.

Next, you're prompted to provide some key information—the site's URL, your name and contact info, and so forth. When you're done with this, Google creates your GA account and displays a block of HTML code. This code block must be inserted into the underlying HTML of each page you want to track; the code goes in the body text section of your page, immediately before the final **</body>** tag. The code looks something like this:

```
<script type="text/javascript">
var gaJsHost = (("https:" == document.location.protocol) ? "https://ssl." :
"http://www.");
document.write(unescape("%3Cscript src='" + gaJsHost + "google-analytics.
com/ga.js' type='text/javascript'%3E%3C/script%3E"));
</script>
<script type="text/javascript">
var pageTracker = _gat._getTracker("trackingID");
pageTracker._initData();
pageTracker._trackPageview();
</script>
```

After the code has been inserted, Google Analytics can start tracking the pages on your site.

Using the Dashboard

When you've set up your site with the Google Analytics code and given Analytics time to crawl your site and assemble the requested data, you can view the reports that Analytics generates about your site. Just go to the main Google Analytics page and click the View Reports link next to your site. This displays the Dashboard page, shown in Figure 16.1. Think of the Dashboard as a summary of the data gathered, as well as a gateway to more detailed reports.

The Dashboard displays the following information:

- Daily site traffic over the past 30 days

- Site usage statistics: number of visits, pageviews, pages viewed per visit, bounce rate, average time on site, and percentage of new visitors

- A Traffic Sources Overview pie chart that shows what types of sites (referring or linking sites, search engines, direct URL entry, and other) generated traffic to your site

SEO Tip

You can configure Google Analytics to track the performance of multiple websites under a single Google account.

◆ The most popular pages on your site, ranked by number of pageviews

◆ A world map that displays where your site visitors are located

Figure 16.1

The Google Analytics Dashboard.

At the top of the Dashboard is an interactive graph that can display a variety of different data—visits, pageviews, pages per visit, average time on site, bounce rate, and percentage of new visitors. Select the data to display from the pull-down list; then click anywhere on the resulting chart to display more information in a pop-up window.

Additional Reports

Google Analytics includes 80 different reports and variations that analyze various aspects of your site traffic. To access these reports, select the appropriate links on the left side of the Dashboard.

What kinds of reports can you generate? Table 16.1 provides an overview of what's available.

Table 16.1   Google Analytics Reports

Report Type	Individual Reports
Visitors	Overview, Benchmarking, Map Overlay, New vs. Returning, Languages, Visitor Trending, Visitor Loyalty, Browser Capabilities, Network Properties, and various user-defined reports
Traffic Sources	Overview, Direct Traffic, Referring Sites, Search Engines, All Traffic Sources, Keywords, AdWords, Campaigns, and Ad Versions
Content	Overview, Top Content, Content by Title, Content Drilldown, Top Landing Pages, Top Exit Pages, Site Overlay, and various Site Search reports—Overview, Usage, Search Terms, Start Pages, Destination Pages, Categories, and Trending
Goals	Overview, Total Conversions, Conversion Rate, Abandoned Funnels, Goal Value, and Funnel Visualization

As noted in our discussion of the Dashboard, the reports in Google Analytics are quite visual, which makes the data easier to grasp. For example, the Traffic Sources Overview, shown in Figure 16.2, provides a visual representation of where your site traffic is coming from—direct traffic, referring sites, or search engines. There's also a list of the top traffic sources, as well as the top keywords used to find your site via Google search.

A lot lies beneath the surface of Google Analytics—more than can be discussed in this chapter—including the ability to create custom dashboards and reports. I recommend that you visit the site, click around the various reports, and check out the help files. I guarantee that you'll find information about your site that will surprise you—and help you increase your site traffic.

Figure 16.2

The Traffic Sources Overview report.

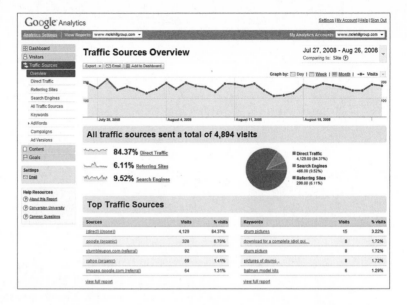

Tracking Google Performance with Webmaster Tools

Google Analytics isn't the only site-analysis tool Google offers. In fact, it may not even be the best tool for determining how well your site is being crawled. For that, I recommend you check out Google's Webmaster Tools, located at www.google.com/webmasters/tools/.

Google's Webmaster Tools, like Google Analytics, is a free service. Unlike Google Analytics, you don't have to insert any code into your web pages to generate Webmaster Tools data. It does help, however, if you've submitted a sitemap of your website to Google beforehand.

The Webmaster Tools Dashboard, shown in Figure 16.3, lists all the websites you've registered with Google to date. You can add websites to the Dashboard via the Add Site box at the top of the page. Once added, Google performs all available analysis.

Viewing Overview Information

To view details about a website, click the site's name in the Dashboard. This displays the Webmaster Tools Overview page, shown in Figure 16.4. This page conveys the following information about your site:

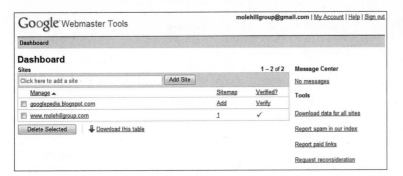

Figure 16.3

The Webmaster Tools Dashboard.

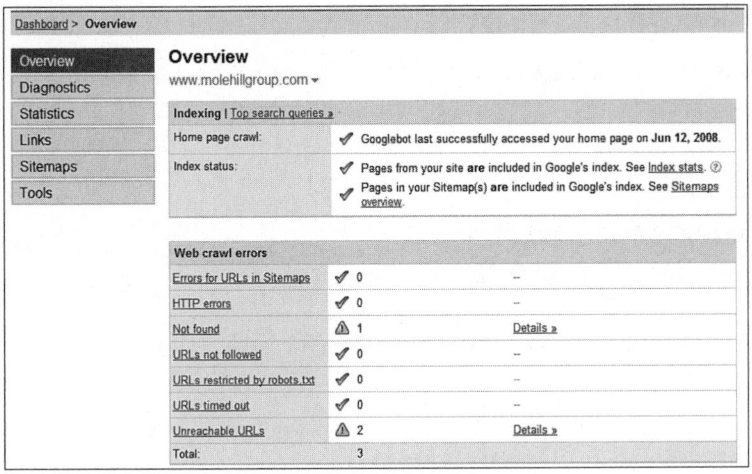

Figure 16.4

Google's Webmaster Tools Overview page.

◆ When Google last crawled your site

◆ Whether pages from your site are included in the Google index

◆ What type of errors, if any, Google found when crawling your site

Additional information is available by clicking the links along the left side of this page, which we discuss next.

Viewing Diagnostic Information

When you click the Diagnostics link, you have access to various types of diagnostic information. Table 16.2 details the available reports.

Table 16.2   Google Webmaster Tools: Diagnostics

Report	Contents
Web Crawl	URLs from your site that Google had trouble crawling
Content Analysis	Problems encountered with your site's **\<META\>** and **\<TITLE\>** tags
Mobile Web	Mobile crawl errors

Viewing Statistical Information

Although Google's diagnostic information is useful, I find its statistical information much more interesting. Here is where you'll get the most information about your site traffic, as detailed in Table 16.3.

Table 16.3   Webmaster Tools: Statistics

Report	Contents
Top Search Queries	The top search queries and search query clicks
Crawl Stats	Your site's PageRank data
What Googlebot Sees	Phrases used by other sites in the anchor text that links to your site
Index Stats	Links to standard Google site linkage and cache info, such as pages that link to your site, related pages, and the like
Subscriber Stats	For sites with site feeds, the number of users who subscribe to those feeds through various services

For example, the Top Search Queries page, shown in Figure 16.5, lists the top search queries that visitors used to find your site, as well as which of those search queries generated the most clicks. (Click any link to view the Google search for that phrase.) The Crawl Stats page, shown in Figure 16.6, lists the average PageRank of your pages. And so forth.

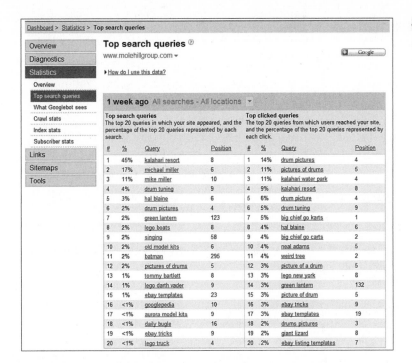

Figure 16.5

Google's Query Stats page.

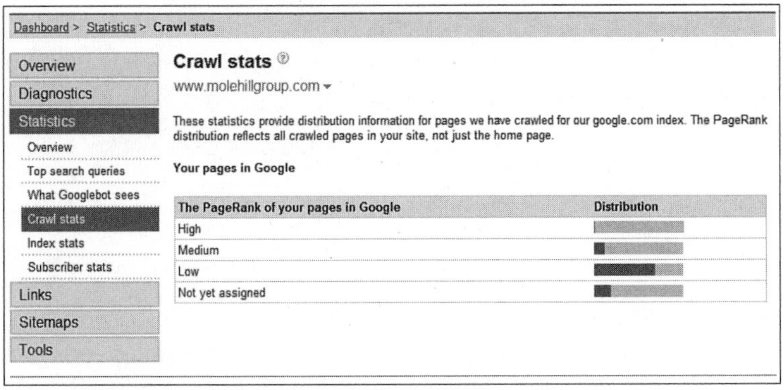

Figure 16.6

Google's Crawl Stats page.

Viewing Link Information

Google offers three reports that help you analyze your site's internal and external (inbound) links. Table 16.4 details these reports.

Table 16.4 Webmaster Tools: Links

Report	Contents
Pages with External Links	Lists the pages on your site that have inbound links to them, along with the number of those external links
Pages with Internal Links	Lists all the pages on your site that are linked to from other pages on your site
Sitelinks	Displays additional links that Google sometimes generates, based on your site content, to help visitors better navigate your site

For example, Figure 16.7 shows the Pages with External Links report. Click the link number to view all the sites that link to that page.

Figure 16.7

Viewing all the pages on your site that have external links, in alphabetical order.

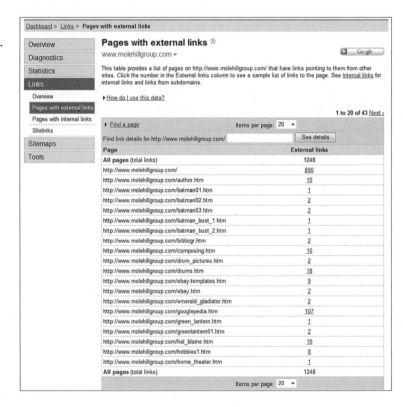

Viewing Sitemap Information

When you click the Sitemaps link, Google displays the page shown in Figure 16.8. This page lists some brief statistics about the sitemaps you've submitted, including the sitemap status and how many pages were included in the sitemap.

Figure 16.8

Viewing information about your submitted sitemaps.

Using Other Webmaster Tools

Google offers additional tools for webmasters, found by clicking the Tools link in the Webmaster Tools Dashboard. Table 16.5 details the available tools.

Table 16.5   Webmaster Tools: Additional Tools

Tool	Description
Analyze **robots.txt**	Determines whether the **robots.txt** file blocks specific URLs
Generate **robots.txt**	Helps you create a **robots.txt** file for your site
Set Geographic Target	Identifies your site to a specific geographic location; great for enhancing mobile search
Enhanced Image Search	Enables Google's Image Search for images on your site; adds advanced labels to your site's images
Manage Site Verification	Displays and reverifies site owners
Set Crawl Rate	Displays how often Google crawls your site—and lets you change the crawl rate
Set Preferred Domain	Associates a preferred domain with this site
Remove URLs	Deletes site pages from the Google Index

You shouldn't gloss over these tools; a few are extremely useful for optimizing your site's performance.

In particular, the Generate **robots.txt** tool, shown in Figure 16.9, is a great way to create a **robots.txt** file for your site. As you learned elsewhere in this book, you use the **robots.txt** file to tell searchbots where your sitemap file is, which pages you don't want crawled, and the like. Google's tool lets you create a **robots.txt** file just by selecting options from a series of pull-down lists. It's much easier than trying to create such a file by hand.

Figure 16.9

Use the Generate robots.txt tool to create a robots.txt file for your site.

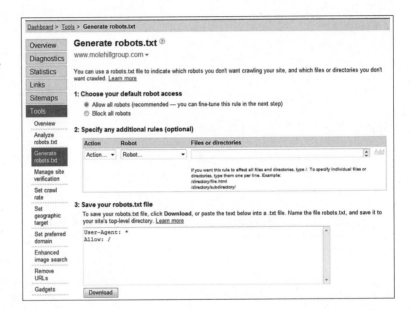

Also useful is the Enhanced Image Search tool. Just by selecting a single check box, you tell Google that you want to enhance your site for Google's Image Search. Google then adds advanced labels to the images on your site, which it uses to assemble its Image Search index; this should improve your images' ranking in Google's Image Search results.

Finally, take note of Google's Set Crawl Rate tool. Not only does this tool show you the number of pages on your site crawled per day, as shown in Figure 16.10, but if you scroll down to the bottom of the page, you can choose a new crawl rate for your site. Select a slower crawl rate to reduce Google's traffic on your server (which results in less-fresh results in Google's search index), or a faster crawl rate to make Google notice newer content quicker.

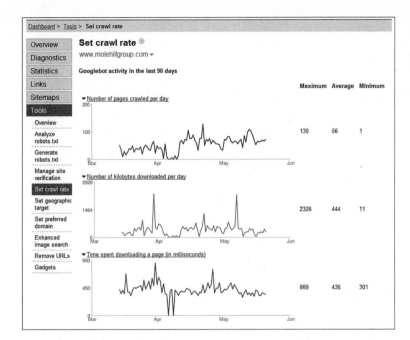

Figure 16.10

Viewing various crawl-related statistics for your website.

Tracking Live Search Performance with Webmaster Tools

Compared to what Google offers in the way of website analysis, both Microsoft and Yahoo! come up short. That said, both of these sites do offer a variety of analytical tools—all of them useful, but just not as many as what Google offers.

Let's examine the Webmaster Tools that Microsoft offers for its Windows Live Search. These tools are accessed from the Live Search Webmaster Center (http://webmaster. live.com). When you first access the tools, you're asked to add your website, via the page shown in Figure 16.11. This is also where you add your site's sitemap, tell Microsoft how you'll verify that you're the site's owner (via either an XML file or a special **<META>** tag), and supply your contact e-mail address. However you choose to authenticate your site, Microsoft next displays the text you need to add in either the file or the tag.

Figure 16.11

Adding your website to Microsoft's Webmaster Tools.

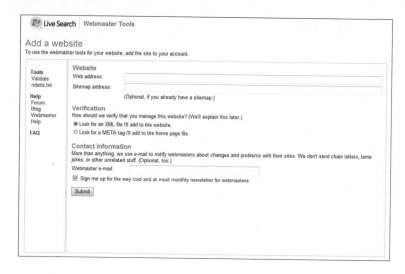

Viewing Summary Information

When your site is authenticated, you have access to the complete set of tools. Click your site name and you see the Summary page, shown in Figure 16.12. This page lists the following information:

◆ When your site was last crawled

◆ How many pages on your site are indexed

◆ Your site's rough rank, on a scale of 1 to 5 bars (5 is best)

◆ The top five pages on your site

Figure 16.12

Viewing summary information about how Live Search sees your website.

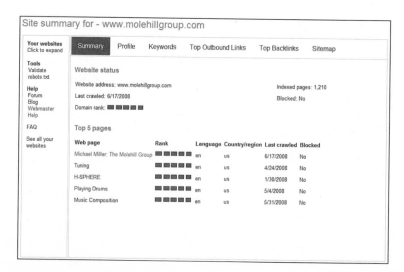

Updating Your Site Profile

Click the Profile tab to see the page shown in Figure 16.13. From here you can provide or edit the following information:

◆ The location of your site's sitemap

◆ How your site is verified to Webmaster Tools

◆ Your contact information

Figure 16.13

Use the Profile tab to add or edit information about your site.

Viewing Keyword Ranking

More useful information is available when you click the Keywords tab. As you can see in Figure 16.14, this page lets you see how your web pages perform in search results for specific keywords. All you have to do is enter a keyword or phrase into the Keyword box and click the Search button; Webmaster Tools lists the top pages on your site for that keyword, along with each page's 1-to-5 ranking.

Viewing Outbound Links

You can also use Webmaster Tools to view the top outbound links from your site to other sites—those links that your site's visitors clicked most. Just click the Top Outbound Links tab to display this list, shown in Figure 16.15.

Figure 16.14

Using Webmaster Tools to view how a keyword ranks.

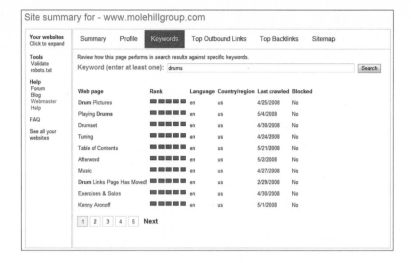

Figure 16.15

Viewing the top sites linked to from your site.

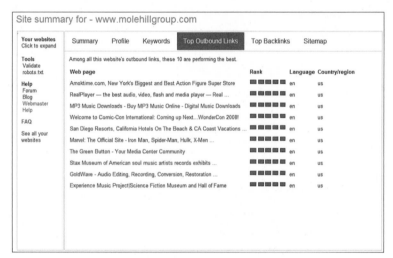

Viewing Inbound Links

If you want to see which sites deliver the most valuable inbound links to your site, click the Top Backlinks tab. As you can see in Figure 16.16, you now see the top 10 sites that link to your site, and the 1-to-5 ranking of those sites.

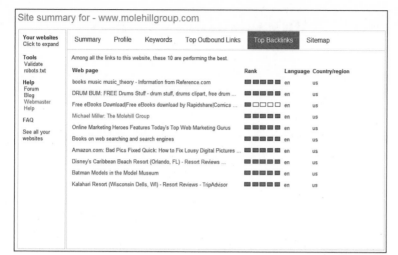

Figure 16.16

Viewing the top sites linking to your site.

Adding a Sitemap

Microsoft's Webmaster Tools is the only way to add your sitemap to the Live Search index. You can do this from the Profile tab or from the Sitemap tab, shown in Figure 16.17. Just enter the full path (URL and file name) of your sitemap file and click the Submit button.

Figure 16.17

Adding your sitemap to the Live Search index.

Tracking Yahoo! Performance with Site Explorer

Yahoo!'s analytical tools are offered as part of Yahoo! Site Explorer (http://siteexplorer. search.yahoo.com). Know, however, that, of the three major search sites, Yahoo! offers the fewest tools and least quantity of data for website analysis. In fact, Site Explorer is a rather limited—but still useful—analytical tool.

The main Site Explorer page, shown in Figure 16.18, is where you add your site for analysis. Just enter your main URL and click the Add My Site button.

Figure 16.18

The Yahoo! Site Explorer home page.

You'll also need to authenticate your site so that Yahoo! knows it's really your site. Click the Authenticate button and follow the instructions to either upload an authentication file to your site or add a **<META>** tag for authentication purposes to your home page.

> **Search Note**
>
> You're not limited to using the search engines' in-house website-analysis tools. Many third-party sites offer their own webmaster tools that you can use to analyze the performance of your website. Learn more about these tools in Chapter 17.

The first bit of useful information available from Site Explorer is a list of pages on your site that Yahoo! crawls; this lets you know what pages appear in the Yahoo! search index. To view this list, click the Explore button; Site Explorer displays the list of crawled pages, with the most popular listed first.

This page can also display all the sites that link to pages on your site. Click the InLinks link to show this list, shown in Figure 16.19. You can filter this list to show links only from other sites (Except from This Domain) and to show links to either the current URL or your entire site.

Figure 16.19

Listing all the external links to a web page.

The Least You Need to Know

◆ When it comes to measuring your site's performance, the key metrics to consider are number of visitors, pageviews and landing pages, visit length, referring sites, queries, and inbound links.

◆ You also want to track your site's ranking on each major search engine site, for each of your most important keywords and phrases.

◆ If you can get your site on Google's first search results page, you can increase visitor count by more than 600 percent in the first two months.

◆ Google offers two robust (and free) analysis tools: Google Analytics and Webmaster Tools.

◆ Use Microsoft's Webmaster Tools to analyze key metrics for your ranking with Live Search.

◆ Use Yahoo! Site Explorer to view which pages on your site Yahoo! crawls, as well as which sites link to your site.

Chapter 17

Using Third-Party SEO Tools

In This Chapter

◆ Analyzing website statistics and performance

◆ Monitoring your search ranking and tracking your competitors

◆ Working with keywords and inbound links

◆ Exploring other SEO tools

In Chapter 16, we examined the website-analysis tools offered by the big three search engines. While these are valuable (and free) tools, they may not offer everything you need to both optimize your site and track your site's ongoing performance.

Rest assured, the technology industry abhors a vacuum. Thus, we have a thriving market for third-party SEO and website-analysis tools, many of which might prove useful for your own site optimization.

While the plethora of such tools makes a complete listing impossible in these pages, we can examine some of the most popular. What follows is this (admittedly brief) overview, which you can use to determine which of these tools are best suited for your site's particular needs.

Analyzing Website Statistics

As you learned in Chapter 16, the big three search engines all offer their own website-analysis tools, some more detailed than others. Of these tools, Google's combination of Google Analytics and Webmaster Tools provides the most comprehensive analysis—and it's all free.

That said, several other firms offer similar tools to analyze your website's performance. Some of these tools offer different or better analysis than what you can get from Google, et al.; we examine some of the most popular of these tools here.

SEO Tip _____

You may not need to invest in a third-party website-analysis tool. Many website hosts offer their own suite of website-analysis utilities, typically for free; check with your site's hosting service to see what's available.

GoStats

GoStats (www.gostats.com) offers free website analysis via a traffic counter you add to your page's underlying HTML code. With the counter installed, you can track visitors and pageviews on your site over the past 12 months. (Figure 17.1 shows a sample GoStats report.)

Search Note

GoStats also offers a paid Professional version that includes additional statistics and analyses.

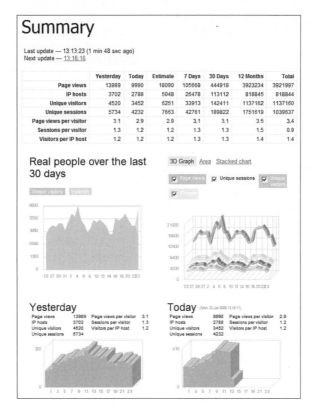

Figure 17.1

Tracking site performance with GoStats.

MindViz Tracker

MindViz Tracker (www.mvtracker.com) is a free website-analysis tool. As you can see in Figure 17.2, MV Tracker offers a variety of statistics about your site, including visitors, pageviews, referring sites, search engine queries, and the like. It even displays a list of the last searchbots to visit your site—and when they last crawled.

Mint

Mint (www.haveamint.com) is a website-analysis suite that is gaining popularity among professional webmasters. It tracks a variety of key metrics, including site visits, referring sites, top searches (keywords that found your site), most popular pages, feed subscription patterns (if your site has an RSS feed), internal searches, outbound clicks, and the like. Mint is available by subscription, at $30 per month. (Figure 17.3 shows a typical Mint tracking report—there's a lot here to look at!)

Figure 17.2

Viewing site information with MindViz Tracker.

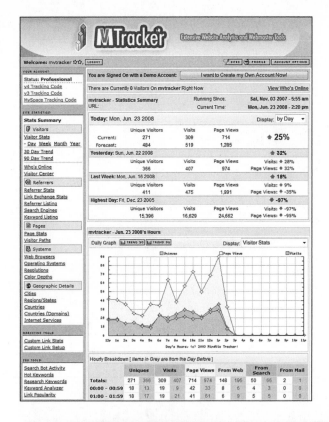

Figure 17.3

Viewing a plethora of site statistics with Mint.

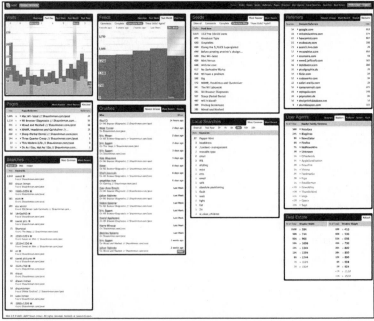

StatCounter

StatCounter (www.statcounter.com) is another traffic counter–based website-analysis tool. Like GoStats, StatCounter is free. As you can see in Figure 17.4, it tracks visitors, pageviews, referring links, keyword tracking, entry and exit pages, and the like.

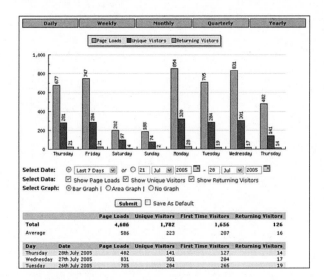

Figure 17.4

Tracking site statistics with StatCounter.

Viewing Site Performance

Beyond analyzing internal website statistics, it sometimes helps to see how other tracking services view your site. To that end, the following tools consolidate information from other sites about your site.

SEO Trail

SEO Trail (www.seotrail.com) is a free tool that monitors the search rankings, indexed pages, inbound links, and social bookmarks from Alexa, Google, Live Search, and Yahoo!—as well as the social bookmarking sites del.icio.us, Digg, and Technorati. (Figure 17.5 shows a sample overview screen that displays each of these results.)

Search Note
Alexa (www.alexa.com), a subsidiary of Amazon.com, compiles traffic data for a large number of public websites.

Figure 17.5

Viewing search and link data from both search engines and social bookmarking sites, thanks to SEO Trail.

Xinu Returns

Xinu Returns (www.xinureturns.com) is another site that generates a slew of information about your website's performance. As you can see in Figure 17.6, Xinu Returns displays your site's ranking at Google, Technorati, Alexa, and DMOZ (Open Directory); the number of pages indexed on Google, Live Search, and Yahoo!; the number of backlinks (inbound links) listed on numerous sites; the number of social bookmarks for your site at del.icio.us, Digg, and other sites; and other interesting information.

Monitoring Your Search Ranking

Of course, the most important indication of SEO success is your site's ranking at Google, Yahoo!, and other search engines. The following tools monitor your search rankings, based on which keywords you select.

Google PageRank Prediction and Search Engine Position

Like many of the sites discussed in this chapter, iWEBTOOL offers a variety of free SEO tools. We focus on two tools that help you monitor and analyze your position in Google's search results.

Use the Google PageRank Prediction tool (www.iwebtool.com/pagerank_prediction) when you want a good guess of how a page might rank within Google's PageRank system. Simply enter the complete URL of the page and click the Check button. The PageRank Prediction tool now returns the page's current and predicted PageRank, along with the estimated accuracy of the prediction and the number of inbound links (backlinks) to the page, as shown in Figure 17.7.

Figure 17.7

Viewing current and predicted PageRank with the Google PageRank Prediction tool.

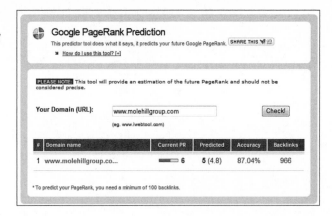

If you want to know where your site places in Google's search results for a particular keyword or phrase, use the Search Engine Position tool (www.iwebtool.com/search_engine_position). Enter your domain and the specific keywords, then click the Check button. The tool returns your site's position and what page of the results it appears on. (If multiple pages on your site rank in the results, they're listed separately.)

GoRank Online Keyword Rank Tracking

If you can get past the long title, GoRank's Online Keyword Rank Tracking (www.gorank.com) is a very useful tool for tracking where your site ranks for various keywords over time. The free report, like the one in Figure 17.8, tracks the ranking of multiple keywords over the past month. It's a great way to see if your site is increasing or decreasing in search engine popularity.

Rank Checker

Here's a great little utility when you want to know where your site ranks in a given site's search results. SEO Book's Rank Checker (http://tools.seobook.com/firefox/rank-checker/) is a free add-in for the Firefox web browser that automatically looks up your ranking at Google, Live Search, or Yahoo! for any keyword you enter.

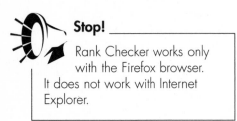

Stop!

Rank Checker works only with the Firefox browser. It does not work with Internet Explorer.

Just click the Rank Checker button at the bottom of the Firefox browser, and Rank Checker opens a new window on your desktop. Enter your site's URL and the keyword you want to check, and Rank Checker displays your site's ranking for that keyword on all three search engines. As you can see in Figure 17.9, you can use Rank Checker to check for multiple keywords and phrases; all the results are displayed in a big list.

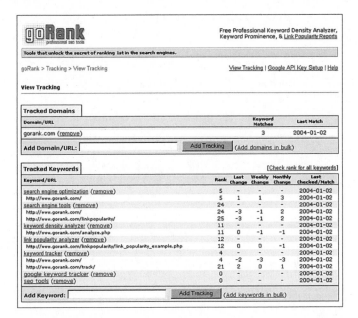

Figure 17.8

Tracking keyword ranking over time with Online Keyword Rank Tracking.

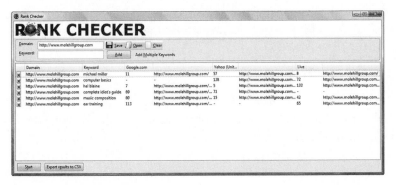

Figure 17.9

Checking search engine ranking with the Rank Checker tool.

SEO Tip

You can use Rank Checker to check the ranking of any website—even those of your competitors. It's a great way to see how you're performing compared to your competitors.

Search Engine Rankings

Internet Explorer users (and Firefox users, too) can use the Search Engine Rankings tool (http://mikes-marketing-tools.com/ranking-reports/) to see where their sites rank vis-à-vis specific keywords on the major search engines. This free tool checks your site against a specific keyword for eight different search sites—Google, Live Search (MSN), Yahoo! Search, AlltheWeb, AOL Search, AltaVista, the Open Directory, and the Yahoo! Directory.

Just enter your website URL and the keyword or phrase you're interested in, and click the Check Rankings button. A new window now opens on your desktop, as shown in Figure 17.10, displaying your ranking at each of these search sites.

Figure 17.10

Viewing rankings at eight different search sites with the Search Engine Rankings tool.

Tracking Your Competitors

Tracking your own site's performance is great, but your site doesn't exist in a vacuum. You also want to see how your site compares with competing sites—which argues for using tools that track your competitors' performance.

Search Analytics

Compete specializes in tools that help you analyze how your competitors are performing. Case in point is their Search Analytics tool (http://searchanalytics.compete.com), available in both free and paid versions. (The free version shows only the top five results for any given analysis.)

Start by entering the URL of a competing website or by selecting the general category in which you compete. Search Analytics then displays the top keywords and phrases that drive traffic to that site or sites in that category, as shown in Figure 17.11. This tool also displays the site share (percentage of all site referrals), engagement (a measure of the amount of time spent on the site after entering the keyword), and effectiveness (a measure of the total number of people referred by the keyword and their engagement) for each keyword listed.

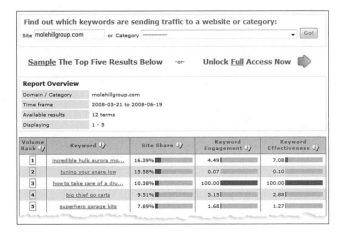

Figure 17.11

Viewing top referring keywords with the Search Analytics tool.

The Search Analytics tool can also show you which sites get the most clicks from a keyword. Just select the Keyword Destination tab and enter a keyword or phrase, and the tool displays the top sites for that keyword. You also see the keyword share, site share, and average monthly referrals for each matching site.

In addition, the Search Analytics tool lets you see how two sites compete in the keyword race. Select the Compare Sites tab, enter the URLs for two sites, and click the Go button. The tool now lists the top keywords the two sites share, along with which of the two sites has the advantage for each keyword.

Site Analytics

Also useful is Compete's Site Analytics tool (http://siteanalytics.compete.com). This is a traditional site-analysis tool tweaked to compare stats for up to three competing sites. Just enter the URLs (for your site and a competing site, for example), and Site Analytics displays a series of graphs that compare the number of site visitors, visit length, traffic growth, and other data for the sites. For example, Figure 17.12 shows a comparison of site traffic for the Salon, Slate, and Daily Koz websites.

Figure 17.12

Comparing traffic for three websites with Site Analytics.

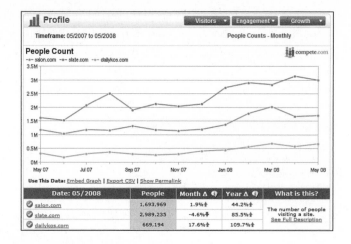

Scrutinizing Inbound Links

Because Google's PageRank puts a high value on inbound links, it's important to know which sites are linking to your sites. Use the following tools to analyze your inbound links—or what many of these sites call *backlinks*.

Backlink Summary

Webconfs.com offers a number of different SEO tools, all free of charge. I draw your attention to three tools that help you monitor and analyze the inbound links to your site. The first of these tools is Backlink Summary (www.webconfs.com/backlink-summary.php). This tool generates a list of the top 10 sites (and the number of inbound links from each) that link to your site, as shown in Figure 17.13.

Backlink Anchor Text Analysis

Next up is Backlink Anchor Text Analysis (www.webconfs.com/anchor-text-analysis.php). This tool displays a list of sites that link to your site, along with the anchor text they use for these links. Use this tool to determine the quality of the inbound links to your site.

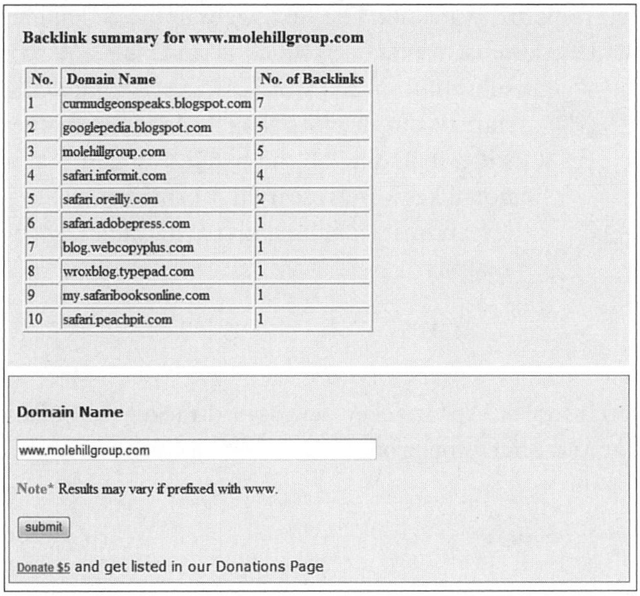

Backlink summary for www.molehillgroup.com

No.	Domain Name	No. of Backlinks
1	curmudgeonspeaks.blogspot.com	7
2	googlepedia.blogspot.com	5
3	molehillgroup.com	5
4	safari.informit.com	4
5	safari.oreilly.com	2
6	safari.adobepress.com	1
7	blog.webcopyplus.com	1
8	wroxblog.typepad.com	1
9	my.safaribooksonline.com	1
10	safari.peachpit.com	1

Domain Name

www.molehillgroup.com

Note* Results may vary if prefixed with www.

[submit]

Donate $5 and get listed in our Donations Page

Figure 17.13

Viewing top linking sites with the Backlink Summary tool.

Backlink Builder

Finally, Backlink Builder (www.webconfs.com/backlink-builder.php) generates a list of websites that are relevant to the keyword or theme you enter. The sites on this list are, presumably, quality sites that you can solicit for inbound links to your site.

Working with Keywords

Keywords are important to the success of your site. You need to choose the right keywords, get the right keyword density, and then monitor the success of the keywords you've chosen. The following tools should help with each of these tasks.

KeywordDiscovery

Let's start with choosing keywords for your site. When it comes time to decide on the keywords and phrases to target, you need a keyword-research tool. These tools ask you to input a description of your site's content and then generate a list of the most popular keywords related to that descriptive phrase.

Several keyword-research tools are available. The first we examine is Trellian's KeywordDiscovery (www.keyworddiscovery.com), which is sold via a $69.95 monthly

Search Note

Learn more about keyword-research tools in Chapter 5, "Optimizing Your Site's Keywords."

subscription. KeywordDiscovery compiles search statistics from more than 180 search engines world-wide, including all the biggies. In addition to traditional keyword research, it provides spelling mistake research, seasonal search trends, and keyword-density analysis.

Wordtracker

Our next keyword-research tool is Wordtracker (www.wordtracker.com). Like similar tools, this one is aimed at and priced for professionals, with a $59.95 monthly subscription.

WordZe

Finally, WordZe (www.wordze.com) is a newer, lower-priced keyword-research tool. It's available for a $35 monthly subscription.

Keyword Density Analyzer

Back in Chapter 5, we discussed the concept of keyword density—the percentage of body text represented by your chosen keywords. To analyze the density of any particular keyword on a web page, use the free Keyword Density Analyzer (www. keyworddensity.com).

Here's how it works. Enter the URL of the page you want to check, along with the keyword you want to analyze. The results page, shown in Figure 17.14, shows the overall density for that keyword (in both raw occurrences and percentage of total words), as well as the density of that keyword in your page's **<TITLE>** and **<META>** tags, anchor text, image tags, and the like.

Keyword Density Checker

Here's a different and more visual way of analyzing keyword density. Keyword Density Checker (www.webconfs.com/keyword-density-checker.php) is a free tool that lets you visually analyze the keyword density of your website, in the form of a keyword cloud.

Figure 17.15 shows just such a cloud; the most frequently appearing words on the site appear bigger than the less-used words. There's also a complete list of words underneath, accompanied by each word's count and density.

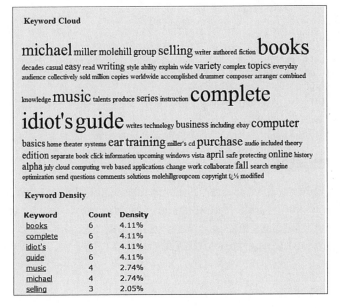

Figure 17.14

Analyzing keyword density with the Keyword Density Analyzer.

SEODigger

SEODigger (www.seodigger.com) is a great little tool (free, of course) that reveals which keywords your site ranks highly for. It does this by building a reverse Google index; enter your URL, and SEODigger displays the keywords and phrases for which your site ranks in Google's top 20 results, like the list in Figure 17.16.

Figure 17.16

Viewing a site's top-ranking key phrases with SEODigger.

Show 1 ... 21 of 21 | Page 1 of 1

Link search in Google database:

ID	Date	Requests	Pos.	WT	OT
1	01.05.2008	building really annoying web site	1	34	0
2	07.05.2008	group michael miller molehill	1	44	0
3	10.05.2008	molehill group	1	0	0
4	30.04.2008	annoying building really site web	2	34	0
5	04.05.2008	mike millers	2	0	0
6	06.05.2008	building really annoying web sites	2	0	0
7	08.05.2008	michael miller	3	29	0
8	04.05.2008	really annoying web pages	4	0	0
9	11.05.2008	really annoying website	5	0	0
10	06.05.2008	annoying web sites	6	0	0
11	08.05.2008	michael miller	6	2083	47
12	04.05.2008	mole hill	10	100	2
13	08.05.2008	michael miller in	10	0	0
14	01.05.2008	building music site web	11	38	0
15	06.05.2008	by michael miller	11	0	0
16	10.05.2008	mike miller	11	1416	53
17	03.05.2008	home mike miller page	14	34	0
18	08.05.2008	mike miller in	14	0	0
19	04.05.2008	mike millar	15	0	0
20	08.05.2008	james michael miller	15	25	2
21	11.05.2008	molehill	15	171	9

Show 1 ... 21 of 21 | Page 1 of 1

Examining Other SEO Tools

Some SEO tools just don't fit into any other category. Here are a few of these unique—but uniquely useful—tools.

Search Engine Spider Emulator

Want to see how a searchbot sees your site? Then check out the Search Engine Spider Emulator (www.webconfs.com/search-engine-spider-simulator.php). As you can see in Figure 17.17, this free tool displays the spidered text on your site, along with the spidered links and the contents of your site's **<META>** tags.

Similar Page Checker

Here's something you need to know: some search engines penalize sites that contain pages with duplicate or even similar content. To that end, use the free Similar Page Checker (www.webconfs.com/similar-page-checker.php) to determine how similar one page is to another on your site, on a percentage basis.

Spidered Text :
Michael Miller: The Molehill Group Michael Miller is a best-selling writer who has authored more than 80 non-fiction books over the past two decades. He is known for his casual, easy-to-read writing style and his ability to explain a wide variety of complex topics to an everyday audience. Collectively, his books have sold more than a million copies worldwide. Michael is also an accomplished drummer, composer, and arranger, and has combined his knowledge of music with his writing talents to produce a series of best-selling music instruction books in the Complete Idiot's Guide series. He also writes on a variety of technology and business topics, including eBay, computer basics, and home theater systems. New Books! Check out the following recently released titles from author Michael Miller: Is It Safe: Protecting Your Computer, Your Business, and Yourself Online Easy Computer Basics: Windows Vista Edition Starting a Successful eBay Business (LiveLessons DVD) Absolute Beginner's Guide to eBay, 5th Edition Online Marketing Heroes Photopedia: The Ultimate Digital Photography Resource Complete Idiot's Guide Ear Training Course Now Available Michael Miller's The Complete Idiot's Guide Ear Training Course on CD is now available for purchase. This is the same audio ear training course included with the best-selling The Complete Idiot's Guide to Music Theory, 2nd Edition, now available for purchase separate from the book. Click here for more information and to purchase. Upcoming Books The Complete Idiot's Guide to Music History (Alpha Books, July 2008) Cloud Computing: Web-Based Applications That Change the Way You Work and Collaborate Online (Que, Fall 2008) YouTube for Business (Que, Fall 2008) Googlepedia: The Ultimate Google Resource, 3rd Edition (Que, Fall 2008) The Complete Idiot's Guide to Search Engine Optimization (Alpha Books, Fall 2008) Send questions or comments to solutions@molehillgroup.com Copyright © 2006 The Molehill Group Last modified: June 21, 2008

Spidered Links :
http://www.molehillgroup.com/easy_computer_basics.htm
http://www.molehillgroup.com/ebay-livelessons.htm
http://www.molehillgroup.com/ebay.htm
http://www.molehillgroup.com/online_marketing_heroes.htm

Figure 17.17

Viewing your site's spidered text and links with the Search Engine Spider Emulator.

URL Rewriting Tool

If your site generates dynamic web pages, those dynamic URLs are tough for searchbots to understand. The solution is to rewrite dynamic URLs as static ones, with the free URL Rewriting Tool (www.webconfs.com/url-rewriting-tool.php). Just enter the dynamic URL, and this tool generates a usable static URL for the page.

Xenu's Link Sleuth

One thing you don't want on your site is broken links; searchbots really don't like trying to crawl links that don't go anywhere. To that end, check out Xenu's Link Sleuth, a free program that checks your site for broken links and generates a report accordingly.

Investigating SEO Tool Suites

We end our discussion of SEO tools by noting that some sites offer not just one or two, but rather a variety of such tools. These sites are good "one-stop shops" for webmasters charged with the complete pre- and post-SEO management. Given the quantity and variety of the tools these sites offer, they're worth checking out.

SEO Chat

When it comes to sheer quantity of SEO tools, you can't beat SEO Chat (www.seochat.com/seo-tools/). This site offers 40 free SEO tools, including the following:

- AdSense Calculator, which lets you test values for a variety of AdSense variables.

- AdSense Preview, to help you determine which AdSense ads should be placed on a given page.

- Advanced Meta Tag Generator, to assist you in adding **<META>** tags to your site.

- Alexa Rank Comparison Tool, which creates a traffic history graph for your site.

- Check Server Headers, which checks your web server to make sure the proper HTTP status codes are being returned in the server headers.

- Class C Checker, which determines whether some sites are hosted on the same Class C IP range.

- Code to Text Ratio, a valuable tool that compares the amount of text on a web page to the amount of HTML code. A higher text-to-code ratio is preferable.

- CPM Calculator, which measures the return on investment (ROI) of the cost per thousands (CPM) advertising model.

- Domain Age Check, which returns the age of any entered web domain.

- Domain Typo Generator, which generates a list of likely misspellings of a given web domain. This is a great way to find profitable new domains to purchase.

- Future PageRank, which checks for Google PageRank changes for a given URL.

- Google Dance, which queries Google's three main servers for a particular keyword, to determine any differences in how that keyword is processed.

- Google Keyword Suggestions, a keyword-research tool specifically designed for the Google search index.

◆ Google Search for Multiple Datacenter, which searches for a given keyword or phrase across all of Google's datacenters.

◆ Google Suggest Scraper, which lets you enter a few initial letters and then generates popular queries starting with those letters.

◆ Google vs. Yahoo!, which compares search results for the same keyword between Google and Yahoo!.

◆ Indexed Pages, which returns the number of indexed pages for your site from each of the major search engines.

◆ Keyword Cloud, which generates a cloud display of a page's keyword density.

Search Note

To serve the needs of its millions of users, Google uses multiple servers across multiple datacenters. While these servers and datacenters theoretically operate from the same search index, the indexes housed on each server may not always be updated at the same time—and thus may sometimes return slightly different search results.

◆ Keyword Density, which displays a more traditional list of keywords and accompanying densities on a given page.

◆ Keyword Difficulty Check, shown in Figure 17.18, which tells you how difficult it would be to rank for specific keywords or phrases.

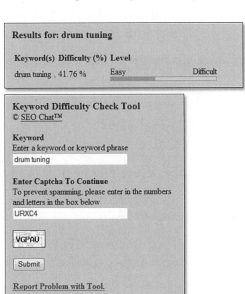

Figure 17.18

Ascertaining the difficulty of choosing a given keyword with SEO Chat's Keyword Difficulty Check.

◆ Keyword Optimizer, which lets you enter a list of keywords and then removes any duplicates.

◆ Keyword Position Check for Multiple Datacenters, which finds the ranking of your site across Google's multiple datacenters.

◆ Keyword Typo Generator, which generates a list of common typos for a given keyword or phrase.

◆ Link Popularity, which returns the total inbound link count for a given URL at all major search engine sites.

◆ Link Price Calculator, which determines what you should be paying per month for a text link.

◆ Meta Analyzer, which examines the contents of your site's **<META>** tags.

◆ Meta Tag Generator, which helps you create effective **<META>** tags for your site.

◆ Multiple Datacenter Link Popularity Check, which counts the number of inbound links for a given URL from multiple Google datacenters.

◆ Page Comparison, a useful tool that compares the page titles, **<META>** information, and common phrases for multiple pages.

◆ Page Size, which returns the total size of the files associated with a given web page, including images and other embedded files.

◆ PageRank Lookup, which returns the Google PageRank value for a list of individual URLs.

◆ PageRank Search, which lets you enter a Google query and then displays the PageRank for each site in the search results.

◆ Robots.txt Generator, which helps you create a **robots.txt** file for your website.

◆ ROI Calculator, which measures the return on investment of a CPC campaign.

◆ Search Engine Comparison, which compares the rankings and comparative positions of web pages in various search results.

◆ Search Engine Keyword Position, which displays the position of your site for a given keyword across the Google, Yahoo!, and Live Search sites.

◆ Site Link Analyzer, which displays the outbound links and anchor text for a given web page.

◆ Spider Simulator, which displays the contents of a web page as seen by a search engine spider.

◆ URL Redirect Check, which checks for valid HTTP redirect headers.

◆ URL Rewriting, a useful tool that converts dynamic URLs into static URLs.

That's a lot of tools, some of them rather narrow in scope, others useful on a more universal basis. Since they're all free, they're definitely worth evaluating.

SEOmoz

SEOmoz is another site that offers a comprehensive suite of powerful SEO tools. While the site does offer some tools only to paid subscribers, the following tools are free for anyone to use:

◆ Crawl Test (www.seomoz.org/crawl-test), which crawls any URL you enter, along with internal pages linked from that URL, and delivers a wealth of useful information—indexed by the major search engines, the last time Google spidered the page, primary keywords on the page, number of internal links on the page, and so on.

◆ GeoTargeting Detection (www.seomoz.org/geotarget), which determines how well your site is optimized for local search.

◆ IP Location Lookup (www.seomoz.org/ip2loc), which looks up the location of a website based on its IP address.

◆ Page Strength (www.seomoz.org/page-strength), shown in Figure 17.19, which analyzes the relative visibility of a web page and its ability to rank high in search engine indexes, based on a variety of factors.

◆ Popular Searches (www.seomoz.org/popular-searches), which aggregates the most popular searches from a variety of search engines and social bookmarking sites for a given day.

◆ Rank Checker (www.seomoz.org/rank-checker), which reports your site's ranking for a given keyword with Google, Live Search, Yahoo!, and Ask.com.

◆ SEO Toolbox (www.seomoz.org/toolbox), a collection of targeted SEO utilities, including Strongest Pages on a Domain, Who Else is Hosted on My IP?, Check Inclusion, Check Backlinks, Outbound Link Checker, Check PageRank, Find Domain Age, Check HTTP Status Code, Check Indexed Pages, and Whois.

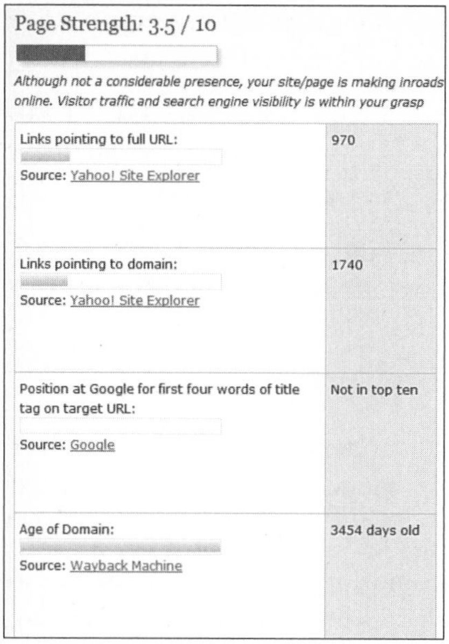

Figure 17.19

Evaluating a site's Page Strength.

Page Strength: 3.5 / 10

Although not a considerable presence, your site/page is making inroads online. Visitor traffic and search engine visibility is within your grasp

Links pointing to full URL: Source: Yahoo! Site Explorer	970
Links pointing to domain: Source: Yahoo! Site Explorer	1740
Position at Google for first four words of title tag on target URL: Source: Google	Not in top ten
Age of Domain: Source: Wayback Machine	3454 days old

◆ Term Target (www.seomoz.org/term-target), a useful tool that determines how well a page is targeting a particular keyword, based on the use of the keyword in the page's text and HTML code.

◆ Term Extractor (www.seomoz.org/term-extractor), which analyzes the content of a web page and extracts the words and phrases that appear to be targeted at search engines.

All useful tools—and even more are available to paid site members.

The Least You Need to Know

◆ Website-analysis tools such as GoStats, MindViz Tracker, Mint, and StatCounter tell you everything you need to know about your site's visitors and pageviews.

◆ Tools such as SEO Trail and Xinu Returns provide an overview of how your site rates with various tracking sites.

◆ You can use tools like Search Engine Position, Rank Checker, and Search Engine Rankings to track your site's position on Google and other search engines. Tracking your competitors is also easy, thanks to tools such as Search Analytics and Site Analytics.

◆ You can analyze inbound links to your site from other sites with Backlink Summary and Backlink Anchor Text Analysis.

◆ Keyword-research tools, such as KeywordDiscovery and Wordtracker, help you choose keywords for your site; Keyword Density Analyzer and Keyword Density Checker help you monitor keyword density; and SEODigger shows which keywords your site ranks highly for.

◆ SEO Chat and SEOmoz both offer comprehensive suites of SEO tools—a lot of useful tools on a single site.

18

Avoiding the Most Common Search Engine Mistakes

In This Chapter

◆ Uncovering approaches that search engines don't like

◆ Avoiding the five most common SEO mistakes

◆ Warning against black hat SEO techniques

So far in this book, we've discussed all the things you can—and should—do to increase your site's ranking with the major search engines. But did you know you can do things to actually *decrease* your ranking? It's true; the search engines despise certain techniques and penalize you for them.

That said, let's take a look at the things you *shouldn't* do when revamping your website. There's a lot more than you might think!

Understanding What Search Engines Don't Like

It's unfortunate and unfortunately common: many website designers work against their own best interest by embracing methods that effectively decrease a site's ranking in a search engine's index. That's right, many techniques that you can employ have a detrimental effect on how Google, Yahoo!, and other search engines view your site.

Obviously, you want to avoid these techniques—no matter how forcefully your designers or technical staff may argue in their favor. SEO is difficult enough as it is without deliberately doing something that you know will cause your site to drop in—or disappear from—the search engine rankings.

So here's a quick look at the most common problems that you're likely to encounter—and that you should avoid.

Long and Complicated URLs

The shorter and more straightforward a page's URL is, the better. Searchbots don't like long URLs, nor do they like URLs that contain special characters.

To that end, don't use **&id=** as a parameter in your URLs. Most search engines don't include pages with this parameter in their indexes.

Similarly, avoid the use of dynamic URLs. Most search engines can index only static URLs, not those that are dynamically generated. If your site does include dynamic pages, use a URL-rewrite tool to turn your dynamic URLs into static ones.

Splash Pages

Here's the thing about splash pages, those introductory pages that appear before users can advance to your site's true home page: nobody likes 'em. Visitors don't like them because they make it longer to get into your site. And searchbots don't like them, for a number of reasons.

First, most splash pages don't include the types of internal links and menus found on a true home page. You might have a link to the site's home page, but that's about it. (If that—some splash pages have no links and are instead programmed to automatically advance to the home page after a specific length of time.) If there are no links to other pages from the first page that the searchbot encounters, the searchbot won't know about the other pages on your site. That's not a good thing.

Second, most splash pages don't contain much content—or, at least, much text content. Many splash pages consist of a Flash animation or big graphic, neither of which registers with searchbots. Thus, the first page searchbots encounter appears empty. And Google isn't going to rank an empty page highly.

The moral of this story, then, is to avoid the use of annoying and practically useless splash pages. Make your site's first page a traditional home page; both your visitors and the searchbots will be much happier.

High Keyword Density

This is one I hope you've learned from previous chapters in this book. While keywords are good, too many of them are bad.

In other words, don't include too many keywords in your content or **<META>** code. If a page has too high a keyword density, most search engines will categorize your page as a doorway page—and penalize you accordingly.

> **Search Note**
>
> When done deliberately, including too many keywords is known as "keyword stuffing," which we discuss later in this chapter.

Hidden Text

You might think you're being tricky by using hidden or invisible text on your page. This is when you disguise keywords or links by making them the same or similar color as the page background, using a tiny font size, or hiding them within the HTML code itself. Many webmasters think this is a clever way to stuff lots of keywords onto a page without looking as if they're doing so.

But you can't trick a searchbot. These spider programs see this text just as easily as they do the regular text on your page—which means they'll see all those keywords you're trying to stuff. And, as you know, searchbots don't like keyword stuffing. You get the picture.

While most major search engines pretty much ignore hidden text, this practice can sometimes decrease your page's ranking. So do yourself a favor, and don't create hidden or invisible text or links on your page. It just won't work.

Duplicate Content

Here's another false trick that too-savvy webmasters sometimes employ, to their own detriment: duplicating content on a site, in the hopes of increasing the number of hits in search engine results. This can be done by putting the same content on multiple pages or using multiple domains or subdomains.

Duplicating content is a bad idea. Google and the other search engines utilize duplicate content filters that will identify and remove duplicate sites from their search results. When you duplicate your content, you run the risk that your main site or page will be filtered out—while the subsidiary content remains!

Bad Outbound Links

You know that the quality of your inbound links matters; did you know that the quality of your *outbound* links can also affect your search rankings?

That's right, most search engines consider the sites you link to as part of their page-ranking process—at least when it comes to overtly low-quality sites. For that reason, you don't want to link to a site that's been dropped or banned from a search engine's index; you could get tarred by relation.

Images, Videos, and Animations

This is another one that I hope you've picked up on from coverage earlier in the book. It's a simple concept: searchbots read text (including HTML code); they can't view images, videos, or Flash animations.

This means, of course, that creating an image- or animation-heavy page renders that page virtually invisible to the search engine spiders. Your page might look great to visitors, but if the searchbots can't see it, it won't get indexed. When in doubt, go with a text-based approach.

Along the same lines, resist the temptation to use graphics for your page headers. Again, this has visual appeal, but you'll get more bang for your SEO buck if you use traditional text-based headers with HTML **<H1>, <H2>,** and **<H3>** tags. (Remember, heading tags have a big impact on your search engine rankings.)

Big Pages

Here's another reason to go easy on web page images. Lots of big graphics increase the size of your web page and increase its download time—especially for visitors with slower Internet connections.

And here's the other thing: searchbots don't like big pages, either. More specifically, searchbots don't like long load times. If it takes too much time for all the elements on a page to load, the searchbot will give up and move on to the next page in its queue—bad for you.

So keep an eye on size, for all the elements on a page. This is one instance in which smaller is better.

JavaScript Code

Searchbots read text and HTML code—well, *some* HTML code. Most searchbots tend to ignore JavaScript code in your HTML, which means anything you have in a script won't be indexed. This is particularly vexing if you use a JavaScript menu system; searchbots may not see all the internal links you have in your menus.

For that reason, try to minimize your use of JavaScript. It's a tempting technology because of its versatility, but it could hurt your search rankings.

Too Much Code

Speaking of HTML code, don't overdo it. Having more code than you do actual text on your page will cause some searchbots to give up before they crawl your entire page. This means you need to avoid employing too many code-heavy effects, such as nested tables or JavaScript effects. If your important text is buried under hundreds of lines of code, you'll be at a disadvantage compared to a well-optimized site.

Messy Code

One last thing when it comes to the coding of your site: don't create messy code. This is one instance in which neatness counts; messy HTML can confuse most searchbots and cause them to miss important content.

Identifying the Five Most Common SEO Mistakes

So now you know what search engines don't like and can penalize you for. But these aren't the only things you can get wrong with revamping your website; you can make a lot of mistakes that will negatively impact your search rankings.

To wit, here are the five most common SEO mistakes. Take particular care to avoid falling into these traps.

Mistake #1: Targeting the Wrong Keywords

SEO starts with identifying the keywords that you want your site to rank for when those words are included in search query. If you target the wrong keywords, potential visitors won't see your site in their search results. If you target the right keywords, you can effectively optimize your site to rank highly for those queries.

In other words, the keywords you choose can make or break your SEO campaign.

Avoid choosing keywords based on your own personal search experience. Just because you search for a particular keyword or phrase doesn't mean that it's the most popular way to find your site. This is where keyword research comes in; tools exist that precisely identify the most effective keywords and phrases for a given topic. Use keyword research to target the best keywords for your site's content, and you'll be glad you did.

Mistake #2: Underusing Keywords in Your Content

Once you choose a target list of keywords and phrases, you have to use them—and not just in your site's **<META> KEYWORDS** tag. You get the best search results when you use your keywords in your site's content—early and relatively often. Your keywords should be used organically, not in a forced or artificial fashion. Write your body text around your keywords—make your site about the keywords you've chosen.

Beyond that, consider highlighting the keywords in your text—use the bold or emphasis tags for this purpose. In addition, put your keywords in your page's header tags, which is another place searchbots look for important content.

Mistake #3: Ignoring the ‹TITLE› Tag

One of the first things searchbots look for is your site's **<TITLE>** tag. If you ignore the title, you miss a great opportunity to feed your chosen keywords to the search engines. Unfortunately, it's all too common for sites to leave the **<TITLE>** tag blank; don't fall into this trap.

Mistake #4: Ignoring Your Site's URL

Here's another one that's easy to get wrong. Many webmasters simply forget that searchbots examine the URL of a page to help determine its content. In fact, Google and the other search engines place significant weight on a page's URL; it's a resource not to be ignored.

Use your page's URL (and the accompanying file name for pages beyond the home page) to feed content and keywords to the searchbots. Don't rely on automatically generated page URLs; similarly, avoid dynamic URLs. Treat your page's URL as an important holder for keyword information.

Mistake #5: Not Maintaining Your Site

Here's the final but perhaps most common SEO mistake—not following through. That's right, search engine optimization is an ongoing process; it doesn't end when you upload your last optimized page. You need to maintain your site, keep it updated, and constantly monitor your site's performance. Watch the competition, keep your content fresh, and continue to tweak your use of keywords, content, and the like. A good site can always get better; a site that's not maintained can—and will—drop in the search rankings.

> **Search Note**
>
> Learn more about maintaining your site in Chapter 19, "Maintaining SEO on an Ongoing Basis."

Avoiding Black Hat SEO Techniques

Yes, you might accidentally do something that can adversely affect your search ranking—and you should avoid making these mistakes. But some sneaky web designers deliberately do certain things to increase their search rankings; Google and other major search engines take issue with these practices and can ban you from their indexes if you're caught.

To that end, here's a quick look at some of the more nefarious outlawed optimization practices—typically referred to as *black hat techniques*. Employ any of these dubious techniques, and you're likely to do your site more harm than good.

> **Search Note**
>
> Any attempt to influence search engine rank via misleading methods is referred to as *search engine spamming* or *spamdexing*. The practice of creating a website solely for the purpose of achieving a high Google PageRank is called *Googleating* (pronounced "Google-ating").

Keyword Stuffing

We touched on keyword stuffing previously in this book. This is when you insert multiple instances of a keyword on a page—often using hidden, random text—in an effort to increase the keyword density and, thus, increase the apparent relevancy of a page. For example, if your page is about trains, you might insert several lines of invisible text at the bottom of the page that repeat the keyword *train* over and over.

Search Note

A related technique to keyword stuffing is *metatag stuffing*, with keywords stuffed into HTML <META> tags.

In the past, some search engines simply counted how often a keyword appeared on a page to determine relevance, which rewarded the practice. Today, however, Google and other search engines view keyword stuffing as a kind of search-related spam and employ sophisticated algorithms to detect the technique.

Link Bombing

Link bombing, sometimes called *link washing*, is an attempt to increase your search ranking by having a large number of sites link to a page with identical anchor text. For example, you might register several domains and have all of them link to a single site, using the same anchor text for the links. Searching for the term used in the link anchor text will return the linked-to site high in the search results.

Search Note

Link bombing often occurs in blogs, where a site owner "bombs" multiple blog postings with replies linking to the owner's site.

Doorway Pages

A doorway page is a web page that is low in actual content, instead stuffed with repeating keywords and phrases designed to increase the page's search rank. Doorway pages contain little or no original content; they're typically optimized for a number of terms that aren't connected to the site's primary content.

Link Farms

A link farm is a group of web pages that all link to one another. The purpose of a link farm is to increase the number of links to a given site; since Google's PageRank is at least partially driven by the number of linked-to pages, using a link farm can make it appear as though a large number of sites are linking to a given site.

Mirror Websites

When you have a group of websites with the same content but individual URLs, you have a group of mirror websites. The goal with mirror websites is to increase the likelihood that any one (or more) of the mirror sites will appear on search results pages.

Scraper Sites

A scraper site is one that "scrapes" results pages from Google and other search engines to create phony content for a website. A scraper site is typically full of clickable ads.

Link Cloaking

Link cloaking is the attempt to mislead a search engine by serving up a different page to the site's crawler than will be seen by human visitors—that is, you show one thing to the searchbots and something different to actual visitors. This is sometimes used for *code swapping*, in which one page is optimized to get a high ranking and then swapped out for another page with different content.

Link Masking

Similar to link cloaking is link masking, in which you mask a link on your site to look like something that it's not. That is, the link's anchor text implies one URL, while the actual URL of the link is something different. This technique is often used to trick visitors into clicking a link for what they think is a particular page, when, in fact, they're taken to a different page altogether.

 Stop!

Link masking is often used with phishing sites or e-mails to trick users into thinking they're going to a legitimate site, when they're actually directed to a phony site that asks for personal information.

The Least You Need to Know

◆ Many things can negatively impact your site's search engine rankings, including long and complicated URLs, splash pages, a too-high keyword density, hidden text, duplicate content, bad outbound links, overuse of images and animations, large page sizes, JavaScript code, a high code-to-text ratio, and messy HTML code.

◆ The five most common SEO mistakes include targeting the wrong keywords, underusing keywords in your content, ignoring the **<TITLE>** tag, ignoring your site's URL, and not maintaining your website.

◆ Black hat techniques are those used to deliberately increase search engine rankings; these include keyword stuffing, link bombing, doorway pages, link farms, mirror websites, scraper sites, link cloaking, and link masking.

Maintaining SEO on an Ongoing Basis

In This Chapter

◆ Maintaining your SEO

◆ Creating an SEO maintenance plan

◆ Discovering how to plan for various contingencies

If you think you're done with SEO after you've followed all the advice in this book and then optimized and submitted all your web pages, you're mistaken. To ensure consistently high search rankings, you must continually track how your site is performing and do SEO tweaks as necessary.

That's right, SEO isn't a one-time thing; it's a continuing process. You must check your pages regularly to make sure that they're listed with the major search engines and that their ranking is not deteriorating. You must stay on the lookout for any signs of trouble and be ready to reoptimize problem pages as they come to your attention. And you must be prepared to undertake either a partial or a complete reoptimization if conditions change—or if your business undergoes a change in direction.

In other words, you need an ongoing SEO maintenance plan—which is what this chapter is about.

Why You Need to Maintain Your SEO

Even if you do a perfect SEO job on your current website, that's not good enough. Oh, maximizing your search rank is a good thing—even better if you end up on the first page of Google's search results for your top keywords. But just because you rank high today doesn't mean that you'll rank quite as high tomorrow. In fact, given the changing nature of the web and the constant influx of new websites, chances are, your ranking will start to slide over time. Unless you take some action at some point in time, your SEO efforts will be old news.

This argues, of course, for making SEO an ongoing process. Your site needs regular tweaks to ensure tip-top performance. That might mean changing the priority of your current keywords, choosing new keywords, modifying your page content or site layout, or even redesigning your site from scratch. It's all in the effort to remain competitive and retain a high search ranking.

It's not that what you did, SEO-wise, suddenly becomes less valuable. It's simply that your website doesn't exist in a vacuum. While your site stays the same, everything around it changes:

- **Your competitors get better.** If you think that competing websites will ignore your site changes, you're engaging in wishful thinking. Your best competitors will react to your changes with their own improvements to site content, layout, and optimization. Some sites will simply improve their sites as part of an ongoing growth process, regardless of what you do to your site. The point is that sites that compete with yours for the same keywords will get better over time—which will negatively impact your search ranking. That's a given.

- **You get new competitors.** Few categories are dormant. New websites pop up every day, some small and amateurish, and others large and professional. Unless you're in a very small, very boring, and very stagnant category, expect new competition at some point in the future—competition that will eat into your search rankings.

- **Your customers evolve.** It happens. Your customers grow older or more sophisticated, or they start making more money, or maybe they start making less money. Their tastes change, their budgets change, their lifestyles change. Bottom line: they start looking—and searching—for something slightly different. As their search needs change, your site starts showing up in fewer and fewer search results. You have to change with your customers or get left behind; after all, the McDonald's menu today isn't identical to the one 20 years ago.

◆ **Your customer base shrinks.** Here's a sad situation. Your customers not only evolve, they leave. Product categories seldom stay stagnant; what do you do if the number of customers who want your product starts to shrink? You'll need to expand your product offerings to attract a wider customer base—which means substantial changes to your website.

◆ **The search engines change how they rank sites.** Here's one that happens with surprising frequency, and it really stinks. Just as you get your site optimized for Google, Yahoo!, et al., one or more of the big search engines tweaks its page rank algorithm; you wake up one morning and find that you've dropped from Google's first page of search results clear to page five. Something in the way Google ranks sites has changed, and you have to figure it out and change your site accordingly—or you may never rank highly again.

For these reasons, at least, you need to constantly stay on top of your site's search engine performance and make any necessary changes to maintain your ranking. You can't afford to drop lower in the search results; the resulting drop in traffic and sales could be catastrophic.

Developing an SEO Maintenance Plan

Knowing that SEO is an ongoing process, you need to develop an SEO maintenance plan for your website. This plan should include performance tracking, competitive analysis, keyword evaluation, content updating, structural analysis, and inbound link–development components. Let's look at what's involved.

Performance Tracking

Before you make any site changes, however minor, you have to know what changes to make—and why. This means tracking your site's performance and being on the lookout for any changes in your site's ranking, traffic patterns, visitor counts, and the like. View performance tracking as an early warning system; when you notice a downward trend, it's time to evaluate what you're doing and consider new optimization efforts.

Start by monitoring your site's search engine rankings for your top keywords. Know, however, that rankings never stay perfectly constant; there will be some day-to-day fluctuations. But if you notice a steady downward trend, you need to look behind the numbers and figure out why. Which sites are starting to rank above yours? Are there new competitors in your space? Have competing sites made any recent changes? Or has something changed regarding your keywords? Don't let lower rankings go unnoticed.

Next, look at your site's traffic—not just raw numbers, although they're important, but also where your traffic is coming from. Look for changes in traffic patterns, new sites suddenly popping up on your referral lists, or older ones becoming less important. Even if your overall traffic count doesn't change, you want to be aware of how visitors find your site—and make any changes necessary due to changes in inbound traffic patterns.

Competitive Site Analysis

Don't be caught unaware by new competitors—or by old competitors with a new look and content. Someone on your team should be assigned to visit competitive sites on a weekly basis so that you know what your competitors are up to. In addition, make sure you search your category regularly so you'll know about any new sites coming into the space.

Your review of competing sites shouldn't be superficial. Analyze how each site is optimized, which keywords it's focusing on, and the like, and watch for any changes in SEO. And don't forget inbound links; follow the links backward from competitive sites to see if any new sites are linking to them.

Keyword Evaluation

Based on your performance tracking, you probably want to reevaluate the keywords you've chosen for your site. Whether it's the market changing, your customers changing, or your category getting more competitive, chances are the keywords you chose a year ago don't pack quite the same punch today as they did back then. You may need to change the order of keyword priority, dump some poorly performing keywords, or choose some completely new keywords; some tweaking is probably in order.

And, of course, once you tweak your keywords, you need to tweak all the parts of your site that are keyword dependent—the site's title, **<META>** tags, heading tags, and content itself. That's right, you may need to rewrite some of your body text to incorporate your latest keywords. It's a bit of work, but it's necessary.

SEO Tip _____

Don't be afraid to triage your keyword list and dump even your most precious keywords. If a keyword isn't working, you need to either find out why or get rid of it.

Content Updating

Speaking of your site's content, if the text on your page is more than a few months old, it doesn't have the same punch as it used to—at least as far as the major search engines are concerned. Most search engines reward fresh content, which means you have to put on your writer's hat and hit the keyboards. Simply put, a stale site ranks lower than a fresh one.

There are other reasons to update your site's content, of course. First and foremost, if you never change your main text, you'll start losing visitors—who are always looking for something new. You have to give your established users something new to keep them coming back. If you never change anything, you'll drive your older visitors to competitive sites.

Structural Analysis

Depending on the severity of the market changes, you may need to revisit your entire site design. Is your current structure working for you? Do some customers land on the wrong page or click to a virtual dead end? Do some pages have trouble holding visitors for an appropriate length of time? Are your competitors' sites easier to navigate?

These are all good reasons to analyze your site structure and make any necessary changes. You may also need to effect a site redesign if your company's mission or strategy changes, or if you make changes to your product mix. In short, don't get married to the way your site works; be ready and eager to change up everything if the need arises.

SEO Tip _____

Remember that you need to update your site's sitemap with every new page you add or old page you delete—and then submit the revised sitemap to the major search engines.

Inbound Link Development

Finally, don't forget those always-valuable inbound links. Even if you change nothing about your site, you still should be working on a regular basis to solicit more and higher-quality inbound links. These links are the invisible keys to improved site rankings.

If you see a competitor's site suddenly jump up in the search rankings even though it has made no major changes to site design or content, chances are it's because the site has scored some high-impact inbound links. For that matter, if your site rankings suddenly slide, check the sites linking to yours; a previous high-traffic link might have changed or disappeared.

As noted in Chapter 8, you'll probably spend more time on link development than you do on site design. That's only fitting, given the importance of inbound links not just to drive traffic, but also to affect your search rankings. It may not be a full-time job (or it may be, depending on your site), but it's a constant job; you must always be on the lookout for high-quality sites that should be linking to yours, and soliciting those webmasters for links.

Planning for Various Contingencies

Under what circumstances should you consider reoptimizing your website? There are many, all of which require slightly different approaches. Read on to discover when and how you should perform SEO anew.

Reoptimizing for New Content on Existing Pages

This one's simple. For some reason, you change the content on one or more of your web pages. Maybe you're just changing things to keep them fresh. Maybe you need to impart some new news. Maybe you've decided that your old content wasn't good enough, and you're creating new and better content for your visitors. (And good for you!) Whatever the case, when your page content changes, you need to engage in new SEO efforts for those pages.

The first thing to examine when you have new page content is the title of the page. If the content changed enough, you may need to change the title to reflect the new content. In addition, it's always good to evaluate the performance of a page title, vis-à-vis keyword placement, content description, and the like. Use this opportunity to give your title a second look—and make it more impactful.

Naturally, you should take a new look at the changed page's **<META>** tags, as well as your use of keywords in the new content. You should also take this opportunity to resolicit related sites for inbound links; let the webmasters know what's changed and why they should rethink their linking policies to include your site.

Reoptimizing for New Pages

Adding new pages to your site is also cause for reoptimization. Here we're talking about your sitemap as the primary focus. For your new page to be crawled, you must update your sitemap to include the page and then resubmit your sitemap to the major search engines.

You also need to be sure that your new pages are included in your site's navigation structure. Are the new pages linked to from your home page or from the next level in your site's hierarchy? They should be, if you want the searchbots to find them.

Finally, don't neglect all the normal SEO techniques for the new pages. Work keywords into the title, first few paragraphs, and **<META>** tags. Solicit inbound links specifically to the new pages. And don't forget your internal links; make sure that several key pages on your site include links to your new pages.

Reoptimizing for New Competition

Now let's examine what you should do in response to new sites that appear on the web. How concerned should you be when a new competitor enters your established space?

The first thing you need to do is seriously evaluate the new competitor. What is the new site doing right, and what is it doing wrong? What's it doing differently from what your site does? Evaluate the content, the layout, the mix of text and images—everything your eye can see.

Then go behind the scenes and evaluate the site's SEO. Look in the site's underlying HTML code and see what keywords are included in the **<TITLE>** and **<META> KEYWORDS** tags. You can do this from within your web browser; for example, in Internet Explorer 7, select Page, View Source to display a code window like the one shown in Figure 19.1. This will tell you what keywords the site is focusing on; you can then do your own search-ranking analysis for those keywords to see how well the site is performing.

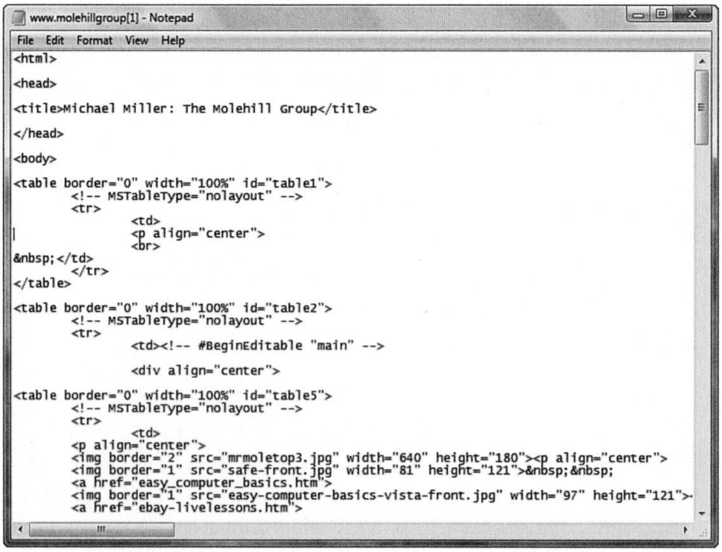

Figure 19.1

Viewing the source code for a web page with Internet Explorer.

You also need to discover which other sites are linking to that site. You can do this from within Google, as Google does a good job of identifying these inbound links. All you have to do is conduct a Google query using the **link:** operator, like this: **link: URL.** For example, to see the pages that link to my own Molehill Group website, enter **link:www.molehillgroup.com,** as shown in Figure 19.2.

Figure 19.2

Displaying inbound links for a specific web page, via Google.

Next, you have to learn from what you've just discovered. Is the new site targeting a keyword or phrase that you should be using, too? Are there sites linking to the new site that should also be linking to your site? Is the new site's content better or fresher or just different from yours? What about the site's layout—is it easier to navigate or crawl?

Take everything you've learned into account and then work on reoptimizing your site in response. Add new keywords, shake up your site design, write fresher content. Do whatever you have to do to keep pace with the new site—and maintain your previous search ranking.

Reoptimizing to Improve Site Performance

Sometimes you reoptimize your site not in response to anything, but simply because you want to improve your site's performance. Maybe you're stuck on page two of Google's search results; maybe you're having trouble generating inbound links. Whatever the motivator, you can always improve your site's performance—which means rethinking your previous SEO efforts.

In most cases, trying to improve your site performance requires a complete SEO reappraisal, starting with your keywords and phrases. Use a keyword-research tool to see if you can be using more effective keywords. Evaluate the keywords your competitors are using. See if you can be using other keywords that are less competitive or that pull more traffic.

With a revised list of keywords, then attack the optimization of each page on your site. Revisit the **<TITLE>** and **<META>** tags, using your new keywords. Make sure the body text of key pages includes your new keywords.

While you're on your site's content, make sure it's effective, well written, and fresh. Compare it to the content of competing sites—is yours the most authoritative? This is an area where you can't settle for second best.

Next, look at your entire site design and navigation. Make sure you have an appropriate number of internal links; don't leave any pages as orphans. If necessary, streamline your navigation. Don't leave things as they are just because that's the way you've always done them; if a new approach is called for, do it.

Work your inbound links. Take the time and effort to notify related sites of your new content and design, and suggest that now's the time for them to add a link to your site. Search the web for new sites that might be inbound link fodder. Make personal appeals.

Finally, when you're ready to launch the reoptimized site, create a new sitemap and post it to Google and the other search engines. Make sure your **robots.txt** file is updated for the new sitemap file. And resubmit your entire site to all the major search engines and directories. There's no point in reoptimizing if nobody knows about it!

Reoptimizing to Correct Problems

If you encounter any problems getting your site listed by the search engines, that's reason enough to revisit the SEO process. If one or more of the search engines refuse to index your site, find out why—and then fix the problem.

Are you committing any of the sins we discussed in Chapter 18? Are you engaging in keyword stuffing, or do you have duplicate content on your site or across the web? Take a cold, hard look at your SEO practices, and wean yourself from those that have even a whiff of black hat about them; you want do everything you can to remove your site from the search engines' blacklists. White hat SEO techniques are always best.

You also want to correct any other issues that may have arisen because of your site. For example, you may have discovered that duplicate content exists not on any site of yours, but rather on somebody else's site. We're talking stolen content here, in the form of content scraping. If you find another site that reuses your content without permission, contact that site's webmaster and ask him to remove that content. (Some will, believe it or not.)

If that doesn't work, you can try contacting the major search engines about the problem and ask them to remove the duplicate sites from their indexes. Here's how you make contact:

- ◆ **Google:** Fill out the form at www.google.com/support/bin/request.py.
- ◆ **Yahoo!:** E-mail ystfeedback@yahoo.com.
- ◆ **Live Search:** Go to webmaster.live.com and click the Feedback link.

Inform the search engines of the URL that contains the infringing content, and ask for those pages to be deleted from their indexes.

Reoptimizing for Changed Goals

Finally, you may need to reoptimize your site if the mission for that site changes. Maybe your company is undergoing a major makeover, maybe your marketing plan is changing, maybe you're changing your product mix. Whatever the case, if your online goals change, your website should also change—as should your target keywords and related SEO strategies. When things change at the top, it's time to undertake a new SEO campaign—from the bottom up!

The Least You Need to Know

◆ SEO isn't a one-off activity; it's a continuing process.

◆ Your site's search ranking can deteriorate for any number of reasons: your competitors may improve, you may get new competitors, your customer base may change, or the search engines may change how they rank sites.

◆ A search engine maintenance plan should include performance tracking, competitive site analysis, keyword evaluation, content updating, structural analysis, and inbound link development.

◆ Consider reoptimizing your site if you add new content on existing pages, add new pages, gain new competition, want to improve site performance, or need to correct problems, or if your company's goals change.

Part 5

Managing a Complete Search Engine Marketing Plan

This final part shows you how SEO fits into your overall marketing mix; this is the business section of the book. You'll learn how to create an SEO strategy for your site, integrate SEO into your online marketing plan, integrate online shopping directories and pay-per-click advertising into your plan, and evaluate your marketing plan's performance.

20

Creating an SEO Strategy for Your Site

In This Chapter

◆ Learning how to plan your project

◆ Discovering the best ways to analyze the situation

◆ Getting ready to implement the optimization

◆ Preparing to monitor the results

◆ Determining whether you should do it yourself—or hire a professional

In the first four sections of this book, we discussed the nuts and bolts of search engine optimization—what elements to focus on, what techniques to adopt, how to measure your results, and the like. Now it's time to take a few steps backward and look at SEO as part of a company's complete online marketing plan.

SEO shouldn't be the sole component of your online marketing efforts. Yes, it's important to attain a high ranking for your site in order to drive traffic from Google and the other search engines, but it's not the only thing you should be doing to promote your website. And, of course, your website shouldn't be the only online component of your overall marketing plan. SEO is just a piece of the whole—an important piece, mind you, but just one component of a holistic plan.

With that in mind, let's address the SEO component of your marketing plan—in particular, the creation of an SEO strategy for your site. In other words, what do you hope to accomplish and how do you plan to do it? This isn't something you want to walk into blindly; as with all business activities, you have to plan for success.

Planning the Project

A successful SEO strategy revolves around four elements: planning, analysis, implementation, and monitoring. We start at the beginning, with your plans for the project.

Why Plan?

The key to achieving SEO success is to sit down beforehand and give serious thought to what you want to achieve. You don't want to rush into this new endeavor without thinking through all the details. While it is possible to stumble into high search engine rankings, accidental success is seldom long-term success. Businesses that successfully achieve higher search rankings do so because they have a plan for success.

> **SEO Tip**
>
> An SEO plan doesn't have to be long and involved. Keep it short and simple, with bullet points and conversational language. Doing it is more important than how you do it.

If you *don't* plan your SEO campaign in advance, chances are you'll run into more than a few surprises. Unpleasant surprises. You don't want to get halfway into your site optimization and then find out that you've chosen a set of ineffective keywords. Everything you do needs to be planned in advance so you'll know exactly what needs to be done and when. No surprises—that's my motto.

An SEO plan also helps you and your company's management set realistic expectations for what you hope to achieve. Without a plan, IT staff might assume they can assign one person a few hours a week to make all the site changes, while senior management might expect a doubling of site traffic the first month—even though the implementation might require several full-time staffers and it might take a year or more to increase the traffic to hoped-for levels. You have to get everyone on the same page, get their total buy-in to the work required and objectives desired, and get a full commitment from all departments involved. A well-written plan, complete with definable and quantifiable goals, is the way to do this.

Finally, an SEO plan is like a to-do list for everything that needs to get done. Define the entire process in advance, complete with schedule goals and definable costs and workloads. Implementing the plan, then, is a simple matter of checking off tasks from the plan's to-do list. It's a roadmap to everything that must be done.

Setting Objectives

The first thing you need to define in your plan is what you seek to achieve—that is, what should be different (better) after the plan is implemented.

Naturally, the goal of any SEO plan should be to increase a site's ranking with the major search engines. But how much of an increase should you aim for—and what else follows if you meet that goal?

Let's break down that overall goal into primary and secondary objectives. Here's what I recommend.

Search Note

What do I mean by quantifiable results? Simple—results that you can measure. That typically means some sort of numeric goal, such as ranking in the top 20 search results, or increasing traffic 50 percent, or something similar. Your results need to be quantifiable so that you can cleanly measure your progress to the defined goals; if you can't measure progress, you won't have a clear, unarguable indication of what you've achieved.

Your primary objective should address your search engine rankings. You need to define which search engines you want to target, what kind of quantifiable results you want to achieve, and when you want to achieve those results.

For example, you may define your primary objective as having your site listed in the top 20 websites (first page of search results) for the top three search engines (Google, Live Search, and Yahoo!) for the search terms that most relate to your website's content, within six months of launch of your SEO campaign. Note that this objective defines what (top 20 search results), where (top three search engines), and when (within six months). That's an easy objective to track.

You also need to define a set of secondary objectives—goals that follow from the achievement of your primary goal. I like to think of these secondary objectives as traditional marketing metrics, focusing on both numeric counts and more lofty goals.

For example, you may set some or all of the following secondary objectives for your campaign:

◆ Increase visitor traffic by XX percent within the first X months

◆ Increase sales from the website by XX percent within the first X months

◆ Increase customer leads generated from the website by XX percent within the first X months

◆ Increase brand awareness for the company or product line among the targeted consumer base

> **Stop!**
>
> Search engine optimization takes time—and achieving desired results takes even longer. Remember, Google refreshes its entire index just once a month, so don't expect instant results. Make sure that all management involved has realistic expectations in this regard.

The first three secondary objectives are numeric and, thus, easily measurable. You either increase site traffic by 50 percent, for example, or you don't; there's no debating the results. The final objective, however, is more nebulous—although you can use traditional market research techniques to measure brand awareness among targeted consumers. In any instance, these goals are achievable only if you achieve your primary goal; the increase in search ranking will drive traffic, sales, leads, and brand awareness.

Setting Budgets

Now that you know what you want to achieve, you need to define how you plan to achieve it. For this, you first need to set a budget for the project; this will tell you just how much work you can afford to do in what time span.

When putting together your budget, make sure that you include both external and internal costs. That is, if you're using your in-house IT staff to do your site coding, budget the internal costs associated with that work—staff salaries, facilities costs, and the like. Also budget for any external expenses, such as the cost of purchasing SEO tools and services, or hiring an SEO consulting firm.

> **SEO Tip**
>
> When calculating costs, don't forget yourself. Make sure your salary (or an appropriate part of it) is included in the SEO budget!

By the way, you should define the time span for your budget. That is, do you have a total of $100,000 to spend over the course of the project, or are you budgeting $10,000 per month? And if it's the latter, how many months are you budgeting for? This all needs to be defined ahead of time so that you don't face any budgetary surprises.

Setting Tasks

With your budget in hand, you can now delineate all the tasks associated with your SEO campaign. This means laying out, in order, all the things you need to do—select keywords, optimize HTML code, rewrite page copy, submit sitemaps, and the like.

Accompanying each task on your list should be who or which department is responsible for accomplishing that task; it's not just a to-do list, but rather a "who does what" list. Naturally, you should consult all involved internal staff and departments to get their buy-in of the task list, as well as to reserve time on their schedules.

Setting Schedules

Speaking of schedules, you need to assign each task to a timeline. That is, each task you define should have a defined end date. Participating staff and consultants need to know when all task items are due, and you need to track progress to plan.

The timeline should include fixed start and completion dates. Allow several weeks after the acceptance of the plan before you start your SEO project; you need time to assign tasks, juggle schedules, and get everything prepped. Then you need to assign a project completion date—that is, the date that the newly optimized site goes live to the public. And, of course, you need to plan for every activity in between the start and stop dates.

Your timeline should also include all follow-up activities to the main plan, particularly results monitoring and any necessary reoptimization. This argues for constructing your timeline all the way through to the results date set in your objectives; naturally, someone has to plan for monitoring the results.

Analyzing the Situation

Once you've put your SEO plan in place, you need to do some preliminary analysis before you start changing things on your site. This analysis will tell you what specific work you need to do and will shape the content of your site.

Current Site Analysis

First, take a good, hard look at your current website. What's working and what's not? What have you done well, and what aspects are you disappointed with?

Look at your current site metrics. Which pages perform best—and why? Where are you currently drawing traffic from? How long are visitors staying on your site? What keywords are currently generating the most traffic?

Seldom do you want to completely scrap an existing site and create a new one entirely from scratch. In most instances, there's something that's working on your current site, something you want to carry over into your new site design. If nothing else, you probably want to maintain some continuity in look and feel, for branding purposes. You don't want your old customers to be completely alienated when you effect your site changes.

SEO Tip

It's sometimes difficult for a company to objectively review its own website. You may want to bring in an outside consultant to do this analysis for you.

In short, analyze your current site to help determine what needs to stay and what needs to be changed. Learn from what you've done in the past, and apply those lessons to your new SEO campaign.

Competitive Analysis

You also need to analyze what your competitors are doing. What are the top competitive sites, and how well do they rank with the search engines (compared to your site's ranking)? What are your competitors doing well, and where do they fall behind?

More specifically, which keywords do your competitors target? How do they use those keywords on their sites? What about inbound links—which sites are linking to your competitors? Equally important, what relevant sites *aren't* linking to them—and why?

Learn from your competitors' efforts to make your new site at least as effective as theirs, if not more so. You want to do everything they're doing right and then go the next step. But to do so, you have to understand what they're doing and how. That's the competitive analysis.

Keyword Analysis

Now we come to keyword analysis—selecting the best keywords and phrases to target. That means choosing keywords that best describe what you do or offer, while at the same time reflecting the most popular queries for that topic at the major search engines.

Choosing keywords might appear to be an art, but it's really a science. A lot of keyword research tools are available to help you select the most effective words and phrases; there's no reason to guess at this.

Given that so much of your SEO efforts depends on which keywords you choose, this should be a very important part of your SEO strategy. It also needs to come before you do any actual optimization.

> **Search Note**
>
> Learn more about keyword analysis in Chapter 5, "Optimizing Your Site's Keywords."

Implementing the Optimization

The three steps of the analysis process should dictate what you need to do to implement your SEO plan. As you've learned throughout this book, a lot is involved in performing SEO; all this work comprises the implementation process.

Design the Navigation Structure

Start by laying out all the pages you have in your site. Determine which are necessary and which aren't; there are arguments for a leaner site, if you can accomplish that. Go for a shallow hierarchy, and make sure all key pages are linked to from your site's main page. And don't forget to examine the names of all your page files; file names are an often-overlooked aspect of SEO.

> **Search Note**
>
> Learn more about the importance of site navigation in Chapter 7, "Optimizing Your Site's Design."

Create the Site Content

With your keyword list at hand, you now have to write the copy for each page on your site. Focus on text over graphics and animations, and work as many keywords as practically possible into the first few paragraphs of each page. Also make liberal use of headings on each page, working important keywords into each heading.

But content is about more than just keywords. Your content makes or breaks your site; authoritative content will attract more traffic and inbound links, while weak or derivative content will cause your site to be seen as a "me, too" site. This argues for hiring a professional web copywriter, someone who knows how to write for web audiences and for search engine optimization.

> **Search Note**
>
> Learn more about the importance of content in Chapter 4, "Optimizing Your Site's Content."

In any case, your site is defined by its content. All the other SEO techniques pale next to the importance of unique, authoritative content.

Rewrite the HTML Code

Your SEO team also needs to address the code behind the content. In particular, the **<TITLE>** and **<META>** tags need to be tweaked to include your site's most important keywords. You should also optimize the heading tags within each page's body text.

> **Search Note**
>
> Learn more about working with your site's HTML code in Chapter 6, "Optimizing Your Site's HTML Tags."

While you're working on your site's HTML, make sure that the code is as clean and efficient as possible. Searchbots have trouble navigating sloppy code, and they definitely don't like pages that have more code than body text. The easier your code is to "read," the easier it is to index it.

Create and Submit the Sitemap

Once you've optimized all your site's pages, your team needs to create a sitemap file that includes the URLs of every page on your site. You should then submit that sitemap (and your site's home URL, of course) to each of the major search engines. It's a simple step, but an important one.

> **Search Note**
>
> Learn more about site submission in Chapter 10, "Submitting Your Site to Search Engines and Directories." Learn more about sitemaps in Chapter 11, "Mapping Your Site for Best Results."

Solicit Inbound Links

The final step in your SEO implementation is to solicit quality inbound links from other sites. For many SEO teams, this is the most challenging component of the plan; it's the one that is least technical and most personal. And you can't automate it; generic "Dear webmaster" requests are most often viewed as spam and are deleted accordingly.

To successfully solicit quality inbound links, you have to manually select relevant sites, establish a personal relationship with the site's webmaster or community, and then politely ask for the link. You may also need to promise a reciprocal link or even pay for the inbound link. But however you do it, garnering quality inbound links is critical to achieving a high Google PageRank; you have to devote an appropriate amount of effort to this process.

> **Search Note**
>
> Learn more about inbound links in Chapter 8, "Optimizing Links to Your Site."

Monitoring the Results

The implementation phase of your plan can take several months, especially on larger and more complex websites. But finishing the implementation isn't the end of the process; once all the pieces and parts are put into place, you have to track the success of your efforts. That means monitoring your site's performance and comparing that performance to both preoptimization metrics and the goals you set as part of your plan.

You should note up front who is directly responsible for monitoring your SEO results, who they report to, and what exactly is to be monitored. I like monitoring metrics that directly relate to plan goals; for example, if your goals include increases in search ranking and traffic count, you should measure your site's search rank and traffic (among other metrics, of course).

Your measurements should be as precise as possible. Don't just report that your search rank is "up" or that you're on the first page of search results. Say how much (how many positions) your rank has increased and what that precise ranking is. Note how you're measuring results—what metrics and measurement tools you're using. And, as much

> **Stop!**
>
> The most common mistake companies make is not analyzing the site's performance post-SEO. While it's tempting to say that the project's done and then move on, you need to plan for ongoing measurement of the revamped site's performance.

as possible, compare apples to apples when tracking your performance versus preoptimization rates.

It's also a good idea to track what your competitors are doing during the measurement period. Track their performance to your key metrics, and note any changes they've made to their sites during the same period. While you need to directly measure the metrics related to your internal goals, your site performance doesn't occur in a vacuum; achieving your goals while losing market share is not a desirable situation.

At the end of the monitoring program, you need to report your results to the SEO planning team, and probably to your company's senior management. Be honest; if you fell short on a particular metric, report it and analyze why. You probably won't precisely achieve every one of your objectives; you may achieve higher search rankings, for example, but still fall behind your goals in terms of traffic count. Site performance is a report card, no doubt about it, but it's also a learning tool. Make sure your entire team knows this.

Finally, know that reporting your site's performance isn't the end of the SEO process. Yes, you're measuring key metrics to determine whether you achieved your goals. But what if the site performed below expectations? You need to use the numbers you generate to help you further optimize your site. As noted in Chapter 19, SEO isn't a one-time activity; it's a continuing process for all involved.

So it's important to review, revise, and then repeat. That's the way SEO works in the real world.

Should You Do It Yourself or Hire a Professional?

When it comes to planning and implementing your SEO strategy, should you try to do everything in-house or should you hire an outside SEO firm to do at least part of the work for you? The answer to this question depends on your own particular situation—including your company's culture and your project's budget.

Advantages of In-House SEO

Let's start with in-house SEO, the way a lot of small companies have to do it. Given the techniques outlined in this book, SEO is certainly something that can be accomplished by anyone with enough time and a modicum of marketing and technical expertise. In fact, many firms prefer to do their own SEO, even when larger budgets are in play. Here's why:

- **Responsibility**—When an outside firm is involved, it's sometimes hard to assign responsibility for parts of the project—or blame if something goes wrong. When you do it yourself, you're personally responsible. That's not a bad thing.

- **Control**—When you do it yourself, you have complete control over each element of your SEO plan's progress. You don't have to worry about whether the outside firm did or didn't do a particular step; you control everything that gets done.

- **Institutional learning**—You'll learn a lot from your first SEO efforts. What you learn stays inside the company, so the next time you optimize your site, you're smarter about what to do and how. It's a lot better than hiring a second SEO firm and trying to get them up to speed about what you've done in the past and what you want to accomplish in the future.

- **Cost**—Let's face it, one of the primary reasons many companies perform their own SEO is that it costs less than hiring an outside firm. Not that the cost is zero (the salary of all internal workers needs to be factored in), but having inside staff do the work is often considerably cheaper than engaging an SEO firm. And, budget constraints being a fact of corporate life, keeping your costs low may be the deciding factor in whether you perform any SEO at all.

When it comes down to it, doing your own SEO is more often a matter of budget and control. If you like to be in complete control of your website and related marketing, in-house SEO is the way to go. Same if your budgets are tight—or if your company has a standing preference for staying in-house versus hiring outside firms.

Advantages of Professional SEO

All that said, there are several reasons why you might want to bite the budgetary bullet and outsource your SEO strategy to a firm that specializes in just that. Here are a few good reasons to hire a professional SEO firm:

- **Experience**—SEO professionals have done it all before; there's no reinventing the wheel here. While you might have a steep learning curve in implementing an effective SEO strategy (that's one of the reasons you bought this book, after all), the pros know exactly what has to be done because that's what they do for a living. They'll be able to jump right into your particular situation and use their prior experience to help you interpret the data, choose the best keywords, and optimize your pages accordingly. Even better, they know what things to avoid; they won't make the same mistakes that you might.

◆ **Industry contacts**—An experienced professional knows a lot of important people in the industry. Need a press release written? They probably know somebody. Want to solicit some inbound links? They might have a previous relationship with the webmaster of a key site. You get the picture—sometimes it's good to have friends who know people.

◆ **Link-building expertise**—While we're touching on building inbound links, expect SEO professionals to be a lot better at that than you probably are. They know which topical communities to address, which sites are likely to be both relevant and interested, and which techniques are most effective. This will save a lot of time—and create the most inbound links to your site.

◆ **Time savings**—Speaking of saving time, the pros know how to do it faster. Let's face it—they do this stuff day in, day out, and they're good at it. That means that they're both effective and efficient; they can do in a day what it might take you a week when you're first starting out. This is especially important when you're on a tight deadline.

◆ **Troubleshooting**—Not all SEO efforts go smoothly. Sometimes you find that the changes you make have a negative impact on your search rankings; sometimes something you do can actually get you deleted from a search engine's index. An SEO expert will know what techniques to avoid, as well as have a head start in fixing anything that might go wrong. Instead of scratching your head when problems arise, it often pays to have a professional figure things out.

Assuming that money isn't an object, you may get better and faster results by engaging an outside SEO firm. It's not that they can do anything you can't; that's not the case, as there are few "secrets" in the SEO world. It's just that they do this sort of thing every day and can probably jump to just the right conclusion a lot faster than you can while you're learning the ropes. It's a matter of time and effort; an SEO professional will be faster and more efficient than someone who doesn't do SEO for a living.

Choosing a Professional SEO Firm

If you decide to hire an SEO consultant to work with your site, how do you decide what firm to use? And how much will it cost?

You can find an SEO professional that best suits your needs in a number of ways. Obviously, if you know another company that has engaged an SEO firm in the recent past, solicit advice. You can also e-mail webmasters of sites you particularly admire to ask who they've used.

Beyond the recommendation approach, you can consult several directories of SEO professionals on the web. These include SEOfinders.net (www.seofinders.net) and the SEO Services Marketplace (www.seomoz.com/marketplace/). You can also search Google or Yahoo! for SEO professionals; you can expect the firms with the best-optimized sites to appear high in the search results.

Beyond that, look for a firm that specializes in your type or size of website. If you need additional marketing services, such as help with PPC or display advertising, take that into account. And if it's important that work be done onsite, look for a firm local to your offices.

As for pricing, it varies. (But you expected that, didn't you?) Some firms charge by the hour (probably somewhere in the range of $100–$400 per hour); others charge by the project. However they charge, ask for an estimate up front—and use that to compare costs between competing firms.

SEO Firms to Avoid

Unfortunately, search engine optimization is an area that attracts a number of scam artists. And given that the topic of SEO is confusing even to experienced web designers, it's easy to be taken in by false claims and unrealistic promises.

When you're evaluating an SEO firm, beware those that promise you specific results or that claim a "special relationship" with Google, Microsoft, or Yahoo!. There's no way to guarantee a number-one ranking in any search engine's search results; all anyone can do is follow the good design practices detailed throughout this book.

A legitimate SEO firm promises to do only what can be done—that is, optimize your site to attempt to achieve a higher page rank. Legitimate firms will not—and cannot—promise specific results, nor will they try to sell you position or placement.

So how can you tell a legitimate SEO firm from a fraudulent one? Look out for some warning signs; in particular, beware any SEO firm that does the following:

- ◆ Guarantees ranking
- ◆ Doesn't distinguish between actual search results and sponsored ads that appear on search result pages
- ◆ Gets traffic from fake search engines or spyware
- ◆ Puts links to its other clients on doorway pages
- ◆ Offers to sell keywords in the address bar

◆ Owns shadow domains (these are registered domains that funnel users to another site by using deceptive redirects)

◆ Is not itself listed in the Google or Yahoo! index, or has had domains removed from either index

◆ Operates with multiple aliases or falsified WHOIS info

No legitimate SEO firm will attempt to falsify results, generate phony results or traffic, or use deceptive spamdexing methods. When it comes to improving your search engine ranking, there is no magic formula; success is directly related to the amount of hard work involved.

In other words, if a firm's promises sound too good to be true, they probably are.

The Least You Need to Know

◆ SEO success isn't accidental; it requires careful planning.

◆ Your SEO plan should include quantifiable objectives, a detailed budget, and a defined schedule.

◆ After you create your plan, you need to conduct analyses of your current site, competitive sites, and the keywords you want to use.

◆ Implementing the plan involves everything we've discussed in this book: designing a navigation structure, creating authoritative content, rewriting HTML code, creating and submitting a sitemap, and soliciting high-quality inbound links.

◆ The final part of your SEO strategy is monitoring your results; you need to review, revise, and then repeat as necessary.

◆ The advantages of keeping SEO in-house are primarily financial and control related; using an outside firm is all about exploiting its speed and experience.

Chapter 21

Integrating SEO into Your Online Marketing Plan

In This Chapter

◆ Discovering the components of an online marketing plan

◆ Learning how SEO fits into an overall online marketing mix

◆ Working with all the elements of your marketing plan

◆ Making online and traditional marketing work together

Search engine optimization is a necessary component of search engine marketing—using organic search engine results to drive traffic to your website, and thus sell your goods and services online. The better your SEO, the more effective your search engine marketing.

Search engine marketing, however, isn't the only kind of online marketing you can or should do. It's only one component of a well-rounded online marketing plan; you need to construct a marketing plan that recognizes the impact of search engine marketing while still mining the benefits of other types of online marketing.

What we're talking about, of course, is creating an online marketing plan for your organization that revolves around search engine marketing but doesn't depend solely on it. That's a challenge for any marketer today, especially with new and exciting channels to exploit.

Understanding the Components of an Online Marketing Plan

How do you market your business online? You can't just put up a website and hope that potential customers will trip over it. No, you have to reach deep into your bag of marketing tricks to attract customers online, sway them in your direction, and persuade them to purchase whatever you're selling (or simply increase your brand awareness, if that's your game).

What marketing tools can you use to promote your business online? Search engine marketing is important, of course, but you have many more tools at your disposal—some you're no doubt familiar with, others that may be new to you. Let's see what you have to work with.

Search Engine Marketing

We'll start with the marketing tool that drove you to read this book—search engine marketing. "Wait," I hear some of you saying, "I bought this book because I wanted to learn about search engine *optimization*, not marketing." But SEO is only a technique, a means to an end. That end is the use of search engine results to drive traffic to your website—otherwise known as search engine marketing.

Search Note
Search engine marketing is effective because it's relatively simple to translate a search query into the ultimate intentions and desires of the customer. They essentially state, in their queries, what they're interested in; nothing is hidden.

Search engine marketing, unlike traditional advertising, doesn't purchase results. A marketer doesn't pay the search engines anything to get listed, nor for specific results. You don't pay for space or rank or clicks.

Instead, search engine results occur organically. If you do your job right designing your website, users searching for the right topic will see your website among the top search results. That results in click-throughs to your site, which you hopefully convert into customers, revenues, and profits.

The key to search engine marketing, then, is ensuring that your site ranks high enough in the search results for potential customers to notice it—higher, most certainly, than your competitors. The higher your site's search ranking, the more traffic you create—and the more effective your search engine marketing.

This, of course, is why search engine optimization is important. You want to optimize your site so that it appears as high as possible in the search engine rankings. Since you can't directly buy your way to the top of the results, you have to improve your rankings organically, by making your site as authoritative and relevant as possible. With search engine marketing, success really is a result of hard work—not how much money you have in your budget.

How important is search engine marketing? For most companies, extremely. That's because, for most websites, the majority of traffic comes not from direct URL entry or even links from other websites, but from queries made at Google, Yahoo!, and the other search engines. Check your own website logs if you don't believe me; it's probably true of your own traffic as well.

So if half or more of most sites' traffic comes from the search engines, you need to maximize the effectiveness of those search engines to maximize your potential site traffic. That means, of course, that you need to increase your site's search ranking for those keywords that drive the most traffic to your site—which you do via SEO.

Search engine marketing is also important because it's a relatively low-cost way to increase traffic and generate revenues. Since you can't buy placement in search engine results, your primary cost is the SEO effort itself. And since SEO isn't that expensive, whether you do it yourself or hire it done, search engine marketing provides a huge bang for your marketing buck.

So for most online marketers, search engine marketing and the attending SEO represent a major component of their online marketing mix. It's not the only thing you should do to market your business online, but it may be the most important thing.

> **SEO Tip**
>
> You can also use SEO and search engine marketing to test various ads, promotions, and approaches. Those items that rank highest in your search engine results are the best candidates for a full-blown promotion.

Pay-Per-Click Advertising

For most companies, the second most important component of their online marketing mix is also related to search engines. Pay-per-click advertising, as it's called, involves purchasing specific keywords or phrases so that your ad appears in the "paid results" section of search engine results pages, as shown in Figure 21.1—and on relevant third-party websites as well. The advertiser pays only when a customer clicks the link in the ad to go to the advertiser's website.

Figure 21.1

PPC ads on the Yahoo! search results page—the "sponsor results" along the top and the right side.

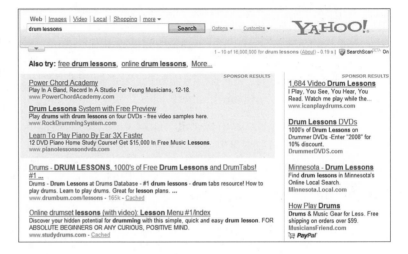

Which are the most important PPC ad networks today? Not surprisingly, they're the same companies that run the three largest search engines:

- ◆ Google AdWords (http://adwords.google.com)
- ◆ Yahoo! Search Marketing (http://searchmarketing.yahoo.com)
- ◆ Microsoft adCenter (http://adcenter.microsoft.com)

Because search engine marketing is so closely related to PPC advertising, many companies, large and small, integrate PPC into their marketing mix. But how much of *your* mix should you devote to PPC advertising?

Search Note
PPC advertising is so important that I devote an entire chapter to the topic. Turn to Chapter 23, "Integrating Pay-Per-Click Advertising into Your Plan," to learn more.

It depends. While it's unlikely that PPC ads will drive as much traffic to your site as will organic search engine results, they can still be an effective part of your mix. Some percentage of searchers will always either confuse paid results with organic results, thus benefiting PPC advertisers, or who trust the paid results much the same way they trust display ads in traditional Yellow Pages directories.

PPC advertising can also be beneficial if you compete in a niche with some very influential targeted websites. Find out which ad networks those sites use, and place your ads with those networks. Purchasing the right keywords will almost guarantee placement for your ads on those sites, which should generate some very targeted traffic.

Display Advertising

PPC ads are text ads, which should not be confused with more traditional display ads. Display ads, like the one in Figure 21.2, are those banner ads that you see at the top (and sometimes along the sides) of web pages. These banner ads combine text and graphics (and sometimes videos and Flash animations), much the same way that display ads work in printed media.

Figure 21.2

A typical online display ad, from the Minneapolis StarTribune.com website.

Of course, display ads don't have to be static. Many display ads, like the one in Figure 21.3, are actually video ads. This type of ad is a lot like a traditional television commercial, typically 30 seconds or less, but with a clickable component so customers can click through to your related website.

Figure 21.3

An Apple video display ad on CNET's News.com website.

While most display ads are clickable, thus facilitating the type of direct marketing common with all-text PPC ads, they're most often used for brand-building purposes or to reinforce aspects of a larger marketing campaign. As such, you tend to see large national advertisers go the display ad route instead of engaging in the guerrilla marketing common with text ads.

That's not to say, of course, that you can't use display ads to drive traffic directly to your website. Of course you can. You just have to design your display ads to encourage clicking, and the link has to be quite obvious within the ad.

The problem with display advertising, compared to search engine marketing or PPC advertising, is that the click-through rates are much, much lower. Most people see a display ad and move right past it. Even if the ad registers, they don't bother to click through, which results in click-through rates in the low single digits. Of course, if you purchase space on enough high-traffic websites, even that low click-through rate can generate significant traffic. And, let us not forget, users can still absorb your ad message even if they don't click the ad.

> **Search Note**
>
> Even though online display ads are less efficient than online text ads, they're so much less expensive than offline ads that the inefficiencies are effectively offset.

That said, display advertising is one of the fastest-growing parts of the online marketing mix, especially as big national advertisers slowly but surely move onto the Internet. If you have a message—and the corresponding budget—for a mass audience, this may be a way to go.

E-Mail Marketing

Many firms also find success with e-mail marketing. An e-mail marketing campaign involves sending targeted e-mail messages to a company's existing customer base; these e-mails can advertise upcoming promotions, new products, and the like.

> **Search Note**
>
> Don't confuse e-mail marketing with spam e-mails. Legitimate e-mail marketing is sent only with prior approval by the customer; spam is unsolicited and typically unwanted e-mail.

Most e-mail marketing is a form of direct marketing. You're using the e-mails not to increase brand awareness or simply drive traffic to your website, but rather to solicit direct sales of a particular product or service. Airlines, for example, use e-mail marketing to notify prior customers of upcoming specials and get them to click through to order tickets; online retailers use e-mail marketing to put today's promotions in front of customers and get them to click through and order products. (Figure 21.4 shows a typical promotional e-mail, complete with a special offer.)

Figure 21.4

A promotional e-mail from Macy's.

E-mail marketing has appeal to many types of companies, especially those with aggressive direct sales operations. Compared to other parts of the marketing mix, e-mail marketing has several advantages. E-mail marketing is ...

◆ **Low cost.** It costs nothing to send 100,000 e-mails, compared to the tens of thousands of dollars it would take to send an equivalent number of postal mails.

◆ **Fast.** You can get an e-mail into the hands of a customer within seconds, compared to the days or weeks it might take to place an offer with traditional media.

◆ **Easily trackable.** All you have to do is create a distinct landing page for the URL in the e-mail and then track traffic coming to that page.

◆ **Proactive.** Compared to search engine marketing, which waits for a user to find you, you're pushing your message to your customer base.

◆ **Targeted.** You can send e-mail promotions only to specified customers in your company's database.

Successful online merchants use e-mail marketing to entice more sales from their existing customer base. If you offer goods or services for sale over the web, e-mail marketing should be an essential part of your marketing mix.

Blog Marketing

Blogs are becoming more important to savvy online marketers—especially those that recognize that a company blog can be an effective channel of communication between a company and its customers. In this regard, blogs let companies talk to and with their customer base; companies can use a blog to convey their message or to solicit input from interested customers. It's a great way to research what's on the minds of your most active customers.

For this reason, many companies, both large and small, are creating their own in-house blogs, like the one in Figure 21.5. These blogs are typically part of the company's master website and feature posts written by a variety of employees in different areas of the company. Company blogs of this sort help to foster a sense of shared community among the customer base.

Figure 21.5

A well-written and well-received company blog from Southwest Airlines.

Since hosting and posting to a blog are relatively inexpensive (the biggest expense is the time to manage the blog), company blogs are especially valuable to small and budget-conscious organizations. As such, an internal blog can be a valuable component of a company's overall online marketing mix.

Social Media Marketing

The newest type of online marketing is social media marketing—exploiting social networks and social bookmarking services to bring visibility to your company, brand, or product. This is a form of public relations; the goal is to get all manner of social websites to include mention of what you're promoting.

Let's start with marketing to blogs, where the goal is to get your company or product in front of influential bloggers. When a well-read blogger mentions your company or product, that's like free advertising to all of that blogger's readers. In fact, it can be even better than that; in some readers' eyes, it's tantamount to a celebrity endorsement.

This type of social media marketing typically utilizes traditional public relations methods; you work influential bloggers much as you'd work reviewers at traditional print newspapers and magazines. But some blogs let you pay for a mention or review. This sort of paid placement is similar to product placement in movies or TV shows and is becoming more common in the blogosphere.

Search Note
If you're interested in exploring product placement in the blogosphere, check out Blogitive (www.blogitive.com), a network of bloggers who accept paid placement.

Generating attention within video-sharing communities is typically accomplished by creating videos for viewing on YouTube (www.youtube.com), the largest such site on the Internet. If you do everything right, a YouTube video can be seen by a potential audience of millions—some subset of which can then be persuaded to visit your website for more information or to purchase whatever you're selling.

The most effective YouTube business video isn't an advertisement; YouTube users don't waste their time watching online what they tend to skip over when they're watching traditional television. Instead, you need to create a video that YouTubers want to watch—something entertaining, educational, or informative. That may be a funny video promoting your brand or product, a how-to video demonstrating how to do something that people really need to do, or a video packed with useful news or information, like the one shown in Figure 21.6. In fact, the most effective YouTube business videos are more like infomercials; they use a light sell to get their message across and entice viewers to ask for more.

Figure 21.6

An informative YouTube video from D-Link.

YouTube videos don't have to be expensive (you can shoot with a typical consumer camcorder) to be effective, which makes them ideal for smaller businesses on a budget. Best of all, posting videos on YouTube is free; you don't have traditional media placement costs.

Then we have the true social networks, exemplified by Facebook (www.facebook.com) and MySpace (www.myspace.com). While you can place display ads on both of these sites (just as you can on YouTube), a more effective approach is to create a profile page for yourself or your business and use that page to announce upcoming products, promotions, and events. Naturally, your profile page should include links back to your company's website—or, even better, a landing page customized for your "friends" on that social network.

> **Search Note**
>
> Learn more about using YouTube videos for marketing in my companion book, *YouTube for Business* (Que, 2008).

Marketing to social networks is low cost but resource intensive. To be effective, you have to spend lots of time on the social network sites, participating in various communities and actively seeking new friends. If you don't work the community, this type of effort is likely to fail.

Online PR

That brings us to the topic of online public relations. In some aspects, online PR is no different from traditional PR; you're trying to get as many outlets as possible to mention your latest product or service. But online PR involves many new and different channels you need to address, from blogs and social networks to topic-oriented communities and message boards. It's not as simple as sending out a hard-copy press release.

To that end, blog and social media marketing are just different types of online PR; when you cultivate relationships with influential bloggers, for example, you're engaging in a public relations activity. You get your best results not by sending out an electronic press release, but by making friends with individual bloggers and actively participating in targeted online communities.

Another way that online PR differs from traditional PR is that actual results are more easily tracked. With traditional PR, about the only thing you can track is mentions in the media. With online PR, however, you can track actual sales that result from mentions on various websites; all you have to do is provide the solicited media with their own dedicated URLs to link back to your site.

 SEO Tip

Savvy companies turn online PR into direct response marketing by including links to product landing pages in all their press releases.

It goes without saying that public relations is always a key part of a company's marketing mix. That remains so when we're talking about the online marketing mix—which has to include online PR.

Where SEO Fits into Your Online Marketing Mix

Knowing all the various components of an online marketing mix, where do search engine marketing and search engine optimization fit in?

For most companies, search engine marketing is one of the most cost-effective components of their online marketing mix. A site goes through the entire SEO treatment for a relatively small one-time cost, with significant and easily tracked results. An effective SEO campaign will increase a site's ranking on Google, Yahoo!, and the other search engines, and the higher rankings will drive more traffic to your website. Few, if any, other components of a marketing plan can have this type of near-immediate impact with minimal investment.

Search engine marketing is especially useful when you have an active customer base—that is, where potential customers are actively seeking information online. Whether they're seeking general information, specific data, or product comparisons, if they go to Google or Yahoo! to find what they want, a well-engineered search engine marketing strategy will put your name in front of their eyeballs. All you have to know is what they're searching for and then optimize your site for keywords that best describe that topic.

That said, search engine marketing isn't ideal for all types of businesses. If you have a new business, for example, or are creating a new product category, people might not know to search for you. When it comes to creating brand or company awareness, search engine marketing isn't that effective. In this situation, you may be better off diverting marketing funds to brand-oriented online display advertising and public relations.

The same holds if you're a retailer in a price-competitive marketplace. In this scenario, customers aren't necessarily looking for the highest-ranking retailer in the search results; they're looking for the one that offers the lowest price on what they're shopping for. Plain-vanilla search engine marketing might not get this message in front of target customers; you may need to shift your focus from the major search engines to the shopping search engines. This is a form of search engine marketing, to be sure, but it doesn't necessarily involve Google, Microsoft, and Yahoo!.

> **Search Note**
>
> Learn more about using the shopping search engines in Chapter 22, "Integrating Shopping Directories into Your Plan."

For most other business situations, search engine marketing more than pulls its own weight. You just need to make sure that your search engine plans are well integrated into your other online and offline marketing activities—and we discuss this next.

Making All the Elements of Your Online Marketing Plan Work Together

For most companies, search engine marketing isn't the only component of their online marketing plan. Most companies also engage in PPC advertising, online display advertising, e-mail marketing, blog marketing, social media marketing, or online public relations—or some combination of these activities.

Knowing this, it's important that all components of your marketing mix mesh with each other. They should all carry the same message; you don't want to present one image to the search engines, another to customers viewing display ads, and yet another to blogs and social media through your PR activities. Your message should be consistent, no matter where customers encounter that message.

What does that mean, in reality?

First, it means that the way you define your business has to be consistent. The key-words you choose as part of your SEO should also be the keywords you purchase for your PPC advertising, the keywords in the copy for your display ads, highlighted text in the promotional e-mails you send to customers, talking points when you communicate with influential bloggers, and part of the electronic press releases you send to online news organizations. You can't describe your business one way in press releases, another way in advertisements, and yet another way to the search engines; you must have a consistent message.

That extends to using themes and images from your display advertising on your website—especially in the landing pages you create for your search engine and e-mail marketing campaigns. When someone clicks the URL in a promotional e-mail, that person should land on a page that not only repeats the message of the e-mail, but also mirrors the look and feel of your display advertising. Again, consistency is the key.

That doesn't mean, however, that you can't adapt the message for the medium. PPC and display ads, for example, demand much less copy than do promotional e-mails and landing web pages. Your message and image have to reflect how they're being delivered; given the unique qualities of each online medium, you can't be a slave to consistency.

You should also strive to exploit the unique features of each medium. Granted, there's not a whole lot you can do with a three-line text PPC ad, but most online media have qualities that reward creativity. For example, you can put together a contest on YouTube that encourages viewers to submit their own videos for your newest product; this is not a campaign that is easily mirrored in other online media. (That contest, of course, should not conflict with the main image and message you convey in other media.)

The point is, all of your online media needs to work together. All channels have to convey a consistent message and image, without sending conflicting messages to your customer base. Your online marketing mix should be a consistent whole that is greater than the sum of its parts.

Driving your consistent message is your intimate knowledge of the market and your customers—your ability to *think like the customer.* This insight helps you select the right keywords for your search engine marketing and PPC advertising, as well as informs the messages and images you send in your display advertising and public relations efforts.

Melding Online and Traditional Marketing

Given all this attention to online marketing, what about your traditional marketing media—print, radio, and television advertising, as well as direct mail and traditional public relations? How do your online and traditional marketing efforts mix?

Stop!

Just because you add search engine marketing to your overall marketing mix doesn't mean that you should abandon any traditional marketing channels. Online marketing and its various components should supplement your existing marketing efforts, not replace them.

The answer is surprisingly simple. Your online and traditional elements should work together in the same way as the components of your online marketing plan. Online and traditional components should complement each other while delivering a consistent message, while at the same time exploiting the unique features of each medium.

Again, this should all be driven by your knowledge of what your customers want. Customer research not only informs the keywords that drive your search engine marketing, but it also determines what traditional media you use and the words and images you use in those media.

The end result is that all your potential customers, however you reach them, receive a powerful and consistent message—even if that message is fine-tuned for the particular aspects of that media. So you should use similar images in your television and online video ads, as well as similar copy in your print and online ads—and, of course, that copy should include many of the keywords you use in your search engine marketing and PPC advertising. One medium relates to and feeds the next; the consistency of your message increases its power and effectiveness.

You can't do this, however, by separating your online and traditional marketing. You can't have one department responsible for the one and not for the other; you can't employ two different ad agencies that might work at cross-purposes. This sort of cross-pollination argues for a centralized marketing effort, all working from the same customer data and with the same drivers and keywords. Your thinking should be holistic, while employing specialists to implement your message and plan for each specific medium.

Success in your search engine marketing efforts is hollow if it isn't accompanied by similar success in other channels. Don't focus on one without focusing on the whole.

The Least You Need to Know

◆ The components of an online marketing plan can include search engine marketing, pay-per-click advertising, display advertising, e-mail marketing, blog marketing, social media marketing, and online public relations.

◆ Search engine marketing is one of the most important components of an online marketing plan, as it is both low cost and highly effective.

◆ Not all types of businesses benefit from SEO; it isn't good for making customers aware of new products or brands.

◆ All the components of your online marketing mix should work together to impart a consistent message to consumers.

◆ Online marketing should supplement your traditional marketing efforts; both should impart a similar message, even if that message is fine-tuned for the unique aspects of each medium.

Chapter 22

Integrating Shopping Directories into Your Plan

In This Chapter

◆ Understanding how online shopping directories work

◆ Getting to know the major online shopping directories

◆ Learning how to submit your listings to the shopping directories

Different types of businesses have different search engine marketing needs. While optimizing your site for Google, Live Search, and Yahoo! works for the majority of sites, other types of sites might get better results (or supplement the big search engine results) by listing with other more specialized directories.

Arguably the most popular type of specialized directory is the online shopping directory—a site that compares products for sale from multiple online retailers. Obviously, if you're selling products online, you need to take advantage of these directories, as they can drive a lot of qualified customers directly to your site's product pages. We examine the major shopping directories in this chapter and show you how to get your products listed—for free.

How Online Shopping Directories Work

What online retailers call an online shopping directory, consumers often refer to as a price-comparison site. Whatever you call it, this type of site maintains a huge directory of products for sale from thousands of online merchants—literally hundreds of thousands of different products, complete with current pricing and availability information. Consumers use the site to find the lowest prices on the products they're shopping for; retailers use the site to garner more visibility for the products they're selling.

Consumers might be under the impression that these sites scour the web for prices from a wide variety of online retailers. That's a false impression; instead, these sites build their price/product databases from product links submitted and paid for by participating retailers. And not only are these product listings submitted by retailers, but they're also (in most cases) paid for by retailers. That's right, most price-comparison sites charge retailers to be included in their listings; that's how the sites make money.

Fortunately for retailers with large inventories, payment isn't on a per-listing basis; instead, they pay when customers click their product listings. This is the old pay-per-click model, and the individual fee is, of course, a cost per click. CPC charges run anywhere from a nickel to more than a buck, depending on the site and the product category.

So if you run a website that offers products for sale, you can often get more visibility by listing with the major online shopping directories than you would relying on organic search results from Google, Live Search, and Yahoo!. Even though you pay for the click-throughs, those clicks are likely to result in sales.

> **Stop!**
>
> While Google and the other major search engines will list product pages in their search results, you can't rely on them to always find the products you have for sale on your site. Most product pages are dynamically generated pages, which are difficult for searchbots to crawl. In addition, the crawl rate may be too slow to grab current pricing and availability data for your products.

> **Search Note**
>
> Even though retailers pay to be listed, price-comparison sites appear to honestly present the lowest prices to consumers—from participating merchants, that is. The prices presented are legitimate, no matter who's paying what.

Examining the Major Online Shopping Directories

When it comes to price-comparison sites, 10 consistently attract the most consumer traffic. We look at each of these sites separately and then provide a list of all the other price-comparison sites available.

BizRate

BizRate (www.bizrate.com), shown in Figure 22.1, is one of the oldest comparison-shopping sites, founded way back in the stone ages of 1996. In addition to product listings, it offers customer reviews of the most popular products, as well as reviews of online retailers. These product and merchant reviews make BizRate an extremely useful comparison-shopping site.

> **Search Note**
>
> BizRate is owned by Shopzilla and shares the same product database as its parent site.

Figure 22.1

The BizRate shopping comparison site.

Google Product Search

Google's online shopping directory, shown in Figure 22.2, is called Google Product Search (www.google.com/products/). This is actually one of the newer online shopping directories on the web—even if it isn't technically a directory.

Figure 22.2

The bare-bones consumer interface to Google Product Search.

Unlike the other sites listed in this chapter, Google Product Search doesn't accept payment for its listing. Instead, it uses its GoogleBot crawler software to independently scour the web for merchants and products.

That's right, Google Product Search is a pure search engine, just like its Google parent. Google Product Search searches all the online retailers it can find and doesn't accept any paid listings. For consumers, that makes Google's price comparisons more legitimate than those at other sites.

> **Search Note**
>
> Google Product Search was formerly known as Froogle—a much more distinctive moniker, in my opinion.

That doesn't mean, however, that you can't submit your products to Google Product Search for inclusion in its index—because you can. In fact, submitting your products ensures inclusion in the index, while relying on Google searchbot is a little dicier. But unlike all the other shopping directories, you don't have to pay to submit or pay when your listing is clicked. Like all things Google, this one is free.

Live Search Cashback

Microsoft's online shopping site, shown in Figure 22.3, is a subset of its Live Search site. Newly dubbed Live Search Cashback (http://search.live.com/cashback/), it's unique: it pays consumers to use the site. More precisely, the site offers cash rebates when users purchase from one of its listings; it's Microsoft's way of buying its way into the shopping directory market.

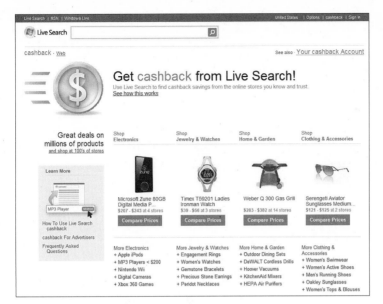

Figure 22.3

Microsoft's unique Live Search Cashback offering.

mySimon

The mySimon site (www.mysimon.com), shown in Figure 22.4, was one of the first price-comparison sites on the web. It's still one of the most popular, even though it doesn't include nearly as many merchants as some competing directories.

Figure 22.4

The mySimon online shopping directory.

For what it's worth, mySimon is part of the CNET network of sites. This enables the site to include product specifications and reviews from the parent CNET site—a distinct advantage over many competing sites.

NexTag

NexTag (www.nextag.com), shown in Figure 22.5, includes listings for everything from computer monitors to airline flights. It has been one of the top five online shopping sites since it was founded in 1999, serving up product listings to more than 17 million consumers each month.

Figure 22.5

The NexTag online shopping directory.

PriceGrabber

PriceGrabber (www.pricegrabber.com), shown in Figure 22.6, is one of the most-trafficked shopping directories on the web, with more than 26 million users. In addition to traditional product listings, it offers an online storefront service for smaller merchants and individual sellers.

Figure 22.6

The PriceGrabber online shopping directory.

Pricewatch

Pricewatch (www.pricewatch.com), shown in Figure 22.7, specializes in computers and consumer electronics products. It's not the directory for you if your business sells clothing or other soft goods, but if you offer any sort of electronic gadget for sale, it's a good place to list.

Shopping.com

All the comparison-shopping sites listed in this chapter are worth your consideration, but my favorite is Shopping.com (www.shopping.com), shown in Figure 22.8. From a consumer's perspective, Shopping.com provides more than just simple price comparisons; it also offers customer reviews of both products and merchants, to help people make better purchase decisions. From a merchant's perspective, Shopping.com hosts 1.5 million customers per day—and delivers 17 million sales leads to participating retailers each month.

Figure 22.7

The Pricewatch online shopping directory—great for selling electronics products.

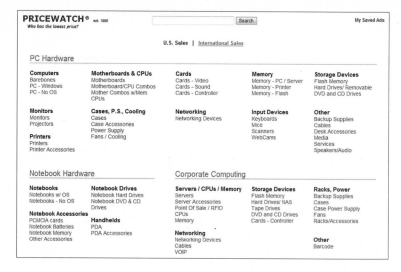

Figure 22.8

Shopping.com—the king of online shopping directories.

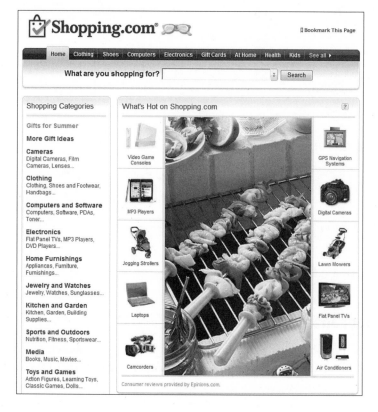

One of the reasons Shopping.com is so popular is that it incorporates product and merchant reviews from Epinions.com (which happens to be my favorite customer review site). But most consumers also find the Shopping.com site extremely easy to use; users seldom have difficulties finding the products they want, as sometimes happens at other sites. If you're an online merchant, it should definitely be at the top of your online shopping directory hit list.

Search Note

eBay acquired Shopping.com in 2005, although there is very little interaction between the online shopping directory and eBay's online auction site.

Shopzilla

As you can see in Figure 22.9, Shopzilla (www.shopzilla.com) offers consumers a more streamlined interface than the category-heavy sites of many of its competitors. That said, it operates from the same product database as its related BizRate site, which is a nice two-fer for participating merchants.

Figure 22.9

Streamlined online shopping at Shopzilla.

Yahoo! Shopping

Yahoo! Shopping (http://shopping.yahoo.com), shown in Figure 22.10, is Yahoo!'s online shopping directory. Previously a simple directory of online merchants, the site was revamped several years ago into one of the leading price-comparison sites on the web, complete with numerous product-comparison features for consumers.

Figure 22.10

Yahoo! Shopping—another big online shopping directory.

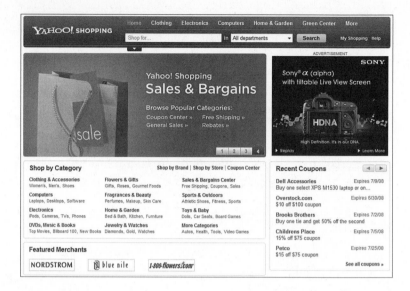

Other Online Shopping Directories

Beyond these top 10 sites, you might want to add other online shopping directories to your online marketing mix. Some of these sites are general in nature; others target specific product categories. Table 22.1 details some of the best of these sites.

Table 22.1   Other Online Shopping Directories

Online Shopping Directory	URL	Product Focus
AimLower	www.aimlower.com	General
Best Web Buys	www.bestwebbuys.com	Books, movies, music, bikes, electronics
CNET Shopper.com	shopper.cnet.com	Computers, cameras, electronics
DealTime	www.dealtime.com	General
DVD Price Search	www.dvdpricesearch.com	Movies
MetaPrices	www.metaprices.com	Books, movies, music
Price.com	www.price.com	Books, movies, music, computers, cameras, electronics

Online Shopping Directory	URL	Product Focus
PriceSCAN	www.pricescan.com	General
PricingCentral	www.pricingcentral.com	General
ShoppingAisles.com	www.shoppingaisles.com	Books, music, movies, video games
ShopSearchEngine.com	www.shopsearchengine.com	General
StreetPrices	www.streetprices.com	General

Search Note

DealTime product listings are also incorporated as part of the Shopping.com site.

Submitting Your Listings to the Shopping Directories

Now that you know which are the most popular online shopping directories, how do you get your products listed on these sites? While the detailed listing process differs somewhat from site to site, the general principles are the same. Read on to learn how.

Signing Up for Merchant Services

Each online shopping directory operates a consumer front end (for shoppers) and a merchant front end (for retailers). You can typically find the link to the merchant page at the bottom of the site's consumer home page.

Before you submit any listings to a directory, you have to sign up for the site's merchant program—sometimes called an advertiser program. This is normally a simple process, with no up-front charge. During this process you'll have a chance to review the site's cost-per-click rates, any additional listing features you can pay for, and the site's data-submission process. Make sure you know what you're signing up for before you commit and send your first data file.

Paying for Your Listings

As noted previously, most online shopping directories don't charge you to submit your product listings—which would be cost-prohibitive if you had a large number of SKUs.

They do charge you, however, when a customer clicks on a product listing to go to your website; you pay whether that customer buys anything or not.

How much will you pay? The cost-per-click rates differ from site to site and from category to category, but typically run from a nickel to a buck per click. For example, Table 22.2 details the CPC pricing at Shopping.com, by product category.

Table 22.2   Shopping.com CPC Pricing

Product Category	Minimum Cost Per Click
Appliance Accessories	$0.15
Books	$0.05
Building Supplies	$0.25
Cars	$0.05–$0.40
Clothing and Accessories	$0.20–$0.35
Computers	$0.70–$1.00
Electronics	$0.40–$1.00
Event Tickets	$0.30
Flowers and Gifts	$0.25
Food and Wine	$0.15
Furniture	$0.25
Garden	$0.25
Health and Beauty	$0.50–$0.70
Home and Garden	$0.15–$0.25
Home Appliances	$0.30–$0.60
Home Furnishings	$0.25
Jewelry and Watches	$0.20–$0.65
Kids and Family	$0.15–$0.50
Kitchen	$0.25
Large Kitchen Appliances	$0.30
Magazines and Subscriptions	$0.15
Miscellaneous	$0.15
Movies	$0.05
Music	$0.05
Musical Instruments and Accessories	$0.05–$0.50

Product Category	Minimum Cost Per Click
Office	$0.40–$1.00
Pets	$0.20
Services	$0.05
Small Kitchen Appliances	$0.15–$0.60
Sports and Outdoors	$0.05–$0.50
Sports Memorabilia	$0.15
Travel	$0.05
Video Games	$0.15–$0.25

Creating a Data File

How do you get your products listed on the shopping directory site? Fortunately, almost all online shopping directories accept bulk uploading of all the items in your inventory. This lets you submit all your products to the site in a single file.

The first step of this process is to create a data file of the products you have for sale. Check the requirements for a given site, but expect most sites to accept information in either tab-delimited text, spreadsheet, or XML (RSS or Atom) formats.

For most businesses, the easiest approach is to use Microsoft Excel to create a spreadsheet file that hosts all the required data. You can then save this file as a tab-delineated TXT file, if that's what a given site requires. While the specific requirements differ from site to site (and you should check with each site to find out exactly what they need—and in what format), most such files include some or all of the following information about each product:

- ◆ URL for the product page on your site
- ◆ Product name
- ◆ Item number or UPC (bar code)
- ◆ Price
- ◆ Quantity available
- ◆ Product category

In your spreadsheet, create one column for each type of data required. Create one row for each product you offer. The result should look something like what's shown in Figure 22.11.

Figure 22.11

Creating an Excel file for your product data.

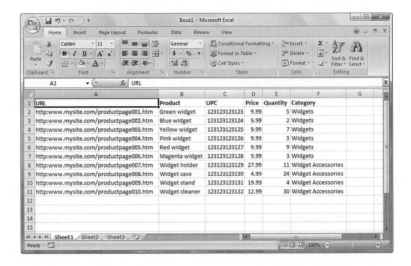

If the shopping site accepts Excel-format XLS files, you're done. If the file requirements are different, you need to save this file in the required file format.

Uploading Product Information

Once you've created your data file, you have to upload it to each of the online shopping directories you work with. This process differs from site to site (of course), so consult the precise instructions for each site. In general, however, it's typically a simple matter of clicking an "upload file" link on the site and then selecting the file to upload.

How often you upload a file depends on the site's requirements and how often your inventory levels change. You may be able to get by uploading a file once a week, or you may need to upload an updated data file daily. Again, check the site's requirements.

> **SEO Tip**
>
> If you have a large number of SKUs, look into automating this process by exporting your inventory listings directly into the spreadsheet file.

SEO Tip

Even though Google Product Search doesn't accept paid listings, it will accept your product data file (for free). You submit your product inventory to Google Product Search via Google's related Google Base service; learn more at www.google.com/base/help/sellongoogle.html.

The Least You Need to Know

◆ If you offer products for sale over the web, you may drive more traffic to your site from an online shopping directory than from the major search engines.

◆ Most online shopping directories (Google excluded) generate their listings via submittals from participating merchants—not by crawling the web.

◆ The 10 largest online shopping directories are, in alphabetical order, BizRate, Google Product Search, Live Search Cashback, mySimon, NexTag, PriceGrabber, Pricewatch, Shopping.com, Shopzilla, and Yahoo! Shopping.

◆ You submit your product listings to a shopping directory by creating a spreadsheet, text, or XML file containing the required product data.

◆ Online shopping directories don't charge for listings, but do charge on a cost-per-click basis for all customers they direct to the product pages on your website.

Integrating Pay-Per-Click Advertising into Your Plan

In This Chapter

◆ Understanding how pay-per-click advertising works

◆ Comparing the PPC ad networks

◆ Launching a PPC campaign

◆ Integrating PPC advertising with search engine marketing

Improving your ranking in a search engine's search results isn't the only way to reach the millions of potential customers who use search engines each day. You can also purchase ad space on the search results pages—text ads that look a lot like the organic search results.

This type of advertising is called pay-per-click (PPC) advertising, because the advertiser pays whenever a customer clicks on the link in the ad. The ads themselves appear on search pages for particular keyword queries; the advertiser "buys" that keyword as part of the ad purchase.

Many companies combine organic search marketing with PPC advertising in a holistic online marketing campaign. They're closely connected, after all—and the combination of the two increases your chances of reaching potential customers through a given search engine.

How Pay-Per-Click Advertising Works

Pay-per-click advertising isn't like traditional display advertising. PPC advertising doesn't buy discrete space on a given web page, nor does it allow for graphics-intensive advertisements. Instead, it's all about getting a text ad onto a specific search results page.

Purchasing Keywords

A PPC advertiser purchases a particular keyword or phrase from the ad network—or, more precisely, ad space that appears on search results pages and other websites that relate to the keywords in question. The advertiser's text ad is linked to that keyword in two different ways.

First, when a user enters a query on that ad network's related search engine site, the advertiser's ad is displayed on the first page of the search results, typically in a "paid results" or "sponsored links" section on either the top or the side of the page. As you can see in Figure 23.1, the ad is designed to look kind of like an organic search result.

Figure 23.1

PPC ads on Google's search results page.

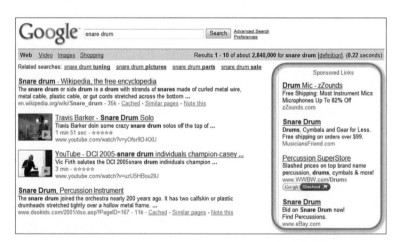

The second place the ad appears is on third-party sites that belong to the ad network. The ad is placed on specific pages that have content that relates to the purchased keyword. These ads, also text-only (as you can see in Figure 23.2), can appear anywhere on the given page; the ad placement is up to the owner of the web page.

Figure 23.2

PPC ads on a third-party web page.

So, for example, if you sell printer ink cartridges, you might purchase the words *printer, ink,* and *cartridges.* When a consumer searches for any of these keywords on the ad network's search engine, your ad will appear. Your ad will also appear when a consumer goes to a third-party website that features content containing these keywords.

Placing Ads in Context

The neat thing about PPC ads is that they use advanced search technology to serve content-focused ads—that is, an ad that relates to the underlying content of the host web page. And an ad that is somehow related to the content of a web page reaches a more targeted audience than a more broadly focused display ad.

The ad networks use the same sophisticated algorithms that they use to create their search indexes to determine the content of pages for sites that participate in their advertising program. They analyze the keywords on the page, word frequency, font size, and the overall link structure to figure out, as closely as possible, what a page is about. Then they find ads that closely match that page's content, and they feed those ads to the page.

For example, my personal website (www.molehillgroup.com) is all about the books I've written. On the page for my book *iPodpedia,* Google AdWords serves up ads titled "iPod Copying Software" and "Rescue Your iPod Music"; on the page for *The Complete Idiot's Guide to Playing Drums,* there are ads for "1,684 Video Drum Lessons" and "Yamaha DTX Drums 40% Off." The right ads for the right content—which greatly benefits the advertisers.

Paying by the Click

Pay-per-click advertising is so named because an advertiser pays the ad network only when customers click on the link in the ad. (The link typically points to the advertiser's website—or, most commonly, a special landing page on the website.) If no one clicks, the advertiser doesn't pay anything. The more clicks are registered, the more the advertiser pays.

Ad rates are on a cost-per-click (CPC) basis. That is, the advertiser is charged a particular fee for each click—anywhere from a few pennies to tens of dollars. The actual CPC rate is determined by the popularity of and competition for the keyword purchased, as well as the quality and quantity of traffic going to the site hosting the ad.

As you can imagine, popular keywords have a higher CPC, while less popular keywords can be had for less.

Advertisers typically bid on the most popular keywords. That is, you might say you'll pay up to $5 for a given keyword. If you're the high bidder among several advertisers, your ads will appear more frequently on pages that contain that keyword. If you're not the high bidder, you won't get as much visibility—if your ad appears at all.

> **Search Note**
>
> Pay-per-click advertising is in contrast to traditional cost-per-thousand-impressions (CPM) advertising, where rates are based on the number of potential viewers of the ad—whether they click through or not.

Sharing Ad Revenue

And here's something interesting about PPC advertising: it's not just the ad network that gets paid. Typically, any third-party site where the ad appears gets a cut of the ad revenues paid by the advertiser—which is why sites agree to put PPC ads on their web pages.

> **Search Note**
>
> Here's something important to know about PPC advertising—your ad probably won't appear on every search engine results page for the keyword you purchase. The page inventory is limited, while advertisers are theoretically unlimited. The big PPC ad networks, then, rotate ads from multiple advertisers on the search results and third-party pages.

Here's the way it works:

1. An advertiser creates an advertisement and contracts with an online ad network to place that ad on the Internet.

2. The ad network serves the ad in question to a number of appropriate websites.

3. An interested customer sees the ad on a third-party site and clicks the link in the ad to receive more information.

4. The advertiser pays the ad service, based on the CPC advertising rate.

5. The ad service pays the host site a small percentage of the advertising fee paid.

Evaluating the Big PPC Ad Networks

The big three PPC ad networks just happen to be run by the big three search engine companies—Google, Yahoo!, and Microsoft (in that order). When you purchase an ad on Google's AdWords network, your ad appears in Google's search results; when you purchase an ad on the Yahoo! Search Marketing network, that ad appears in Yahoo! search results; and when you purchase an ad from Microsoft Advertising, that ad appears in Live Search results.

In this respect, AdWords and its competitors essentially serve as ad brokers. They arrange ads from individual advertisers, then place those ads on their own and on third-party websites. Their payment comes from a cut of the PPC revenues.

> **Search Note**
>
> Not surprisingly, the three top online ad networks are run by the three top Internet search engine companies. You see, Google and Yahoo! (and, to a lesser extent, Microsoft) do not make money from their search engines. (Nobody pays for search results, remember—nor do users pay to conduct searches.) Instead, these companies make money from the ads they place in their search engines' search results pages—and from other sites in their network across the web. The search engines are merely containers for revenue-generating advertising, much as the articles in traditional magazines and newspapers are just filler between the advertisements that actually pay the rent.

Google AdWords

Just as Google is the largest search engine, Google AdWords (www.google.com/adwords/) is far and away the largest PPC ad network. Google sells ads on its own search results pages, throughout its entire network of sites, and on participating third-party sites. Google claims that its AdWords program reaches more than 80 percent of all Internet users; most advertisers confirm that AdWords generates the overwhelming majority of PPC traffic to their sites.

Advertising with Google AdWords isn't like a traditional advertising buy; there are no contracts and deadlines and such. You pay a one-time $5 activation fee and then are charged on either a cost-per-click (CPC) or

> **Search Note**
>
> The Google Network includes all of Google's sites (Google Maps, Gmail, YouTube, and the rest), the hundreds of thousands of small and medium-sized sites that participate in the Google AdSense program, and a number of major websites, including Amazon.com, AOL, and About.com.

cost-per-thousand-impressions (CPM) basis. (You can choose either payment method.) You control your costs by specifying how much you're willing to pay (per click or per impression) and by setting a daily spending budget. Google will never exceed the costs you specify.

How much does AdWords cost? It's your choice. If you go with the cost-per-click method, you can choose a maximum CPC click price from $0.01 to $100. If you go with the CPM method, there is a minimum cost of $0.25 per 1,000 impressions. Your daily budget can be as low as a penny, up to whatever you're willing to pay.

If you go the CPC route, Google uses AdWords Discounter technology to match the price you pay with the price competing advertisers are offering for a given keyword. The AdWords Discounter automatically monitors your competition and lowers your CPC to 1¢ above what they're willing to pay.

Creating an AdWords ad is as easy as following these steps:

1. Write the ad (a title line and two lines of text).

2. Enter the URL on your site you want to link to.

3. Choose the keyword(s) you want to purchase—up to 20 keywords or phrases.

4. Set the maximum you're willing to pay per click.

5. Set your monthly AdWords budget—Google recommends a $50 monthly minimum.

Once your ad campaign starts, you can monitor performance from the main AdWords page, shown in Figure 23.3. From here you can view your campaign's performance, generate various reports, create new ads, and access Google Analytics for additional performance tracking.

Figure 23.3

Tracking Google AdWords performance.

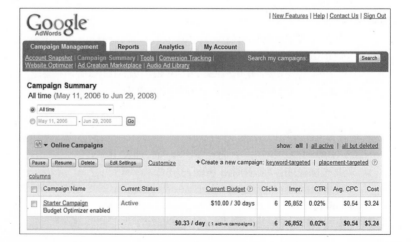

Yahoo! Search Marketing

Yahoo! Search Marketing (http://searchmarketing.yahoo.com) is a distant number two in the PPC advertising game. It works pretty much like Google AdWords: you purchase specific keywords and your ad appears in Yahoo! search results for that query, on related sites in the Yahoo! network, and on third-party pages that participate in the Yahoo! Search Marketing program.

Once you sign up for Yahoo! Search Marketing, you can start creating your ads. As with AdWords, the process is fairly straightforward:

1. Choose the keywords you want.

2. Specify your maximum bid per click ($0.10 minimum).

3. Set a daily budget.

4. Write your ad (title, description, and URL).

Yahoo! then matches your keywords with keyword queries of its search engine users and displays your ad on those search results pages. Your ad also gets displayed on third-party pages that contain content similar to the keyword(s) you've purchased.

You monitor your Yahoo! campaigns through the Dashboard, shown in Figure 23.4. You can track multiple campaigns, view campaign performance, generate various reports, and create new campaigns.

> **Search Note**
>
> Yahoo! Search Marketing is the new name for Overture, a large PPC ad network that Yahoo! acquired in 2003.

Microsoft adCenter

Most advertisers designate the bulk (75 percent or more) of their PPC ad budgets to Google AdWords, with the remaining amount split between Yahoo! and Microsoft. Microsoft adCenter (http://adcenter.microsoft.com) is Microsoft's answer to Google and Yahoo!, currently the number-three player in the PPC ad space.

After you sign up for the program, you start creating your adCenter ads the same way you create similar ads with Google and Yahoo!. You can create both Search Ads and Content Ads; the former appear in Live Search results pages, the latter on editorial pages on the Microsoft content network.

Figure 23.4

Tracking Yahoo! Search Marketing campaigns.

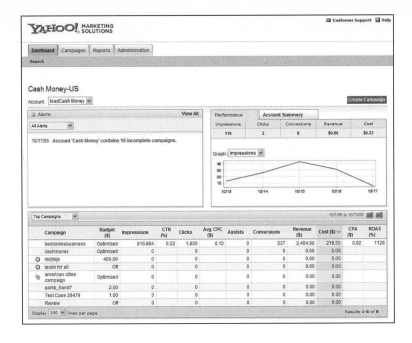

The process of creating an ad is similar to the process with the other PPC ad networks:

1. Write the ad, including a title, one-line description, and URL.

2. Pick your keywords—up to 100.

3. Set the maximum CPC rate ($0.05 minimum).

4. Set a monthly budget.

When you're done, your ad appears on relevant search and content pages. You manage your account via adCenter Analytics, shown in Figure 23.5. This reporting tool lets you view all sorts of data about your ad campaigns, as well as manage your existing ads and create new ones.

Other PPC Ad Networks

The big three PPC ad networks are just that—three ad networks. There are more than three ad networks selling ads on the web, however, often at prices much lower than what Google, Microsoft, and Yahoo! charge.

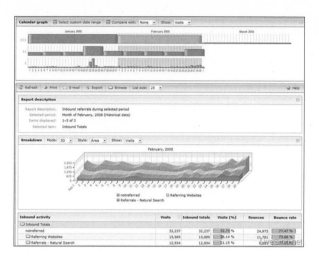

Figure 23.5

Tracking Microsoft adCenter campaigns.

While these lower rates typically accompany much lower traffic, these second-tier ad networks may still be checking out—primarily because of their lower costs. If it's not much more work on your end (and it probably isn't), it's easy enough to carve out a few bucks from your larger budget to divert to these smaller networks. And the smaller networks might actually deliver a higher return on investment for your ad dollars.

Who are these additional players? Here's a short list:

- 7Search (www.7search.com)

- ABC Search (www.abcsearch.com)

- Ask Sponsored Listings (http://sponsoredlistings.ask.com)

- ePilot (www.epilot.com)

- Marchex Adhere (www.marchex.com/product/adhere/)

- MIVA (www.miva.com)

- Search123 (www.search123.com)

- SearchFeed (www.searchfeed.com)

Creating a PPC Campaign

Okay, you think that you need a PPC component to your online marketing plan. What do you need to do to get started?

Selecting the Best PPC Ad Networks

The first step is to select which ad network or networks to use. If you're just starting out, I recommend going exclusively with Google AdSense; it's easy to use and will far and away deliver the most traffic of all current ad networks. Once you get the hang of the PPC thing, and if your budget allows, you can expand to include Yahoo! Search Marketing and Microsoft adCenter. Then, if you have the time, you can always add a few of the second-tier players to see how well they deliver. But it's okay to start simple, and AdSense is as simple as it gets.

Choosing Keywords

Choosing keywords for PPC advertising is exactly the same as choosing keywords for SEO. In fact, if you've already selected your SEO keywords, these are the keywords you want to purchase for your PPC campaign. If you haven't yet selected keywords, use the keyword-research tools discussed in Chapter 5 to determine which keywords are most effective for your site's particular content.

Calculating Optimal Cost Per Click

Now we come to the money part of the equation. Most PPC networks require you to bid on the keywords you select, typically in the form of a maximum CPC price you're willing to pay. How do you know how high to go?

Here's where a little research and performance tracking are in order. Basically, you have to determine what a lead—a single click-through—is worth to you.

Start by determining how much profit you make off a sale from your website. As an example, let's say you sell an item for $100 retail that costs you $60 to purchase or manufacture; you generate $40 profit on each sale.

Next, determine your conversion rate from your PPC campaign; you can find this metric in the reports section of most ad network dashboards. For most sites, expect your conversion rate to be in the low single digits. For our example, let's say that your conversion rate is 1 percent, meaning that 1 out of every 100 people who click your ad ends up buying your product.

Now it's math time. Each sale you make is worth $40 to you, and it takes 100 clicks to make one sale. Divide $40 by 100, and you discover that each visitor you attract costs you $0.40. This means you can afford to spend a maximum of $0.40 per click before you start losing money on each click. So, in this example, you'd set your maximum price per click to $0.40.

This calculation works only when you're selling products or services directly from your website, and it requires a little post-launch calculation. (That is, you won't know your conversion rate until you get some experience under your belt.) On the other hand, if you're using PPC advertising to generate nonsales leads or build your brand image, the value of each click is much more difficult to determine—so difficult, in fact, that each company must determine this on its own.

Writing the Ad

Of course, the effectiveness of the ad you write will, to some degree, determine your conversion rate and, thus, your maximum CPC rates. It takes a lot of talent to drive sales from a simple three- or four-line text ad, but that's what you need to develop.

A PPC ad typically consists of three or four lines of text. The first line is the title, with a relatively short character count. The next one or two lines contain the description, which can hold more characters but still not a lot. And the final line is typically the name and URL of the site where you're driving traffic.

Figure 23.6 shows a typical PPC ad. The title, "Books by Michael Miller," is the short and sweet grabber that gets the customer's attention. The second and third lines in this example, "How-to books by popular author; Computers, music, eBay, and more!" describe the product you're selling. The final line, "www.molehillgroup.com," is the URL for the product page.

Books by Michael Miller
How-to books by popular author
Computers, music, eBay, and more!
www.molehillgroup.com

Figure 23.6

A four-line PPC text ad.

In this example, note how keywords are placed in both the title and the description. The keyword *books* appears twice, while other keywords (*computers*, *music*, and *eBay*) also make their appearance. It's tight and punchy, not at all wordy, and keyword dense. That's all you have room for.

If you're not comfortable writing this sort of supertight ad copy, it's worth hiring a

> **Stop!**
>
> Don't even think about putting puff words (*lowest* or *best*) or punctuation (*) in your PPC ads. You simply don't have space to waste on these unnecessary words and characters!

copywriter. This is the toughest kind of copywriting, and it's well worth using a pro to implement it effectively.

How PPC Advertising Integrates with Search Engine Marketing

If you're in the middle of performing SEO on your website, it's a short step from there to PPC advertising. Since they both target search engine users, search engine marketing and PPC advertising have a lot in common.

First, both SEO and PPC revolve around keywords. When you do your keyword research for SEO, you now have a list of keywords you can purchase for your PPC ads. There's no difference between which keywords work for SEO and which work best for PPC advertising. An effective keyword for one is an effective keyword for the other.

Second, both organic page listings and PPC ads appear on the same search engine results pages. When someone is searching for a keyword, he will see both the pages that best match the query and the paid ads for that purchased keyword. If you have both an organic listing and a paid listing on the same page, that reinforces the quality of your site in the mind of the user, making it more likely that he will click on one of them. On the other hand, if your organic result didn't make it onto the first page of search results, you at least have the paid ad as a backup.

Beyond the commonalities, PPC advertising supplements your organic search results. When you use Google AdWords and the other PPC ad networks, your ad appears on more than just search results pages; it also appears on content pages throughout the ad network's affiliate sites. This adds countless impressions to what you receive organically and helps to drive additional traffic to your website.

So how important is PPC advertising to your online marketing campaign? I like to view it as supplemental to search engine marketing—it can't replace SEO and organic search results, but it can work in addition to your normal search engine marketing. This is why most larger websites engage in both search engine marketing and PPC advertising; they work together to maximize your visibility online.

The Least You Need to Know

- Pay-per-click advertising serves up context-sensitive text ads on search engines and other sites for the keywords you purchase.

- When you purchase a keyword, you specify the maximum cost per click you're willing to pay.

- The largest PPC ad networks are Google AdSense, Yahoo! Search Engine Marketing, and Microsoft adCenter.

- PPC advertising should supplement, not replace, your search engine marketing plan.

Chapter 24

Evaluating the Performance of Your Online Marketing Plan

In This Chapter

◆ Setting goals

◆ Evaluating plan components

◆ Evaluating the overall plan

◆ Defining success

We end our discussion of online marketing plans with the topic of evaluation—that is, determining whether your plan is working. We've already discussed how to evaluate the success of your SEO campaign (back in Chapter 16), so there's no need to revisit those specifics. Instead, we look at what metrics are important for measuring the success of your overall online marketing plan.

Remember, however, that measuring results is only part of the equation; you also have to understand the events that led to those results. Only by learning from both your mistakes and your successes can you continue to improve your online marketing activities—including your search engine marketing.

Setting Goals Beforehand

To measure the success of your online marketing plan, you must have set some goals beforehand. After all, you can't measure a change in performance without a baseline for that performance. You have to know what you want to accomplish before you can determine whether you accomplished it.

Your plan should include objectives for both discrete activities (search engine marketing, e-mail marketing, site traffic, and so on) and the overall plan. It is possible, of course, to meet some individual objectives while missing your overall goal; it's also possible to hit your big goal without meeting all your individual goals. That's why you have to set objectives for and then measure everything you do.

Interestingly, you can measure many of the individual components of a marketing plan using the same metrics. For example, website traffic can be used to measure the success of your search engine marketing, display advertising, e-mail marketing, blog marketing, social media marketing, and public relations efforts. For this reason, it's important to track the source of each metric—in this example, the source of the traffic coming to your website. This way, you can give credit to the correct component of your plan.

Evaluating Individual Components of Your Plan

It's important that you evaluate each individual part of your marketing plan separately from the whole. That's because you may be doing some things right and some things wrong, and you don't want to lose individual successes behind an overall failure, or hide individual failures behind an overall success. You want to find out what you're doing right (so you can repeat your successes) and what you're doing wrong (so you can improve your performance next time).

This means looking at each component of your marketing mix individually. Don't lump multiple components into a big bucket; segregate out all your activities and measure how they contributed to your overall numbers.

Search Engine Marketing

Search engine marketing—the fruits of your SEO efforts—is easily measurable. You want to track the number of clicks you get on each of your chosen keywords; in essence, this measures the traffic generated by each keyword. You can get even more granular by measuring performance per keyword per search engine—that is, determine which search engines are driving the most traffic to your site.

You can go behind simple traffic or pageview monitoring to determine how long each search visitor stayed on your site, which pages they visited, and whether they purchased anything while on your site. Tracking click conversions, direct sales, and profits from those sales is the ultimate in search engine marketing analysis.

> **SEO Tip**
>
> You can also measure your search engine ranking for your chosen keywords, and any increase in ranking you see resulting from your campaign.

Pay-Per-Click Advertising

You measure PPC advertising in much the same way you measure search engine marketing. You want to measure the number of clicks you get on each keyword you purchase, as well as the conversion rate and how many actual conversions you get—that is, how many people who clicked on your ad continued on and actually purchased what you were selling.

It's more important to measure conversions and direct sales with PPC advertising than it is with search engine marketing. That's because PPC advertising costs you for each click generated, whereas search engine marketing has no costs, per click or otherwise, beyond the initial SEO efforts.

> **Stop!**
>
> Be on the lookout for *click fraud*, where third parties click repeatedly on an ad (to generate higher ad placement revenues) but never purchase anything. If you see a marked increase in clicks without a corresponding increase in purchases, notify your advertising network about the suspected click fraud.

Display Advertising

Display advertising effectiveness is less easy to track than PPC performance. That's because much display advertising is meant to increase brand awareness, not necessarily to generate direct sales.

For those display ads that do exist to drive sales on your website, performance is relatively easy to track; just measure click-throughs, conversion rates, and identifiable direct sales. For those display ads that exist to drive brand awareness, you can measure website traffic, although that won't tell you a whole lot; you can also use standard market research tools to identify any changes in brand awareness and determine what activities those changes are attributable to.

E-Mail Marketing

E-mail marketing exists, almost universally, to drive direct sales. Thus, you can measure the effectiveness of e-mail marketing by tracking direct sales that result from each e-mail. Click-throughs (from the e-mail) and site traffic are also important, but it's the sales that count.

Blog Marketing

Blog marketing is more ephemeral. It's more of a public relations activity and, thus, doesn't necessarily drive corresponding sales. This argues for traffic tracking and traditional market research over any sort of direct sales tracking.

Social Media Marketing

Social media marketing is much like blog marketing. It's difficult, if not impossible, to track direct sales resulting from social media marketing campaigns—although, if you're trying to drive sales from a social media site, those sales should be tracked. It's more important to track brand awareness and individual product mentions.

Public Relations

Thus, we come to online public relations. Here you want to track product mentions or placements, resulting impressions, and (assuming inserted URLs into each press release) direct clicks resulting from those placements.

Evaluating the Plan as a Whole

It's possible to meet all your individual goals and still have a failing campaign. That's why you need to have one or two universal metrics you measure to determine whether the campaign as a whole was a success or a failure.

How do you measure the overall performance of your marketing plan? Three related metrics are involved:

- **Overall sales**—Total company sales (not just direct website sales) over the course of the campaign. More precisely, you should measure sales increases, with the additional sales likely resulting from your online marketing efforts.

- **Overall profits**—The additional sales you make minus the cost of those sales.

- **Return on investment**—The additional profit you generate compared to the marketing investment you made to generate that profit.

The key to remember when measuring your total campaign is that its impact can—and probably will—extend beyond the Internet. That is, someone viewing an Internet display ad can remember what he saw the next time he's in a bricks-and-mortar store, resulting in an offline sale driven by online marketing. An effective online marketing campaign will lift your sales everywhere, both online and off, so you need to measure your company's total sales, not just your online sales for that period.

> **SEO Tip**
>
> If your campaign is more of a brand-awareness effort, measuring sales or profits might not provide the full picture. In this instance, you'll also need to measure consumer brand awareness, pre- and post-campaign.

What Constitutes Success?

What metrics are key for measuring the success of your online marketing plan? Let's look at some of the most important things to measure—and what, for each metric, constitutes success.

Return on Investment

The overall success of a marketing campaign is measured in big numbers—overall sales or profits, as well as return on investment (ROI). This last metric is perhaps the most important; given the costs you incurred, how much additional profit did you really generate?

You measure ROI by dividing the additional profit generated (that's sales minus costs on the new sales you made above and beyond your previous level) by the amount of money you spent on your marketing campaign. Here's what the formula looks like:

Sales for the campaign period

MINUS Precampaign level sales

MINUS Cost of sales for campaign period

MINUS Marketing costs

DIVIDED BY Marketing costs

The final number will be a percentage; the higher the percentage, the greater your return on investment.

Let's work through an example.

Let's say that before initiating your campaign, you averaged $100,000 in sales each month. During the course of a two-month campaign, however, your sales increased to $150,000 per month. That's $50,000 in additional sales per month, or $100,000 for the two months of the campaign.

If you average a 40 percent profit margin on each sale, you earned $40,000 gross profit for the additional sales made during the campaign period. But that's not your total profit. You next have to subtract the amount of money you spent on the marketing campaign. Let's say that you spent $30,000 in advertising, SEO, and related costs. Subtract that $30,000 from your $40,000 gross profit, and you get a $10,000 net profit for your campaign.

Finally, you need to divide that net profit by your investment. For our example, that means dividing the $10,000 net profit by the $30,000 marketing investment; your return on investment is 33 percent.

What's a good ROI? That totally depends on what your company wants to achieve and is happy with. In any instance, a positive ROI means that you earned more money than you spent. If your ROI is a negative number—if your additional profit was lower than your marketing expenses—then you lost money on the campaign.

Traffic

ROI is perhaps the best way to judge the effectiveness of your overall marketing campaign. But several components of your campaign can be measured by the amount of additional site traffic they generate.

For this, you want to measure the increase in site traffic. That means subtracting your average monthly visitor precampaign from your monthly visitor count during the campaign. The difference is the number of new visitors you attracted because of the campaign.

The math looks like this:

Monthly traffic during the campaign

MINUS Precampaign monthly traffic

You can get even fancier and express your increased traffic as a percentage of your previous traffic level. To do this, divide the monthly traffic count for the campaign by the precampaign monthly traffic level.

Here's an example. If you were averaging 100,000 visitors per month before your campaign and you attracted 125,000 visitors per month during the campaign, the campaign generated 25,000 new visitors per month. Divide that 25,000 number by 100,000, and you get a 25 percent increase.

Sales

Measuring online sales is important for many online marketing activities, especially those with a direct sales component, such as PPC advertising and e-mail marketing. When you measure your direct sales, make sure you assign (as much as possible) sales to their proper generators; this is typically done by creating different landing pages (with unique URLs) or products with unique sales codes for each source.

You can also measure overall company sales to track the success of the overall marketing campaign—not just offline sales, but also sales generated via traditional channels. That's because a marketing campaign is a holistic thing that has impact beyond its immediate online channels; your online marketing has an offline effect.

Market Share

This next metric is more nebulous and somewhat difficult to measure. But if you can measure it, any increase in market share over the course of a campaign is an excellent measure of the campaign's effectiveness.

You can measure many types of market share, including these:

◆ Share of website traffic in your chosen category

◆ Share of online sales in your chosen category

◆ Share of total sales (online and off) in your chosen category

Whereas you can easily generate your own company's metrics, it's much more difficult to get comparative data about your competition. Still, if such data exists, it will tell you how well you're doing compared to competing companies and websites.

Brand Awareness

Finally, all of your online marketing activities should have an impact beyond immediate short-term sales and website traffic. If your marketing is effective, it should increase the awareness of your company and brand. This is typically measured via traditional market research (surveys, polls, and the like); track your brand awareness over time to see the impact of specific online marketing campaigns.

The goal of online marketing, after all, is a long-term goal. Yes, you want to increase your search rankings, increase site traffic, and drive online sales. But you also want to make your company, your brand, and your products stronger and more relevant. This is what marketing is all about, and it all derives from your ability to *think like the customer.* Get inside the customer's head and use that knowledge to drive all your marketing activities, online and off.

Remember, search engine marketing is just one component of your overall marketing activities. Use SEO to make your search engine marketing as effective as possible—and an important part of your marketing mix.

The Least You Need to Know

◆ To measure the success of your online marketing plan, you need to set goals beforehand.

◆ You must measure not only your overall plan goals, but also objectives for individual plan components.

◆ The success of your overall marketing plan can be measured in terms of sales, profits, and return on investment (ROI).

◆ You can also measure the success of your plan by tracking your company's market share and brand awareness.

Appendix

Glossary

\<ALT\> tag   An HTML tag used to provide alternative text for images; this is how searchbots identify the content of image files on a web page.

\<META\> tag   An HTML tag used to provide various data to searchbots, through the use of the **KEYWORDS** and **DESCRIPTION** attributes.

\<META\> tag stuffing   The act of inserting numerous keywords—and often multiple instances of the same keyword—into the **\<META\> KEYWORDS** tag. Inserting too many keywords in this fashion is regarded as black hat behavior by many search engines.

\<TITLE\> tag   An HTML tag used to provide a title for a web page.

anchor text   The text that accompanies a link on a web page; the text that is linked.

Atom   One of two similar site feed schemes, used to provide notice of updated content to feed subscribers and search engines.

backlink   See *inbound link*.

black hat   The use of SEO techniques that search engines do not approve of.

blog   A web log; a web page that serves as a private or professional journal, consisting of regular posts by the blogger.

blog marketing   The act of using blogs as a marketing medium. Blog marketing can involve soliciting third-party blogs for product mentions or creating your own company blog.

body text   The main text in a document or web page. On a web page, the body is located directly following the head of the page.

broken link   A link on a web page that no longer points to an active web page; clicking a broken link does not take a visitor anywhere.

Cascading Style Sheet (CSS)   A type of HTML (actually XML) coding that gives developers more control over web page elements.

click-through rate   The percentage of users who click a link in a PPC or display ad.

content scraping   The act of copying content from one website to display on another, typically unauthorized, website.

context sensitive   The placement of an item directly related to the content of a particular website.

conversion rate   The percentage of click-throughs that either purchase the item offered for sale or otherwise complete the desired action.

cost per click (CPC)   A form of advertising payment based on a specified fee for each time a site visitor clicks on the link in an ad.

cost per thousand (CPM)   A traditional means of charging for advertisements; a specified fee is charged for each thousand impressions.

CPC   See *cost per click.*

CPM   See *cost per thousand.*

crawler   See *searchbot.*

CSS   See *Cascading Style Sheet.*

Dashboard   A summary or overview page, typically used to monitor and manage a particular set of controls or settings.

directory   See *web directory.*

doorway page   A web page that is low in actual content, instead stuffed with repeating keywords and phrases designed to increase the page's search rank. Doorway pages typically contain little or no original content and exist purely to generate search results.

dynamic drill-down navigation   A process in which the pages on a website are placed on the same level but accessed through different virtual paths.

dynamic page   A web page generated via specific user input, such as using a search form; dynamic web pages typically have unique URLs that are difficult to spider.

e-mail marketing   The act of using opt-in e-mail messages to deliver promotional messages, typical of the direct sales variety.

Extensible Markup Language (XML)   A more versatile extension of the HTML web programming language.

faceted navigation   See *dynamic drill-down navigation.*

Flash   A technology used to deliver animations and other graphic content over the web. Searchbots do not recognize Flash animations, so they are not included in search indexes.

gateway page   The entry page to a website.

geotargeting   The act of targeting a specific geographic area in search results or advertising.

Google   The web's largest and most popular search engine.

Google AdSense   The program that enables independent websites to place Google AdWords ads on their pages.

Google AdWords   Google's PPC advertising program.

Googleating   The black hat technique of creating a website solely for the purpose of achieving a high Google PageRank.

header tags   HTML tags (**<H1>, <H2>,** and so on) used to designate different-level headers on a web page.

hidden text   Web page text that is hidden from human view (typically via small size or special coloring) but still readable by searchbots. Use of hidden text is a black hat technique frowned upon by the search engines.

HTML   See *Hypertext Markup Language.*

hyperlink   See *link.*

Hypertext Markup Language (HTML)   The underlying code language used to create web pages.

impression   A single viewing of an advertisement.

inbound link   A link from another site to a given web page.

internal link   A link from one page on a website to another page on the same site.

JavaScript   A scripting language used to create dynamic content on web pages; JavaScript is typically invisible to searchbots.

key phrase   A phrase entered as part of a query by users of a search engine.

keyword   A word entered as part of a query by users of a search engine; SEO revolves around optimizing pages to target and emphasize keywords and phrases.

keyword density   The percentage of a particular keyword to the total number of words on a web page.

keyword-research tool   A tool used to generate relevant and effective keywords for a given topic.

keyword stuffing   The black hat technique of artificially cramming multiple instances of a keyword into the text of a web page.

landing page   The web page that a user lands on after clicking a specific link.

link   A way of navigating from one web page to another by clicking underlined text or a highlighted image.

link bombing   A black hat technique to increase search ranking by having a large number of sites link to a page using identical anchor text.

link cloaking   A black hat technique to mislead a search engine by serving up a different page to the site's searchbot than human visitors will see.

link farm   A group of web pages that all link to one another, with the purpose of increasing the number of links to a given site. A black hat technique.

link masking   The black hat technique of making a link on a page look like something it's not, typically by changing the name of the URL in the link's anchor text.

link trading   The act of trading a link from your website to another in exchange for a reciprocal link from that website to yours.

link washing   See *link bombing*.

linkworthy   Content that is worthy of being linked to from another site.

Live Search   Microsoft's search engine, formerly known as MSN Search.

local search   Search that is optimized to find local businesses.

Microsoft adCenter   Microsoft's PPC advertising network.

mirror website   A website that duplicates the content of another site; a black hat technique designed to place multiple identical sites in the same search results.

mobile search   Search designed for use on cellular phones and other mobile devices.

online display advertising   The banner and sidebar ads found on many web pages; display ads can contain text, graphics, and video.

online shopping directory   A price-comparison website that contains information about products for sale from multiple online merchants.

organic   "Pure" search results, not influenced by paid listings.

outbound link   A link from your website to another website.

PageRank   Google's search results ranking algorithm.

pageview   A single view of a web page; the request to load that web page.

pay-per-click (PPC)   A form of online advertising in which the advertiser is charged when a user clicks on the link in an ad. Most PPC ads are text-only ads.

PPC   See *pay-per-click*.

PPC ad network   An advertising service that sells PPC ads on its own search engine and related network sites. The major PPC ad networks are Google AdSense, Yahoo! Search Marketing, and Microsoft adCenter.

PR   See *public relations*.

public relations   The practice of communicating news about a company and its products to the public, typically via nonpaid vehicles.

Really Simple Syndication (RSS)   A method of broadcasting website or blog content via syndicated site feeds.

referring site   A website that links to or sends visitors to your website.

return on investment (ROI)   The profit (or loss) on an initial investment, typically expressed as a percentage. ROI is calculated as the net profit divided by the amount invested.

robots.txt   A file placed in a website's root directory that contains information used by searchbots to determine what is or isn't indexed on the site. The **robots.txt** file can also contain a pointer to the site's sitemap file.

ROI See *return on investment.*

RSS See *Really Simple Syndication.*

scraper site A site that consists solely or primarily of content scraped or copied from another website.

search engine marketing (SEM) The act of using organic search engine results to drive traffic to a website.

search engine optimization (SEO) The act of optimizing a website to rank as high as possible in search engine results.

search engine A website that indexes sites on the web and enables users to search for particular sites within that index.

search engine rank The position of a web page in a search engine's results for queries that contain a particular keyword.

search engine results page (SERP) A page of relevant results from a search engine query.

search engine spamming Any black hat optimization of a web page, with intent to deceive a search engine's spider and result in a higher or misleading ranking. This is typically accomplished by adding keywords and **<META>** data that does not reflect the actual content of the site.

search index The list of web pages cataloged by a search engine site.

searchbot The automated software that crawls the web to discover web pages for listing in a search engine index. Also called *spider* or *crawler* software.

SEM See *search engine marketing.*

SEO See *search engine optimization.*

SERP See *search engine results page.*

site feed A way to notify users and search engines of frequently updated web page or blog content. Site feeds are syndicated using either the Atom or the RSS standard.

sitemap A map of a website's pages; literally, a list of the URLs for all the pages on a website.

SKU See *stock keeping unit.*

social bookmarking A website or service that enables users to bookmark or tag web pages and content; those bookmarks can then be shared with friends and colleagues via the social bookmarking website.

social media marketing   The act of using blogs, forums, social networks, social bookmarking services, and other online communities to promote a company, brand, or product.

social network   A website that helps create online communities of people with shared interests.

spam   Unsolicited commercial e-mail.

spamdexing   See *search engine spamming.*

spider   See *searchbot.*

splash page   A web page, typically containing a large graphic or Flash animation, that appears before a website's home page.

spoofing   See *search engine spamming.*

stock keeping unit (SKU)   A unique identifier for a product offered for sale.

tag   A piece of HTML code that inserts or formats a particular element. HTML tags are enclosed within angle brackets, like this: **<TAG>.**

uniform resource locator (URL)   The address of a web page.

URL   See *uniform resource locator.*

visit length   The amount of time a visitor spends on a website before leaving for another site.

web directory   A listing of web pages, assembled and edited by human hands and typically organized by category.

website-analysis tool   A software tool or web service that tracks and analyzes website traffic patterns.

white hat   The use of SEO techniques approved and recommended by the major search engines.

XML   See *Extensible Markup Language.*

Yahoo!   The web's number-two search engine.

Yahoo! Search Marketing   Yahoo!'s PPC advertising network.

YouTube   The web's largest video-sharing community.

Index

X–Y–Z

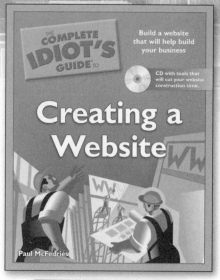

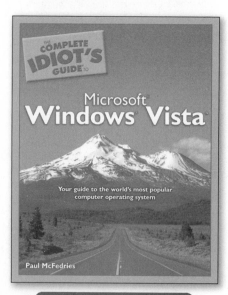